C000103493

303 Impressive Cake Recipes

(303 Impressive Cake Recipes - Volume 1)

Eva Taylor

Copyright: Published in the United States by Eva Taylor/ © EVA TAYLOR

Published on November, 19 2020

All rights reserved. No part of this publication may be reproduced, stored in retrieval system, copied in any form or by any means, electronic, mechanical, photocopying, recording or otherwise transmitted without written permission from the publisher. Please do not participate in or encourage piracy of this material in any way. You must not circulate this book in any format. EVA TAYLOR does not control or direct users' actions and is not responsible for the information or content shared, harm and/or actions of the book readers.

In accordance with the U.S. Copyright Act of 1976, the scanning, uploading and electronic sharing of any part of this book without the permission of the publisher constitute unlawful piracy and theft of the author's intellectual property. If you would like to use material from the book (other than just simply for reviewing the book), prior permission must be obtained by contacting the author at author@chardrecipes.com

Thank you for your support of the author's rights.

Content

CHAPTER 7: SPONGE CAKE RECIPES 102

CHAPTER 8: BAKED CHEESECAKE RECIPES.....................................115

CHAPTER 9: EASY CAKE RECIPES....... 129

Chapter 1: Banana Cake Recipes

***

1. Banana Cake

Serving: 10 | Prep: 25mins | Cook: 60mins | Ready in: 85mins

Ingredients

- 2 tbs butter softened
- 1/2 cup caster sugar
- 1 egg
- 3 banana roughly chopped
- 1 3/4 cup self-raising flour
- 1 tsp mixed spice
- 1 tsp ground cinnamon
- 3 tsp low-fat natural yoghurt
- 1/3 tsp mixed nuts optional

Direction

- Preheat oven to 180°C and line a 23 cm x 13 cm loaf tin with baking paper.
- Cream butter and sugar, then add egg and banana and mix until well combined.
- Add half the flour, spices, yoghurt and mix well.
- Stir in remaining flour as needed. Fold in nuts and pour batter into tin.
- Bake for 35-45 minutes or until the loaf is a pale golden brown and an inserted skewer comes out clean.
- If not eating straightaway, wrap the tin in foil and allow the cake to cool in the tin before removing.

2. Banana Cake Recipe

Serving: 8 | Prep: 15mins | Cook: 60mins | Ready in: 75mins

Ingredients

- 50 g margarine
- 100 g sugar
- 3 egg
- 225 g plain flour sifted
- 1 tsp baking powder
- 1/3 tsp bicarbonate of soda
- 3 banana mashed
- 50 g walnuts chopped

Direction

- Preheat the oven to 180C.
- Mix the margarine and sugar with a mixer until smooth.
- Gradually add the eggs while mixing.
- Add the flour, bicarbonate of soda and baking powder, and continue mixing.
- Finally, add the mashed bananas, glazed cherries, choc bits and walnuts, and mix.
- Pour the mixture in a greased cake mould or loaf tin, and bake for about 1 hour.

3. Banana Cake Supreme Recipe

Serving: 10 | Prep: 10mins | Cook: 50mins | Ready in: 60mins

Ingredients

- 125g soft butter
- 1 cup caster sugar
- 1 cup banana large mashed
- 1 tsp vanilla essence
- 2 egg
- 100ml buttermilk
- 1 1/2 cup self-raising flour
- 1/2 tsp bicarbonate of soda

Direction

- Preheat oven to 180C (160C fan-forced). Grease and line a 22cm springform pan.
- Place butter, sugar, banana, eggs and vanilla into a food processor. Process for 2 minutes.
- Scrape down the sides, then add buttermilk using the pulse button to combine.
- Sift flour and bicarbonate of soda together into a bowl. Add flour mixture to food processor and process until just combined.
- Pour mixture into tin.
- Bake for approximately 50 minutes or until a skewer inserted into the centre of the cake comes out clean.
- Cool cake on a wire rack. Store in airtight container in refrigerator.

4. Banana Cake With Lemon Frosting

Serving: 8 | Prep: 10mins | Cook: 40mins | Ready in: 50mins

Ingredients

- 185 g self-raising flour
- 100 g sugar
- 125 g butter
- 2 egg beaten well
- 4 banana mashed ripe
- 2 tsp lemon juice
- Icing
- 185 g icing sugar sifted
- 60 g butter
- 1 tsp lemon rind
- 2 tsp lemon juice
- 1/2 cup walnuts *to decorate

Direction

- Cream butter and sugar together.
- Gradually add eggs. Mix well.
- Stir in the mashed banana mixed with lemon juice.
- Fold in the sifted flour.
- Place in a 20 cm cake tin. Bake at 175C for approximately 40 minutes.
- Cake is ready when it springs back. Leave to cool on a wire rack. Ice when cold.
- Icing: Cream together icing sugar, butter, extra lemon juice and lemon rind.

5. Banana Cake With Lemon And Coconut Icing Recipe

Serving: 0 | Prep: 10mins | Cook: 30mins | Ready in: 40mins

Ingredients

- 125 g butter softened
- 1/2 cup caster sugar
- 2 eggs
- 2 bananas large mashed ripe
- 1 tsp bicarbonate of soda
- 1 1/2 cups self-raising flour
- 1/4 cup milk
- Icing
- 1 1/2 cups icing sugar
- 30 g butter melted
- 2 1/2 tbs lemon juice
- 1 tbs desiccated coconut *to decorate
- 2 drops yellow liquid food colouring

Direction

- Banana cake: Preheat oven to 170C with fan, 185C without fan.
- Cream butter and sugar until light and fluffy. Add eggs one at a time, mixing well in between. Stir in mashed bananas until combined.
- Put in half of the sifted dry ingredients and stir to combine. Add the rest of the dry ingredients and the milk, and stir until smooth.
- Pour mixture into a greased 20cm round cake pan.
- Bake for 30 minutes, stand for 5 minutes in tin then transfer onto a wire rack to cool.

- Icing: Combine icing sugar and lemon juice in a bowl and mix well, making sure no lumps remain.
- Add the melted butter and mix thoroughly.
- Add a few drops of yellow food colouring for extra richness in colour. Spread over cake and sprinkle with coconut.

6. Banana Cake With Sour Cream Recipe

Serving: 10 | Prep: 15mins | Cook: 60mins | Ready in: 75mins

Ingredients

- 115g butter
- 1 1/4 cups brown sugar
- 2 eggs
- 1 1/2 cups self-raising flour
- 1 tsp baking soda
- 3/4 cup sour cream
- 1 tbs milk
- 1 cup banana mashed

Direction

- Preheat oven to 180C.
- Grease and line a loaf pan.
- Cream butter with brown sugar.
- Add eggs, one at a time, and beat well.
- Sift flour and baking soda into mixture and combine.
- Add sour cream, milk and mashed banana.
- Stir until combined.
- Bake in loaf pan for 50-60 minutes.

7. Banana Tarte Tatin Recipe

Serving: 6 | Prep: 10mins | Cook: 40mins | Ready in: 50mins

Ingredients

- 1/3 cup brown sugar firmly packed
- 40 g butter cold finely chopped
- 3 bananas halved lengthways
- 1 sheets puff pastry partially thawed
- 1 egg whites
- 1 tbs caster sugar
- 1 tsp ground cinnamon
- 1 cup macadamias
- 125 g vanilla ice cream *to serve

Direction

- Preheat oven to 220C/200C fan-forced. Grease a 6cm deep, 20cm round (base) cake pan. Line base with baking paper. Line a baking tray with baking paper.
- Sprinkle brown sugar over base of prepared pan. Dot with butter. Arrange banana over top, trimming to fit. Cut a 22cm circle from pastry. Place over banana, tucking in edges around banana. Bake for 20 minutes or until golden and puffed.
- Meanwhile, whisk egg white, sugar and cinnamon in a bowl. Add macadamias. Toss to coat. Spread onto prepared tray. Bake for 8 to 10 minutes, or until golden. Roughly chop.
- Place a serving plate with sides on top of pan, then carefully invert tarte onto plate. Sprinkle with macadamias. Serve with ice cream.

8. Banana And Carrot Cake Recipe

Serving: 8 | Prep: 20mins | Cook: 60mins | Ready in: 80mins

Ingredients

- 1 1/2 cup self-raising flour
- 1/2 cup plain flour
- 1 cup brown sugar
- 1 tsp ground cinnamon
- 2 banana medium ripe
- 1 carrot grated

- 2 egg
- 1/3 cup canola oil
- 1/3 cup milk

Direction

- Preheat oven to 180C.
- Place flours, sugar and cinnamon in a large bowl and stir to combine.
- In a separate bowl, mash banana, add grated carrot, then add eggs, milk and oil. Stir to combine.
- Add wet ingredients to dry ingredients and stir to combine.
- Pour mixture into a greased loaf pan and bake for 1 hour.
- Stand in pan on wire rack for 5-10 minutes. Serve cake warm with butter, if desired.

9. Banana, Pear And Walnut Cake

Serving: 12 | Prep: 10mins | Cook: 90mins | Ready in: 100mins

Ingredients

- Cake
- 2 cup self-raising flour
- 1 cup brown sugar
- 1 tsp ground cinnamon
- 1/2 tsp allspice
- 3 banana mashed
- 100 g walnuts finely chopped
- 3 egg
- 1 cup olive oil
- 2 pear
- 1 tbs caster sugar
- 1/2 cup sour cream

Direction

- Preheat oven to 180C. Grease and line a 22cm round cake tin with baking paper.

- Sift flour, cinnamon and allspice into a mixing bowl. Stir in brown sugar and walnuts. Set aside.
- In a separate bowl whisk eggs, oil, sour cream and mashed banana until combined. Make a well in the centre of the dry ingredients and add the wet ingredients. Mix until just combined. Spoon mixture into prepared cake tin and smooth top.
- Quarter and remove cores of pears. Thinly slice pears lengthways. Arrange pears over cake mixture, slightly overlapping. Sprinkle with caster sugar.
- Bake for 1 1/2 hour or until skewer inserted comes out clean. Stand for 10 minutes before carefully turning out on a wire rack to cool.

10. Beautiful Banoffee Pie Recipe

Serving: 8 | Prep: 60mins | Cook: 0S | Ready in: 60mins

Ingredients

- 250 g Granita biscuits crushed
- 100 g butter melted
- 760 g Top 'n' Fill Caramel
- 3 banana large sliced
- 300 ml cream
- 1 tbs milk chocolate grated

Direction

- Mix together biscuit crumbs and butter in a bowl, then press into a pie dish.
- Chill for 30 minutes.
- Pour Top'n'Fill onto base and smooth over.
- Add bananas.
- Whip cream until stiff peaks appear and smooth over bananas.
- Top with grated chocolate.
- Refrigerate until ready to serve.

11. Best Banoffee Pie Recipe

Serving: 8 | Prep: 15mins | Cook: 0S | Ready in: 15mins

Ingredients

- 800 g condensed milk
- 3 bananas large thinly sliced
- 300 g chocolate biscuits crushed
- 300 ml double cream
- 50 g milk chocolate
- 3 tbs butter melted

Direction

- Caramelise the condensed milk, by filling the saucepan ¾ full with water on high heat.
- When the water boils place the tins into the saucepan with tongs.
- Place lid on saucepan and leave to gently boil for 2 hours.
- Remove after the two hours and leave to cool.
- Place the biscuit crumbs in a bowl and pour over melted butter. Stir well.
- Pour the crumbs into a spring form cake tin, press down and refrigerate for 15 minutes.
- Spread the banana slices over the base and evenly pour condensed milk over the banana.
- Refrigerate for 20 minutes.
- Whip the cream until stiff and cover the condensed milk mixture.
- Cover with grated chocolate and refrigerate.

12. Best Hummingbird Cake Recipe

Serving: 0 | Prep: 15mins | Cook: 45mins | Ready in: 60mins

Ingredients

- Cake
- 3 cups self-raising flour
- 1/2 tsp salt
- 2 tsp ground cinnamon
- 1 tsp allspice
- 4 bananas overripe
- 1 cup brown sugar firmly packed
- 445 g canned pineapple
- 2 eggs lightly beaten
- 60 g walnuts chopped
- 1/2 cup vegetable oil
- Icing
- 100 g cream cheese
- 55 g butter
- 1 cup icing sugar
- 1 dash vanilla essence

Direction

- Preheat your oven to 180C.
- Spoon mixture into your pre-prepared cake tin.
- Sift flour, salt, cinnamon and salt into a large mixing bowl.
- Add brown sugar and combine thoroughly with a knife.
- Using a blender, emulsify half of your pineapple and your bananas.
- Using a manual/hand potato masher, mash the remainder of your pineapple and bananas roughly.
- Create a well in the centre of your dry ingredients and pour in crushed walnuts, oil, lightly whisked eggs, bananas, pineapple juice and pineapple.
- You could go rustic and smother your cake in the icing using a spatula, or if you feel like you have a little extra patience for this step today and a decorative piping nozzle, you can pipe your icing on in in a pretty pattern.
- Place into a preheated oven for 45 minutes, or until a skewer inserted into the centre of the cake comes out clean.
- Remove from oven, then place in the fridge to chill while you prepare your icing.
- Place cream cheese, vanilla essence and butter into a small mixing bowl.
- Cream together with electric beaters until you see a slight colour change, then gradually add your icing sugar. Beat on high until your icing is smooth in consistency.

- If the top of your cake isn't already flat, use a bread knife and take the top off to ensure you have a flat surface to work with.
- Line a cake tins and set aside. The tin I've used is 20cm in diameter, however you can use cake tins of any diameter to create the desired effect, you will just have to adjust the cooking time of your cake accordingly.

13. Best Ever Banana Cake Recipe

Serving: 10 | Prep: 15mins | Cook: 75mins | Ready in: 90mins

Ingredients

- 1 1/2 cups self-raising flour
- 1 tsp bicarbonate of soda
- 3/4 cup sugar
- 3 bananas mashed
- 1/2 cup oil
- 2 eggs lightly beaten

Direction

- Grease a ring tin and line base with baking paper.
- Sift flour and soda into a bowl. Add sugar.
- Make a well in centre and add bananas, eggs and oil.
- Stir until mixture is smooth.
- Pour into cake tin and bake at 150C for 1 hour.
- Ice with cream cheese or lemon icing if desired.

14. Boiled Banana Cake Recipe

Serving: 10 | Prep: 30mins | Cook: 75mins | Ready in: 105mins

Ingredients

- 125 g margarine
- 1 cup sugar
- 1 tsp cinnamon sugar
- 1 tsp bicarbonate of soda
- 1 cup water
- 3 bananas mashed
- 2 eggs lightly beaten
- 2 cups self-raising flour sifted

Direction

- Preheat oven to 180C.
- Grease a 19cm x 19 cm square cake tin.
- Bring margarine, sugar, spices, bicarbonate of soda and water to the boil, then simmer for 2-3 minutes.
- Cool, then mix in eggs and sifted flour, and fold through bananas.
- Pour into cake tin and bake for approximately 1 hour or until a skewer inserted in middle of cake comes out clean.

15. Choc Chip Banana Cake Recipe

Serving: 8 | Prep: 10mins | Cook: 40mins | Ready in: 50mins

Ingredients

- 3 bananas mashed ripe
- 2 tbs butter
- 3/4 cup sugar
- 1 egg
- 1 1/2 cups self-raising flour
- 1 tsp bicarbonate of soda
- 2 tbs milk
- 3/4 cup chocolate chips

Direction

- Preheat oven to 180C.
- Cream butter and sugar together.
- Add the remaining ingredients and beat well.
- Pour mixture into a greased doughnut tin or 2 greased long tins.
- Bake for 35-40 minutes.

16. Cinnamon Banana Cake

Serving: 10 | Prep: 45mins | Cook: 55mins | Ready in: 100mins

Ingredients

- 2 cup plain flour
- 1 tsp salt
- 1 tsp ground cinnamon
- 1 tsp bicarbonate of soda
- 1/2 tsp ground ginger
- 1/2 cup grapeseed oil
- 1 cup brown sugar
- 2 egg
- 1/2 cup milk
- 3 banana ripe
- 1/2 cup pecans optional roughly chopped

Direction

- Preheat oven to 180C. Grease cake pan.
- Sift flour and baking soda into a large bowl and combine with cinnamon, ginger and salt.
- Mash bananas in separate bowl, combine oil and sugar then add to bananas and mix. Combine with dry ingredients, add eggs and milk and mix well.
- Add pecans, then pour mixture into cake tin.
- Bake for 30 minutes, until an inserted skewer comes out clean.

17. Crunchy Malteser And Banana Cake

Serving: 10 | Prep: 10mins | Cook: 40mins | Ready in: 50mins

Ingredients

- 125 g butter
- 1/2 cup caster sugar
- 2 egg lightly beaten
- 2 tbs milk
- 1/2 tsp bicarbonate of soda
- 1 1/2 cup self-raising flour sifted
- 2 banana mashed
- 2 tbs vanilla sugar
- 1 cup Maltesers

Direction

- Cream butter and sugar until light and fluffy.
- Gradually add eggs, mixing at low speed.
- Blend bicarbonate of soda with warm milk. Alternately fold in milk and dry ingredients.
- Stir in mashed banana, vanillin sugar and Maltesers.
- Pour into a lightly greased oven proof 20 cm ring pan.
- Bake at 180C for 30-40 minutes or until cooked through. Cake should spring back when touched lightly.

18. Easy Banana Cake Recipe

Serving: 12 | Prep: 15mins | Cook: 45mins | Ready in: 60mins

Ingredients

- 125g unsalted butter
- 3/4 cup caster sugar
- 1 tsp vanilla essence
- 1 egg
- 2 bananas mashed ripe
- 1 1/2 cups self-raising flour
- 1/4 cup milk

Direction

- Melt the butter, sugar and vanilla in a medium-sized saucepan.
- Remove from the heat.
- Add mashed bananas and stir through until just combined.

- Add egg and mix well. Stir in the flour, then pour in the milk and fold in lightly.
- Bake at 170C for approximately 40 minutes.

19. Easy Chocolate And Banana Cake

Serving: 10 | Prep: 30mins | Cook: 75mins | Ready in: 105mins

Ingredients

- 3 banana mashed ripe
- 2 egg
- 2 cup brown sugar
- 2 tbs golden syrup
- 1/2 cup canola oil
- 1/2 cup milk
- 1 pinch salt
- 3 cup plain flour
- 4 tbs cocoa powder
- 2 tsp baking powder
- 2 tsp bicarbonate of soda
- 1/2 cup pecans optional

Direction

- Mix or blend all ingredients together.
- For a large cake, bake at 180C for 50-60 minutes, testing with a skewer to ensure it is cooked.
- For muffins, bake at 180C for 20 minutes. Muffins are cooked when the top springs back up when pressed.

20. Easy Flourless Banana And Walnut Cake

Serving: 8 | Prep: 15mins | Cook: 40mins | Ready in: 55mins

Ingredients

- 2 cup almond meal
- 1/2 cup walnuts crushed
- 2 banana mashed
- 1/2 cup extra virgin olive oil
- 1/2 cup rice milk
- 2 extra-large egg lightly beaten
- 1 tsp bicarbonate of soda
- 1 pinch salt

Direction

- Preheat oven to 175C.
- Mix all ingredients in a mixing bowl until well combined.
- Pour into a 20 cm square cake tin lined with baking paper.
- Bake for 40 minutes.

21. Egg Free Banana Cake

Serving: 10 | Prep: 10mins | Cook: 40mins | Ready in: 50mins

Ingredients

- 1 1/4 cup plain flour
- 1/4 cup cornflour
- 1 tsp bicarbonate of soda
- 1/2 tsp salt
- 1/2 cup sugar
- 1 tsp vanilla essence
- 1 cup banana mashed
- 1/2 cup macadamia oil
- 1 tbs white vinegar
- 1/4 cup milk

Direction

- Preheat oven to 165C (fan forced). Line a 20cm x 11cm loaf pan.
- Sift flours, bicarbonate of soda and salt, add sugar and mix well.
- Combine mashed banana, oil, milk, vinegar and vanilla in jug.
- Combine with dry mix, until just mixed.

- Place into prepared pan and bake for approximately 40 minutes or until cooked.
- Ice as desired.

22. Hummingbird Cake Recipe

Serving: 6 | Prep: 45mins | Cook: 90mins | Ready in: 135mins

Ingredients

- 450g (crushed) canned pineapple
- 1 cup plain flour
- 1/2 cup self-raising flour
- 1/2 tsp bicarbonate of soda
- 1/2 tsp ground cinnamon
- 1 cup brown sugar firmly packed
- 1/2 cup desiccated coconut
- 1 cup banana mashed ripe
- 2 eggs lightly beaten
- 3/4 cup vegetable oil
- Cream cheese frosting
- 50g butter softened
- 250g cream cheese softened
- 2 tsp vanilla essence
- 1 cup icing sugar

Direction

- Grease a deep 23cm round cake pan and line base with baking paper.
- Drain pineapple in a fine sieve, pressing out as much syrup as possible, reserving ¼ cup syrup.
- Sift flours, soda and cinnamon in a large bowl. Stir in sugar and coconut. Make a well in the centre.
- Add combined bananas, eggs, oil, pineapple and reserved syrup. Mix until combined. Pour mixture into prepared pan.
- Cook at 180C for about 1 hour, or until cooked when tested with skewer.
- Cover with foil if top is over browning.
- Stand cake in pan for 5 minutes and turn out onto wire rack to cool.

- Cream cheese frosting: Beat butter, cream cheese and essence in a small bowl with electric mixer until light and fluffy.
- Gradually beat in icing sugar until smooth.
- Spread on top and sides of cake

23. Low Fat Banana And Coconut Cake Recipe

Serving: 10 | Prep: 5mins | Cook: 70mins | Ready in: 75mins

Ingredients

- 1 cup desiccated coconut
- 0.6 cup caster sugar
- 1 1/4 cups self-raising flour
- 1/4 cup wholemeal self-raising flour
- 1 cup banana mashed
- 1 tsp vanilla extract
- 1 cup light coconut milk
- 1 egg
- 100 g milk chocolate chips *optional

Direction

- Preheat oven to 170C. Grease a large loaf pan and line with baking paper.
- Place coconut in a dry frypan over medium heat, stir for a minute or 2 until lightly coloured. Remove from heat and cool slightly while mixing other ingredients.
- Beat banana, coconut milk, egg and vanilla in a bowl.
- In another bowl, combine flours, sugar and toasted coconut and chocolate chips if using.
- Pour wet ingredients into dry and gently stir to combine.
- Bake for 1 hour 5 minutes or until a skewer comes out clean.
- Ice when cold if desired.

24. Malteser And Banana Cake Recipe

Serving: 8 | Prep: 15mins | Cook: 40mins | Ready in: 55mins

Ingredients

- 125 g butter
- 1/2 cup caster sugar
- 2 egg
- 2 tbs milk
- 1/2 tsp bicarbonate of soda
- 1 1/2 cup self-raising flour
- 2 1/2 banana mashed ripe
- 2 tbs vanilla sugar
- 165 g Maltesers
- 1 tbs icing sugar *to decorate

Direction

- Preheat oven 180C.
- Cream butter and sugar until light and fluffy with electric mixer.
- Gradually add eggs on a low speed. Blend bicarbonate of soda with warm milk.
- Fold through butter mixture with dry ingredients.
- Stir through mashed bananas, vanilla sugar and Maltesers.
- Pour into a greased ring tin lined with baking paper.
- Bake 30-40 minutes or until skewer comes out clean.
- Let sit in tin for 5 minutes then turn onto wire cake rack to cool.
- Dust with icing sugar when cool.

25. Moist Banana Cake Recipe

Serving: 10 | Prep: 15mins | Cook: 45mins | Ready in: 60mins

Ingredients

- 250g soft butter
- 1 cup caster sugar
- 3 eggs
- 3 bananas ripe mashed
- 2 cups self-raising flour

Direction

- Cream butter and sugar in small bowl with electric mixer until light and fluffy.
- Add eggs one at a time, beating well after each addition. Stir in bananas, then sifted flour.
- Pour into a well-greased, 20cm baba or ring pan. Bake at 180C for about 45 minutes.
- Stand a few minutes before turning cake onto wire rack to cool.

26. Moist Banana Cake Recipe

Serving: 8 | Prep: 15mins | Cook: 40mins | Ready in: 55mins

Ingredients

- 1/2 cup butter
- 2 eggs
- 3 bananas small
- 1 tsp vanilla extract
- 1 tsp bicarbonate of soda
- 50 ml milk
- 1/2 cup caster sugar
- 1 1/2 cups self-raising flour

Direction

- Cream butter, sugar and vanilla.
- Add eggs separately, beating well.
- Mash bananas and add to mixture.
- Dissolve soda in milk and add flour and milk alternately.
- Bake in 2 greased tins or 1 large tin at 180C for 35-40 minutes or until cooked.

27. Moist Chocolate Banana Cake Recipe

Serving: 10 | Prep: 30mins | Cook: 45mins | Ready in: 75mins

Ingredients

- 4 egg
- 1/4 cup butter
- 1 1/2 cup sugar
- 1 tsp vanilla custard powder
- 2 cup plain flour sifted
- 1 1/2 tsp baking powder
- 1 pinch salt
- 1/3 cup milk
- 1 cup banana mashed ripe
- 1 cup white chocolate chopped

Direction

- Whisk eggs and vanilla.
- Add sugar, milk, butter and mix well.
- Add flour, baking powder and salt to mixture and mix.
- Finally add the chocolate and bananas.
- Pour the mixture in a greased cake pan and bake at 200C for 25-35 minutes or until cooked.

28. Nan's Banana Cake

Serving: 0 | Prep: 5mins | Cook: 40mins | Ready in: 45mins

Ingredients

- 2 tbs butter
- 1 cup sugar
- 2 tbs milk
- 1 1/2 cup plain flour
- 1 tsp bicarbonate of soda
- 1 tsp baking powder
- 3 banana mashed
- 1 egg beaten well
- 1/2 cup icing sugar *to decorate

Direction

- Preheat oven to 190C.
- Cream butter and sugar.
- Add milk, flour, bicarbonate of soda, baking powder and banana.
- Add well beaten egg.
- Mix together and pour into a greased cake tin.
- Bake for 40 minutes or until skewer comes out clean.
- Allow to cool and dust with icing sugar, or icing of choice.

29. Quick Mix Banana Chocolate Cake

Serving: 10 | Prep: 15mins | Cook: 40mins | Ready in: 55mins

Ingredients

- 1 1/2 cup self-raising flour
- 3/4 cup sugar
- 1/2 cup cocoa
- 1/2 cup oil
- 1/4 cup milk
- 3 banana mashed ripe

Direction

- Preheat oven to 180C and grease bundt tin.
- Place all ingredients into a bowl and give it a good mix.
- Pour mixture into prepared tin and bake at 180 degrees for 40 minutes.

30. Quick And Easy Banana Cake Recipe

Serving: 8 | Prep: 5mins | Cook: 30mins | Ready in: 35mins

Ingredients

- 3 bananas small
- 3/4 cup sugar
- 1 egg
- 1 cup self-raising flour
- 1 pinch salt

Direction

- Preheat oven to 190C.
- Grease a cake tray or line with baking paper.
- Mash the bananas and sugar together.
- Add remaining ingredients.
- Bake for 30 minutes or until golden.

31. Slow Cooker Banana Cake Recipe

Serving: 10 | Prep: 10mins | Cook: 240mins | Ready in: 250mins

Ingredients

- 100g butter
- 1/3 cup caster sugar
- 1/3 cup Greek yoghurt
- 1 egg
- 2 bananas ripe
- 1 tsp vanilla essence
- 1 1/2 cups self-raising flour
- 1 cup water

Direction

- Pour water into the base of a slow cooker. Grease and line a 20cm cake tin.
- Cream butter and sugar together. Add egg, vanilla, bananas and yoghurt. Mix until smooth.
- Gradually mix in flour, stirring until smooth.
- Spread batter into cake tin, carefully lower into slow cooker.
- Place lid on slow cooker and cook on high for 3-4 hours.

- Cake is cooked when a bamboo skewer inserted into the middle come out clean.

32. Sugar Free Banana Cake Recipe

Serving: 6 | Prep: 15mins | Cook: 30mins | Ready in: 45mins

Ingredients

- 2 cups wholemeal plain flour sifted
- 2 tsp baking powder
- 1/2 tsp bicarbonate of soda
- 60 g butter
- 1 egg
- 1/2 cup pitted dates finely chopped
- 4 banana mashed ripe
- 1/3 cup milk

Direction

- Preheat oven to 180C.
- In a mixing bowl, cream the butter and egg with 1 tablespoon of sifted flour.
- Beat well, then stir in dates and bananas.
- In a separate bowl, sift remaining flour, baking powder and soda.
- Fold in the flour mixture alternatively with the milk to the banana mixture.
- Spread the mixture into a greased loaf tin and bake for 25-35 minutes.

33. Tuckshop Banana Cake Recipe

Serving: 8 | Prep: 15mins | Cook: 40mins | Ready in: 55mins

Ingredients

- 3 bananas large ripe
- 1 cup self-raising flour sifted
- 1 egg brought to room temperature
- 1/2 cup sugar

- 1/4 cup canola oil

Direction

- Preheat oven to 180C and lightly grease a loaf tin.
- Peel bananas, place in a mixing bowl and mash.
- Add the flour and then the remaining ingredients.
- Mix well until combined and pour into the loaf tin.
- Bake for 40 minutes until golden.

34. Upside Down Banana Cake Recipe

Serving: 8 | Prep: 15mins | Cook: 45mins | Ready in: 60mins

Ingredients

- 50g butter
- 1/3 cup brown sugar
- 6 bananas cut into pieces large ripe
- 125g butter softened
- 1 1/4 cups brown sugar *extra
- 2 eggs lightly beaten
- 1 1/2 cups self-raising flour
- 1 tsp baking powder
- 2 bananas large mashed *extra

Direction

- Preheat the oven to 180C. Grease and line a 21cm circle cake tin. Pour the melted butter over the base of the tin and sprinkle with the sugar. Arrange the bananas over the sugar.
- Cream the butter and extra brown sugar until light and fluffy. Then add eggs gradually, beating well.
- Sift the flour and baking powder into a bowl, then fold into the cake mixture with the mashed banana. Carefully spread into the tin, and bake for 45 minutes, or until a skewer

comes out clean. Turn out whilst warm, but not boiling.

35. Upside Down Banana Maple Custard Cake Recipe

Serving: 10 | Prep: 10mins | Cook: 45mins | Ready in: 55mins

Ingredients

- 1 banana mashed ripe
- 1/3 cup coconut oil melted
- 1/4 cup sugar
- 3 tbs maple syrup
- 2 eggs beaten
- 1/2 cup Pauls thick vanilla custard
- 2 tsp baking powder
- 1/2 tsp salt
- 1 1/4 cups plain flour
- Upside down topping
- 4 tbs butter
- 1/4 cup brown sugar
- 1/4 cup maple syrup
- 2 1/2 bananas sliced

Direction

- Preheat oven to 170C. Line cake pan with baking paper.
- To make the upside down topping, melt the butter, brown sugar and maple syrup together. Spread evenly on the bottom of lined pan. Slice the bananas and lay over top of the maple-caramel mixture in a circular overlapping pattern.
- In a large bowl, mix together the mashed banana, coconut oil, egg, custard, sugar and maple syrup until combined. Stir in the baking powder, salt and flour until evenly combined.
- Pour this mixture over the sliced bananas in pan and bake for approximately 45 minutes (the maple~caramel mixture should start to "bubble" up the sides of the pan).

- Allow cake to cool 10 – 15 minutes before flipping onto a serving plate. Best served warm with a big dollop of custard or vanilla ice-cream.

36. White Chocolate And Banana Mud Cake Recipe

Serving: 0 | Prep: 10mins | Cook: 60mins | Ready in: 70mins

Ingredients

- 250 g butter
- 250 g Nestle* white chocolate melts
- 150 ml hot water
- 1 cup caster sugar
- 1 3/4 cups plain flour
- 1 cup self-raising flour
- 1 tsp vanilla essence
- 2 eggs
- 4 bananas mashed

Direction

- Preheat oven to 150C.
- Melt chocolate and margarine in microwave for 1-2 minutes.
- Add water and sugar, stir and put in microwave until sugar has dissolved. Set aside to cool.
- Line and grease the base and sides of a cake pan.
- Mash bananas, eggs and vanilla together in a separate bowl until it has a paste-like consistency.
- When cool add sifted flours to the chocolate mixture. Add the egg and banana and mix well, using a whisk.
- Pour into prepared pan and cook for approximately 45 minutes to 1 hour, depending on size of tin.
- Cake is cooked when skewer comes out clean and the sides should be a light golden color.

37. Wholemeal Banana, Coconut And Walnut Cake Recipe

Serving: 0 | Prep: 10mins | Cook: 30mins | Ready in: 40mins

Ingredients

- 2/3 cup grapeseed oil
- 2/3 cup brown sugar
- 4 eggs
- 1 cup banana mashed
- 1/2 cup milk
- 1 tsp baking soda
- 2 tsp vanilla essence
- 2 tsp ground cinnamon
- 3 cups wholemeal self-raising flour
- 1/2 cup sultanas
- 1/2 cup walnuts
- 1/2 cup walnuts *to decorate *extra
- 1/4 cup shredded coconut
- 1/4 cup shredded coconut *to decorate *extra
- 1/2 cup pecans *to decorate
- 1 tsp butter for greasing

Direction

- Preheat oven to 165C. To prepare your baking tin, tear off a piece of baking paper to fit your pan. Hold it under your tap to wet the paper and scrunch it up into a ball, shake off excess water, grease the tin with a small amount of butter and place in the paper into the tin and press firmly.
- To make the cake, using an electric mixer beat together the oil and brown sugar on a medium speed. Add in the eggs one at a time and beat well until pale and creamy, then add in the mashed banana and milk and beat until well combined.
- Turn the mixer down to the lowest speed and add in the baking soda, vanilla, salt, cinnamon and the flour, 1 tablespoon at a time, and mix until just mixed. Turn off the mixer, then add in the 1/2 cup walnuts, sultanas and 1/4 cup coconut and fold through.

- Fill the prepared tin and bake for 20 - 30 minutes, or until a skewer inserted comes out clean. Cut into even pieces and enjoy warm.

Chapter 2: Lemon Cake Recipes

***

38. Bunny Lemon And Thyme Ice Cream Sandwiches Recipe

Serving: 0 | Prep: 10mins | Cook: 30mins | Ready in: 40mins

Ingredients

- 2 cups plain flour
- 125 g butter
- 1 1/4 cups caster sugar
- 3 tbs fresh thyme
- 1 pinch salt
- 3 egg yolks
- 3 eggs
- 2 lemons juiced zested
- 300 ml Pauls lactose-free Zymil regular thickened cream

Direction

- To make the ice cream: Whisk together 1/4 cup sugar, 3 eggs and 2 egg yolks until combined. Place over a pan of simmering water and whisk until the mixture thickens and light in colour. Slowly mix through lemon juice and zest. Pour into a lined lamington pan and place in the freezer for 3 hours to set.
- To make the biscuit: Combine all remaining ingredients in an electric mixer to form a soft dough. Refrigerate in GLAD Wrap for 15

minutes to firm up before rolling out and cutting into your preferred shapes. Place on a lined tray and bake for 12 - 15. Remove and set aside to cool.
- Once ice cream has set, remove from freezer and gently remove from the tin. Using the same cookie cutter as the biscuits to cut ice cream. Transfer back to the freezer until ready for assembly.
- Place ice cream in-between two biscuits to make a sandwich and enjoy!

39. Cheat's Lemon Puffs Recipe

Serving: 0 | Prep: 5mins | Cook: 30mins | Ready in: 35mins

Ingredients

- 80g butter, melted
- 2 sheets butter puff pastry
- 1/4 cup caster sugar
- 1 egg, beaten
- 1/2 cup cream
- 1/2 cup lemon curd
- Icing sugar, to serve

Direction

- Preheat oven to 180C. Brush 8 holes of a 12-hole muffin pan with some of the melted butter.
- Place a sheet of pastry on a floured bench. Dust the top with more flour. Use a rolling pin to roll the sheet into a 40cm square. Brush liberally with butter and sprinkle with a little caster sugar. Roll up into a large log, then cut into 2 equal-sized pieces.
- Cut each piece in half lengthwise, then turn each half on its side to reveal the layers of pastry. Form into a spiral and place gently into a muffin pan. Repeat with the remaining three pieces, and then repeat with the second sheet of puff pastry until you have 8 puffs.

- Brush with beaten egg and bake for 30 minutes until puffed and golden. Allow to cool.
- Beat cream until stiff and fold through lemon curd. Carefully cut puffs in half and spoon lemon curd cream onto the bottom half, then replace the top. Dust with icing sugar and serve.

40. Coconut Lemon Bars Recipe

Serving: 0 | Prep: 15mins | Cook: 35mins | Ready in: 50mins

Ingredients

- 4 lemons juiced
- 6 eggs
- 1/4 cup plain flour
- 2 tbs coconut milk
- 3/4 cup caster sugar
- Base
- 100 g unsalted butter
- 150 g Arnott's Milk Arrowroot biscuits
- 1/2 cup desiccated coconut
- 1 lemon zested
- 1 1/2 tbs lemon juice
- 2 tbs white granulated sugar

Direction

- Preheat your oven to 180C. Line a slice tin and set aside.
- Base: In a food processor, blitz together sugar, lemon rind and 150g Milk Arrowroot biscuits until they resemble fine crumbs. Add 100g of butter, desiccated coconut and lemon juice. Blitz until well combined and mixture holds together when compressed.
- Evenly spread and press down the mixture into the base of your slice tin to form a level base for your bars. Set aside in the fridge.
- Lemon filling: In a large mixing bowl, combine the juice of four lemons, eggs, coconut cream and caster sugar, and beat on high with electric beaters until smooth.
- Add 1/4 cup of plain flour and beat on low until just combined.
- Retrieve your slice tin from the fridge, and pour your mixture through a sieve and into the slice tin over your biscuit base.
- Tap your slice tin lightly on the bench to dislodge any bubbles and place in the centre of your oven to bake for 30-35 minutes or until set.
- Leave the oven door open slightly and allow to cool in the oven for 1 hour to avoid cracking.
- Move your slice to the fridge and allow to chill before slicing.

41. Condensed Milk Lemon Tart Recipe

Serving: 8 | Prep: 20mins | Cook: 50mins | Ready in: 70mins

Ingredients

- 1 1/2 sheets frozen shortcrust pastry
- 395g tin condensed milk
- 2 eggs
- 2 egg yolks
- 1 tbs lemon zest
- 1/2 cup lemon juice
- Whipped cream *to serve

Direction

- Preheat oven to 180C. Line a 24cm loose-bottomed flan tin with defrosted shortcrust pastry. Place in the freezer for 10 minutes to rest. To blind-bake, top pastry with a sheet of baking paper and pour in some rice or lentils to act as weights. Bake for 10 minutes. Remove baking paper and rice, then return to oven for a further 5-10 minutes until pastry is golden and cooked through.

- Reduce oven temperature to 160C. Meanwhile, in a medium bowl, whisk together remaining ingredients until smooth. Pour into pastry shell and bake for 25-30 minutes until just set.
- Allow to cool, then remove from tin and slice. Serve with whipped cream.

42. Delicate Lemon Cake Recipe

Serving: 10 | Prep: 15mins | Cook: 65mins | Ready in: 80mins

Ingredients

- 4 lemons juiced
- 200g butter melted
- 3 eggs lightly beaten
- 1 cup caster sugar
- 1 1/2 cups self-raising flour

Direction

- Preheat oven to 180C. Grease a 20cm cake tin and line with baking paper.
- Combine all ingredients in a medium bowl. Mix well.
- Pour into a prepared tin. Bake for about 50 minutes or until cooked when tested.
- Cool for 10 minutes of a wire rack.
- Ice with lemon icing or serve with ice-cream or cream.

43. Easy Lemon Meringue Recipe

Serving: 12 | Prep: 45mins | Cook: 50mins | Ready in: 95mins

Ingredients

- Base
- 1 cup self-raising flour
- 1 cup desiccated coconut
- 125 g butter

- 1/2 cup icing sugar
- Lemon filling
- 395 g condensed milk
- 2 egg yolks
- 1/3 cup lemon juice
- 1 tsp lemon rind
- Meringue topping
- 2 egg whites
- 1/3 cup caster sugar
- 1 tsp cream of tartar

Direction

- Grease and line an 18cm x 28cm slice tin. Preheat the oven to 180°C.
- Put the self-raising flour, coconut, icing sugar and melted butter in a large bowl and mix it until it all comes together.
- Press the base mixture into the bottom of the pan. Put it in the oven and cook for about 12 minutes, or until lightly golden. Cool for 5 minutes.
- In a large bowl whisk together the egg yolks, condensed milk, lemon rind and lemon juice.
- Pour the filling on top of the base. Return it to the oven and cook until the filling is just set (about 20 minutes).
- Beat the egg whites in the bowl of an electric mixer until soft peaks form. Add half the sugar, one tablespoon at a time, ensuring the sugar dissolves well between each addition.
- Once you've added half the sugar, add the cream of tartar, then continue adding the sugar gradually until it's all dissolved. (Test it by rubbing the mixture between thumb and forefinger to check for graininess.)
- Keep beating the meringue on a medium speed until stiff peaks form.
- Spread the meringue on top of the lemon filling and return it to the oven. Cook for about 10 minutes or until the top becomes lightly browned.
- Let it cool in the pan, then cut it into squares and serve.

44. Frozen Lemon Cream Pie Recipe

Serving: 8 | Prep: 30mins | Cook: 5mins | Ready in: 35mins

Ingredients

- 12 arrowroot biscuits
- 1/4 cup caster sugar
- 1/4 cup melted butter
- Filling
- 1 cup thickened cream
- 1/4 cup icing sugar, plus extra to dust
- 2 tsp vanilla extract
- 280g jar of lemon curd
- 250g cream cheese
- 1/2 cup condensed milk
- 1 lemon, zest only *to serve

Direction

- Preheat oven to 180C.
- Break biscuits into pieces, place in a food processor and process until fine crumbs. Add melted butter and sugar and process until well combined.
- Press the crumbs firmly into a 24cm round pie dish. Place on a baking tray and bake for 5 minutes until slight golden. Set aside to cool.
- To make the filling, whip the cream, icing sugar and vanilla until stiff peaks. Set aside.
- In a clean bowl, add lemon curd, cream cheese and condensed milk and beat until smooth. Gently fold in 3/4 cup of the whipped cream into the lemon curd mixture until combined.
- Pour the filling into the cooled pie shell. Top with remaining whipped cream and use the back of a spoon to spread it out. Freeze uncovered for at least 2 hours.
- Serve with a dust of extra icing sugar and lemon zest.

45. Lemon Almond Cake Recipe

Serving: 8 | Prep: 20mins | Cook: 30mins | Ready in: 50mins

Ingredients

- 100 g unsalted butter
- 1/2 cup white granulated sugar
- 1 tsp vanilla essence
- 1/2 tsp almond essence
- 2 eggs separated
- 125 g almond meal
- 1/2 tsp baking powder
- 1/4 tsp salt
- 1 lemon juiced
- 2 lemons zested

Direction

- Preheat your oven to 180C.
- Line the base and grease the sides of a 10cm diameter cake tin.
- Cream 100g butter, lemon zest and sugar together with electric beaters until light in colour and smooth in texture. Add your lemon juice, vanilla essence, almond essence and 2 egg yolks to mixing bowl and continue to mix until well combined.
- In a separate bowl, beat your egg whites on medium speed until they form soft peaks.
- Gently fold your lemon mixture into your egg whites. Once loosely combined, add in baking powder, salt and 1/2 your almond meal. Once combined, add the rest of your almond meal and fold until well combined.
- Transfer your batter into your pre-prepared cake tin and place in the centre rack of the oven to bake for 30 minutes, or until the top is golden brown.

46. Lemon Cake

Serving: 10 | Prep: 20mins | Cook: 60mins | Ready in: 80mins

Ingredients

- 1 cup Greek yoghurt
- 1 cup sugar
- 1 tsp vanilla essence
- 3 egg lightly beaten
- 1 lemon juiced zested
- 1/2 cup vegetable oil
- 1 1/2 cup self-raising flour
- 1/2 tsp salt
- 1 tsp baking powder
- Lemon syrup
- 1/3 cup lemon juice
- 1/3 cup sugar

Direction

- Whisk yoghurt, sugar, essence, eggs, lemon zest and juice in a bowl.
- Add the vegetable oil and whisk again well.
- In another bowl, stir together the sifted flour, salt and baking powder. Add this to the wet ingredients. Stir to blend.
- Place in greased cake tin and bake at 180C for approximately 40 minutes. Allow to cool.
- Lemon syrup: Dissolve lemon juice and sugar in a pot over low heat, stirring until sugar has dissolved.
- Pour syrup over cake.

47. Lemon Cake With Coconut Frosting

Serving: 10 | Prep: 45mins | Cook: 115mins | Ready in: 160mins

Ingredients

- 445 g plain flour
- 2 cup sugar
- 2 tsp bicarbonate of soda
- 1 tsp salt
- 1 1/2 cup hot water
- 1/2 cup lemon juice
- 2/3 cup rice bran oil
- 2 tsp apple cider vinegar
- 1 lemon rind
- Lemon Drizzle
- 1/4 cup sugar
- 1/4 cup water
- 1/4 cup lemon juice
- Coconut Frosting
- 270 ml coconut cream
- 2 1/2 cup icing sugar
- 1 cup margarine

Direction

- In a large bowl, whisk together flour, sugar, baking soda and salt.
- Add liquid ingredients and mix until smooth.
- Line a cake tin with baking paper and pour cake batter into tin
- Bake at 180C for ½-¾ hours or until an inserted knife comes out clean.
- Leave in cake tin and use a toothpick to poke holes all over the top.
- Spoon over lemon drizzle to taste.
- Leave to cool in tin.
- Spread with coconut frosting.
- Lemon Drizzle: Combine sugar, water and lemon juice in a small saucepan and bring to a boil over low heat.
- Coconut Frosting: In a large saucepan bring coconut cream to the boil and reduce liquid down until syrupy. Refrigerate to cool.
- In a mixer, whip the margarine until fluffy, add ½ cup of cold reduced coconut cream and beat until combined.
- Add icing sugar one cup at a time. Only add enough to achieve desired consistency for frosting.

48. Lemon Cheesecake And Blueberry Mille Feuille Recipe

Serving: 4 | Prep: 15mins | Cook: 5mins | Ready in: 20mins

Ingredients

- 4 slices puff pastry thawed
- 1 cup thickened cream
- 1/2 cup lemon butter
- 250 g Philadelphia lite cream cheese
- 1 punnet fresh blueberries
- 1/2 lemon zested
- 1 tbs icing sugar

Direction

- Cut 16 heart shapes from the puff pastry sheets using a cookie cutter.
- Preheat a sandwich press, layer 4 hearts between two sheets of GLAD BAKE and cook, checking regularly, until golden and cooked through. Repeat to cook the remainder of the hearts, then set aside to cool before filling.
- Beat cream cheese and lemon butter until smooth. In a separate bowl, whip the cream until stiff, then fold 1/4 of the cream into the cream cheese mixture. Repeat until all the cream is combined.
- Prepare a GLAD Bake piping bag with a star tip. Place one heart on a plate and then pipe cream cheese rosettes to form four layers, ending with a pastry layer.
- Sift icing sugar over the top, then scatter with blueberries and extra icing sugar to serve.

49. Lemon Crepe Cake Recipe

Serving: 8 | Prep: 60mins | Cook: 60mins | Ready in: 120mins

Ingredients

- 8 eggs beaten well
- 720 ml milk
- 480 ml water
- 600 g plain flour
- 170 g butter melted
- 1 cup pouring cream
- 1/4 cup Anathoth Farm lemon curd

- 1 tsp icing sugar *to serve
- 30 g fresh raspberries *to serve
- 30 g fresh blueberries *to serve
- 30 g fresh strawberries *to serve

Direction

- To make the crepes combine all of the crepe ingredients in a blender and pulse for 10 seconds. Place the crepe batter in the refrigerator for at least 1 hour. (This allows the bubbles to subside so the crepes will be less likely to tear during cooking.) The batter will keep for up to 48 hours.
- Heat a small non-stick pan. Add butter to coat. Pour 2-3 tbs of batter into the center of the pan and swirl to spread evenly. Cook for 30 seconds and flip. Cook for another 10 seconds and remove to the cutting board. Lay them out flat so they can cool, you can stack the crepes, they will not stick to each other.
- Whip the cream until stiff peaks form (be careful not to over whip, or you'll make butter!)
- Gently fold the Lemon Curd into the whipped cream. Refrigerate for 1 hour. Stir before using.
- To assemble, place 1 crepe on a flat serving dish. Spread about 1 heaped tablespoon of the whipped lemon cream on top of the crepe. Continue layering the crepes and whipped lemon cream, ending with a plain crepe on top. Refrigerate for about 1 hour or until firm.
- To serve, dust icing sugar of the top of the assembled crepe cake, and top with fresh berries.

50. Lemon Custard Pie Maker Doughnuts Recipe

Serving: 0 | Prep: 10mins | Cook: 24mins | Ready in: 34mins

Ingredients

- 2 cups plain flour

- 1 tbs baking powder
- 1 1/3 cup caster sugar
- Pinch salt
- 1 cup milk
- 1 egg
- 60g butter, melted
- 1 tsp ground cinnamon
- 1 tbs lemon zest
- Oil spray
- Lemon custard filling
- 1/4 cup cornflour
- 1/3 cup caster sugar
- 1/3 cup lemon juice
- 1 egg yolk
- 25g butter
- 1/2 cup water

Direction

- To make lemon custard filling, whisk cornflour and sugar together in a small saucepan. Whisk in 1/2 cup water and egg yolk. Stir continually over low heat until mixture thickens. Remove from heat and whisk in lemon juice and butter. Allow to cool in a bowl covered with plastic wrap.
- Make doughnut batter by whisking together flour, baking powder, 1/3 cup sugar and salt in a large bowl. In another bowl or jug, whisk together milk, egg and melted butter. Add to dry ingredients and whisk until smooth.
- Preheat pie maker according to manufacturer's instructions. Grease the plates with spray oil or a little butter on a paper towel. Scoop 1/3 cup measures of batter into plates, close lid and cook for 8 - 10 minutes until a skewer inserted into the doughnut comes out clean.
- Meanwhile, combine 1 cup sugar with cinnamon in a shallow dish.
- When doughnuts are cooked, use a small sharp-pointed knife to tunnel a hole in the side. Toss doughnuts in cinnamon sugar then fill the hole with lemon custard. Garnish with lemon zest.
- Repeat with remaining batter.

Serving: 0 | Prep: 20mins | Cook: 15mins | Ready in: 35mins

Ingredients

- 300g flour
- 150g butter
- 1 1/2 tbs sugar
- Splash of cold water
- Filling
- 3 egg yolks
- 1/3 cup sugar
- 1 tbs custard powder
- 1 cup full cream milk
- 2 tbs sour cream *optional
- 1/3 cup lemon juice

Direction

- To make the pastry, place the flour into a bowl and add small cubes of butter. Use your fingers to rub the butter into the flour until it resembles fine grains of sand.
- Add 1 1/2 tbs sugar, stir to combine, and then add a splash of water. Mix and then knead to form a ball. Place in a bowl with a lid on it and rest the dough in the fridge for up to 30 minutes.
- Meanwhile, whisk the egg yolks and 1/3 cup sugar together in a large bowl until thick and creamy. Add the custard powder and mix through.
- Heat the milk and sour cream if using in the microwave for 50 seconds. Gradually add the dairy mixture to the egg mixture while continuing to whisk. Gradually add in the lemon juice. Pour into a jug.
- Turn on the pie maker to allow it time to heat up. Roll out the pastry so that it is around 2-3mm thick. Cut into rounds large enough to cover the base of the pie maker.

- Gently press pastry rounds into the pie maker. Pour in the custard mixture so that it comes 3/4 of the way up to the lip of the pastry.
- Close the pie maker and cook for around seven minutes.

52. Lemon Custard Puffs Recipe

Serving: 0 | Prep: 20mins | Cook: 25mins | Ready in: 45mins

Ingredients

- 60g butter
- 1/4 cup milk
- 1/4 cup water
- 1 tsp caster sugar
- Pinch of salt
- 1 lemon, zest only
- 1/2 cup plain flour
- 2 eggs, beaten
- Lemon Custard
- 2 cups milk
- 4 tbs custard powder
- 2 tbs caster sugar
- 4 tbs lemon butter

Direction

- To make the custard, mix a splash of milk in a bowl with the custard powder and caster sugar to form a smooth paste. Heat the remaining milk to just simmering, then add to bowl with custard powder mixture and whisk to combine. Return custard to the saucepan and slowly bring to the boil, then reduce heat and simmer for 2 minutes, stirring continuously, until custard has thickened.
- Pour into a bowl and allow to cool, then whisk through lemon butter. Cover with cling film, pushing it down to touch the top of the custard to prevent it from forming a skin. Refrigerate until you are ready to serve.
- Preheat oven to 180C. Line two trays with baking paper.

- Place butter, milk, water, sugar, salt and lemon zest in a medium saucepan and gently heat to melt the butter. When the mixture is just about to boil, remove from heat and add flour, stirring with a wooden spoon to combine. Return to heat and beat vigorously for 1 minute to cook flour. Place in a bowl and allow to cool for a few minutes, then gradually add the eggs, beating continuously, until you have a smooth, thick batter.
- Place tbs-sized balls of batter onto the prepared baking trays a few centimetres apart. Dampen fingers and carefully smooth over the tops.
- Bake for 20 - 25 minutes until golden brown and cooked through. They should feel hollow when tapped. Allow to cool.
- Cut pastry puffs in half and spread with lemon custard and then top with the other pastry half.

53. Lemon Dutch Baby Cake Recipe

Serving: 8 | Prep: 10mins | Cook: 25mins | Ready in: 35mins

Ingredients

- 3 eggs
- 1/2 cup plain flour
- 3/4 cup almond milk
- 1 lemon zested
- 1 pinch salt
- 1 tsp vanilla essence
- 2 tsp white granulated sugar
- 1/2 lemon juiced *to serve *extra
- 40 g unsalted butter
- 200 ml coconut cream
- 1 tbs icing sugar

Direction

- Preheat oven to 220C.
- Place 200ml coconut cream in the fridge.

- Combine eggs, flour, almond milk, lemon zest, salt, vanilla essence and 2tsp sugar in a blender. Blitz until well combined and aerated.
- Place 40g of butter in a saucepan over high heat. Heat until melted. While still on the heat, pour your batter into the centre of the saucepan and immediately transfer saucepan to oven.
- Bake for 25 minutes or until golden brown.
- Meanwhile, retrieve coconut cream from the fridge and combine with 2tbs icing sugar in a mixing bowl. Using electric beaters on high, beat coconut cream until it forms stiff points. Set aside in the fridge.
- Remove from oven, pour over 1/2 lemons worth of lemon juice and top with coconut cream.

54. Lemon Pavlova Pie Recipe

Serving: 8 | Prep: 45mins | Cook: 120mins | Ready in: 165mins

Ingredients

- 3 lemons juiced zested
- 1/2 cup cornflour
- 1/2 cup white granulated sugar
- 6 eggs
- 250 ml water
- 1 1/2 cup caster sugar
- 2 tbs cornflour
- Base
- 2 cups self-raising flour
- 125 g unsalted butter
- 2 tbs white granulated sugar
- 1 egg
- 2 tbs water

Direction

- Preheat oven to 180C. Grease and dust a pie tin with flour and set aside.

- Base: Combine self-raising flour, 2tbs sugar and 125g butter in a food processor and blitz until the mixture resembles a crumble.
- Add one egg and water to the food processor and blitz until your pastry forms into a ball.
- Remove your pastry from the food processor, press into a ball, wrap in plastic wrap and place in the fridge for 30 minutes.
- Filling: Meanwhile, separate 6 eggs. Set your egg whites in the fridge and place the yolks into a medium saucepan. Add the zest and juice of 3 lemons, 1/2 cup of cornflour, 1/2 cup sugar and 1 cup of water to the saucepan, and whisk until smooth. Set aside.
- Retrieve your pastry from the fridge, lightly flour your bench, and using a rolling pin, roll your pastry out thin, to around 2mm-3mm thick.
- Carefully drape your pastry over your pie tin, press it into the base and using a sharp knife, cut off any excess pastry overhanging the tin. Pierce the pastry in the base of the tin with a fork 10-12 times.
- Cover with baking paper, fill your pie tin with pie weights and place in the oven to bake for 15 minutes.
- Remove your crust from the oven, remove pie weights and set aside.
- Drop oven temperature down to 170C.
- Place the medium saucepan with your filling mixture over a medium heat and whisk until thickened. Set aside to cool for a few minutes, then pour into your pie base and return to the oven for 15 minutes. Set aside to cool.
- Reduce oven to 120C.
- Line a baking tray with baking paper and sift a generous layer of cornflour on top.
- Meringue: Place 6 eggs whites into a large mixing bowl and using electric beaters, beat on a high speed. Gradually add in 1 1/2 cups of sugar, a tablespoon at a time, and 2tsp cornflour. Continue to beat on high until mixture is smooth, glossy and holds semi-stiff peaks.
- Scrape meringue mixture out onto your pre-prepared baking tray, allow it to natural form

a circular shape by pouring the mixture into a central position and letting it spread outwards.
- Place meringue in the oven to bake for 1 1/2 hours.
- Remove meringue from oven and allow to cool slightly.
- Gently crack open your pavlova and separate the crunchy crust from the gooey middle.
- Scrape the gooey middle onto the top of your lemon tart and arrange the pieces of crust on top.

Serving: 8 | Prep: 20mins | Cook: 45mins | Ready in: 65mins

Ingredients

- 2 sheets Pampas shortcrust pastry thawed
- 4 eggs
- 180 ml thickened cream
- 110 g caster sugar
- 2 tsp lemon rind
- 2 tbs lemon juice
- 2 tbs lime juice
- 1 whipped cream *to serve
- 1 handful fresh blueberries *to serve
- 1 sprinkle lemon zest *to serve
- 1 sprinkle lime zest *to serve

Direction

- Preheat oven to 200°C conventional or 180°C fan-forced. Place an oven tray in oven.
- Line an 11.5cm x 34cm fluted rectangular loose base tart tin with pastry, overlapping sheets to fit. Fold excess pastry over the edge and prick the pastry base with a fork. Line pastry with baking paper and fill with pastry weights or beans. Place tin on hot oven tray and bake for 15 minutes. Remove weights and paper. Bake for another 18 minutes or until pastry is light golden.

- Meanwhile, whisk eggs, cream, sugar, lemon and lime rind and lemon and lime juice in a large bowl until combined. Stand for 5 minutes. Pour into tart shell. Reduce oven to 130°C conventional or 110°C fan-forced. Bake for 45 minutes or until just set. Cool, then refrigerate until chilled.
- Serve with whipped cream, blueberries and lemon and lime zest.

56. Lemon Butter Shortbread Slice Recipe

Serving: 0 | Prep: 10mins | Cook: 30mins | Ready in: 40mins

Ingredients

- 250g butter, softened
- 1/2 cup caster sugar
- 1/2 tsp salt
- 1 tbsp lemon zest
- 1/4 cup lemon juice
- 1 1/2 cups plain flour
- 1/2 cup self-raising flour

Direction

- Preheat oven to 160C. Grease and line a 20cm square cake tin.
- In the bowl of a stand mixer, or using hand-held beaters, cream butter with sugar and salt until pale. Add lemon zest and juice and beat to combine. Add flours and beat until it comes together, scraping down the sides of the bowl as necessary.
- Press into the base of the prepared tin and smooth out evenly. Bake for 30 minutes until golden.
- Allow to cool. Make icing by sifting icing sugar into a bowl. Gradually add the lemon juice until you reach a spreadable consistency. Pour over cooled slice and spread out evenly. Allow to set before slicing into squares.

57. Lemon Sour Cream Slice Recipe

Serving: 0 | Prep: 10mins | Cook: 15mins | Ready in: 25mins

Ingredients

- 125g butter, softened
- 3/4 cup icing sugar
- 1 lemon, zest and juice
- 1/2 cup sour cream
- 1 1/2 cups self-raising flour
- For the icing
- 100g butter, softened
- 1/2 cup sour cream
- 3 cups icing sugar, sifted
- 2 tbs lemon juice

Direction

- Preheat oven to 190C. Grease an 18cm x 27cm slice tin and line with baking paper.
- Cream butter and icing sugar until pale. Add zest, lemon juice and sour cream and beat well. Add flour and beat until just combined. Spoon mixture into prepared tin and press into an even layer.
- Bake for 15 mins. Remove from the oven and allow to cool in the tin.
- Make icing by beating butter and sour cream until smooth. Add icing sugar gradually until it has fully incorporated, then add lemon juice. Beat at high speed for 4 minutes until icing is pale and thick. Spread over the slice base in the tin and refrigerate for up to an hour to set icing. Slice into squares and serve.

58. Monica's Lemon Cake Recipe

Serving: 12 | Prep: 15mins | Cook: 65mins | Ready in: 80mins

Ingredients

- 125 g butter
- 185 g sugar
- 185 g self-raising flour
- 4 tbs milk
- 2 eggs large
- 2 lemons zested
- Syrup
- 6 tbs fresh lemon juice
- 6 tbs icing sugar heaped

Direction

- Preheat oven to 160C.
- Grease and line a loaf tin with baking paper.
- Cream butter and sugar, beat in eggs.
- Add flour, lemon rind and milk and mix well.
- Pour into tin and smooth top.
- Bake for 30-40 minutes.
- Syrup: Mix lemon juice and sugar.
- After removing cake from oven, prick the top with a metal skewer.
- Pour over the lemon juice while cake is still hot.
- Leave until cold before removing from tin.

59. No Bake Lattice Lemon Cheesecake Slice Recipe

Serving: 0 | Prep: 15mins | Cook: 0S | Ready in: 15mins

Ingredients

- 2 tsp gelatine
- 1/4 cup boiling water
- 1 pkt Lattice biscuits
- 250g cream cheese
- 100g butter, softened
- 1/2 cup caster sugar
- 1/2 cup thickened cream
- 1 tbs lemon zest, finely grated
- 1/4 cup lemon juice

Direction

- Combine gelatine and boiling water in a small bowl and whisk until gelatine has dissolved. Set aside to cool slightly.
- Line a square cake tin with baking paper, leaving plenty of overhang. Place Lattice biscuits shiny side in a single layer in the base of the tin.
- Using hand-held beaters or a stand mixer, beat cream cheese, butter, caster sugar and cream for 4 minutes until smooth and thick. Add lemon zest, juice and gelatine mixture, and beat for a further 4 minutes.
- Spread cream cheese mixture over Lattice biscuits in tin in a smooth layer. Arrange more biscuits shiny side up on top. Refrigerate for 4 hours or overnight to set. Cut into squares to serve.

60. No Bake Lemon Cheesecake Slice

Serving: 0 | Prep: 40mins | Cook: 0S | Ready in: 40mins

Ingredients

- 2 packets Lattice biscuits
- 250 g unsalted butter
- 250 g caster sugar
- 250 g cream cheese
- 1 sachet gelatine powder
- 1/3 cup lemon juice

Direction

- Cream the butter, sugar and cream cheese.
- Heat the lemon juice (microwave is fine) and stir in gelatine. Add to creamed mix and mix until completely smooth.
- Line a rectangle baking tray with grease-proof paper, leaving some flapping out the sides of the tray so you can lift the slice out once set.
- Lay Lattice biscuits in bottom of tray (shiny side down), cutting biscuits to fit right to the sides.

- Spread the creamed mix evenly over the layer of biscuits. Add another layer of biscuits to finish (shiny side up this time). Refrigerate until set. Cut into slices.

61. Nonna Rita's Lemon Sour Cream Cake Recipe

Serving: 8 | Prep: 10mins | Cook: 80mins | Ready in: 90mins

Ingredients

- 250g butter, softened
- 2 tbs grated lemon rind
- 440g cups caster sugar
- 6 eggs
- 1/4 cup self-raising flour
- 2 cups plain flour
- 200g sour cream

Direction

- Preheat oven to 160C.
- Grease a deep 25cm round cake pan with baking paper.
- Beat butter, rind and sugar in a large bowl with an electric mixer. Stir in half the self raising flour, half the plain flour and half the sour cream.
- Once mixed add the remaining sour cream and remaining flours.
- Spread mixture into pan. Bake for 1 hour and 20 minutes or until cooked.
- Allow to cool on a wire rack. This cake can be served plain or top with icing sugar and strawberries.

62. Nonna's Lemon Ricotta Cheesecake Slice Recipe

Serving: 0 | Prep: 10mins | Cook: 50mins | Ready in: 60mins

Ingredients

- 250g digestive biscuits
- 80g butter, melted
- 500g ricotta
- 250g cream cheese
- 1/2 cup caster sugar
- 2 eggs
- 1 tbsp lemon rind
- 1/3 cup lemon juice

Direction

- Preheat oven to 180C. Grease an 18x28cm slice pan and line it with baking paper.
- In a food processor, blitz biscuits to form a fine crumb. Add melted butter and pulse to combine. Pour into prepared tin and press to form an even layer. Bake for 8 minutes.
- Reduce oven temperature to 160C. Wipe out food processor bowl, then add ricotta, cream cheese and caster sugar. Process until smooth. Add eggs, lemon rind and lemon juice. Process again until thoroughly mixed.
- Pour mixture over base and return to oven. Bake for 40 minutes until just set. Turn off oven and leave cheesecake to cool for 1-2 hours.
- Once cheesecake has cooled completely, slice into squares and serve.

63. Pink Lemonade Jelly Slice Recipe

Serving: 12 | Prep: 30mins | Cook: 10mins | Ready in: 40mins

Ingredients

- 250g butternut snap biscuits crushed
- 100g butter melted
- Filling
- 2 tsp gelatine powder
- 1 1/2 tbs water
- 375 g cream cheese softened
- 1 cup condensed milk
- 2 tbs lemon juice
- Jelly
- 3 tsp gelatine powder
- 2 tbs water
- 2 1/2 cups lemonade room temperature
- 1 tbs lemon juice
- 1 splash pink food colouring

Direction

- Line a 20cm square cake pan with plastic wrap. Combine crushed biscuits and melted butter in a bowl. Stir to combine. Press over base of pan. Refrigerate for 30 minutes or until firm.
- Filling: Sprinkle gelatine over water in a heatproof cup. Stand cup in a pan of simmering water, until dissolved and then cool slightly. Using electric beaters, beat cream cheese until smooth. Beat in condensed milk, lemon juice and then gelatine mixture. Spread mixture into pan and smooth the surface. Refrigerate for 3 hours or until just set.
- Jelly: Sprinkle gelatine over water in a heatproof cup. Stand cup in a pan of simmering water, until dissolved. Combine lemonade and lemon juice in a bowl. Tint with food colour. Whisk in gelatine mixture until combined. Pour jelly over filling. Refrigerate for 3 hours or until set. Serve slice cut into squares.

64. Quick Lemon, Coconut And Yoghurt Mini Muffins Recipe

Serving: 0 | Prep: 10mins | Cook: 20mins | Ready in: 30mins

Ingredients

- 1 1/2 cups self raising flour
- 1 cup Greek yoghurt
- 2 eggs
- 1 lemon
- 1/4 cup maple syrup
- 1/2 cup desiccated coconut

Direction

- Preheat oven to 160 degrees. Grease and set aside a mini muffin tray.
- In a large mixing bowl add the flour, yoghurt and eggs. Mix well.
- Continue to ass the zest and juice of the lemon as well as the maple syrup and coconut.
- Once you have given the ingredients a thorough stir through, evenly divide the mixture into the muffin holes. Pop them in the oven and cook for 15-20 minutes, or until the tops are golden and the centres are fluffy.

Chapter 3: Chocolate Cake Recipes

***

65. Beryl's Chocolate Cake Recipe

Serving: 8 | Prep: 15mins | Cook: 25mins | Ready in: 40mins

Ingredients

- 1 3/4 cups self-raising flour
- 2 eggs
- 1/2 cup butter
- 3 tbs cocoa
- 1 tsp cochineal
- 1 1/4 cups sugar
- 1/2 tsp bicarbonate of soda
- 1 cup milk
- 1 tsp vanilla extract

Direction

- Mix all ingredients together.
- Pour mixture into two greased sandwich tins.
- Bake at 180C for 25 minutes or longer if necessary.

66. Best Chocolate Dessert Cake Recipe

Serving: 8 | Prep: 10mins | Cook: 45mins | Ready in: 55mins

Ingredients

- 125 g butter
- 375 g dark cooking chocolate
- 1 cup brown sugar
- 1/4 cup plain flour
- 1 cup ground almonds
- 2 tbs milk
- 5 eggs
- 2 tbs cocoa powder *to serve

Direction

- Preheat oven to 170C.
- Line a 22 cm spring form tin with baking paper.
- Melt butter and chocolate together over a double boiler until melted and smooth.
- Add the sugar, flour, ground almonds, milk and eggs. Mix together well.
- Pour into prepared tin.
- Cover with tin foil, to stop over-browning.
- Bake for 40 minutes.
- Serve sprinkled with cocoa.

67. Best Moist Chocolate Cake Recipe

Serving: 10 | Prep: 20mins | Cook: 75mins | Ready in: 95mins

Ingredients

- 2 cups water
- 3 cups caster sugar
- 250 g butter chopped
- 1/3 cup cocoa sifted
- 1 tsp bicarbonate of soda
- 3 cups self-raising flour sifted
- 4 eggs lightly beaten
- Fudge frosting
- 90 g butter chopped
- 1/3 cup water
- 1/2 cup caster sugar
- 1 1/2 cups icing sugar sifted
- 1/3 cup cocoa sifted

Direction

- Cake: Grease a deep 26.5cm x 33cm, 14-cup capacity baking dish.
- Line base with baking paper.
- Combine water, sugar, butter, cocoa and bicarb soda in a large saucepan.
- Stir over heat, without boiling, and until sugar is dissolved.
- Bring to the boil, and then simmer, uncovered, for approximately 5 minutes.
- Transfer to a large bowl of an electric mixer and cool for approximately 10 minutes.
- Add flour and eggs, and beat until mixture is smooth.
- Pour mixture into prepared dish.
- Bake at 180C for approximately 50 minutes.
- Stand cake for approximately 10 minutes before turning onto a wire rack to cool.
- Fudge frosting: Combine butter, water and caster sugar in a pan, stirring over heat, without boiling, until sugar is dissolved.
- Add icing sugar and cocoa into a separate bowl, gradually stir in hot butter mixture. Cover and refrigerate until thick.
- Beat with wooden spoon until mixture is spreadable.
- Spread cake with frosting.

68. Chocolate Cake In The Rice Cooker Recipe

Serving: 6 | Prep: 7mins | Cook: 0S | Ready in: 7mins

Ingredients

- 1 cup self-raising flour sifted
- 1/3 cup cocoa sifted
- 1 cup caster sugar
- 1/3 cup butter softened
- 1/2 cup milk
- 2 eggs lightly beaten

Direction

- Grease and flour the bowl of the rice cooker (unless it is non-stick).
- Place all ingredients into a mixing bowl and using a mixer, mix on high for 4 minutes or until combined.
- Pour mixture into the rice cooker bowl.
- Press cook on your rice cooker. If you have a standard rice cooker, you will have to push the cook button several times until this cake is cooked. You may need a rest between each push so the temperature sensor can cool down. If you have an advanced rice cooker you can choose the cake selection. Test your cake with a skewer to see if it is cooked.
- Turn out onto a cooling rack to cool and serve with raspberries and cream.

69. Chocolate Custard Cake With Strawberry And Orange Compote

Serving: 12 | Prep: 21mins | Cook: 70mins | Ready in: 91mins

Ingredients

- 250 g butter softened
- 1 tsp vanilla extract
- 1 cup caster sugar
- 3 egg
- 2 1/4 cup self-raising flour
- 1/4 cup milk
- 150 g dark chocolate cooled melted
- Strawberry and Orange Compote
- 1 punnet fresh strawberries quartered
- 1 cup fresh orange juice
- 2 tbs sugar
- Custard
- 1/2 cup sugar
- 3 tbs cornflour
- 1/4 tsp salt
- 2 cup milk
- 2 egg
- 2 tsp vanilla extract
- Chocolate Ganache
- 1/2 cup thickened cream
- 100 g dark chocolate
- Decorations
- 12 fresh strawberries
- 80 g white chocolate melted

Direction

- Pre-heat oven to 170C. Line two round 22cm baking tins with baking paper on the base and grease the sides with butter.
- In a mixer beat the butter, sugar and vanilla until light and fluffy. Beat in eggs 1 at a time until mixed through. Add slightly cooled melted chocolate, milk and flour and use fold function on mixer until well incorporated. Do not over beat.
- Distribute cake into the 2 pans evenly and bake for 35 minutes or until skewer comes out clean in the centre. Allow to cool in pans before turning on the racks.
- While the cakes are in the oven put strawberries, sugar and orange juice in a small saucepan on low heat. Simmer for 10-15 minutes stirring occasionally and pushing strawberries down with fork. When you are left with a quarter of the liquid it is ready to take off the heat and place in a clean bowl until you are ready to assemble the cake. You want it to be thick enough that you can spread on a cake but liquid enough that the cake can absorb the liquid.
- Add 3 tbs of cold milk to the cornflour and mix until absorbed. To make the custard heat remaining milk in a small saucepan on low heat until it is hot. Add cornflour mix, sugar, salt and vanilla and whisk until the custard begins to thicken. Pull the pan off the heat.
- Add 1/2 cup of custard to the eggs and mix thoroughly before adding the eggs back into the custard/pan. Put the saucepan back on low heat and beat with a wooden spoon until the custard becomes nice and thick. Place custard on a clean deep plate or bowl and cover with cling film. Cool in the fridge.
- As the cakes are cooling make your chocolate ganache. Heat the cream until very hot in a small pan. Take off the heat and add broken dark chocolate into the cream. Allow to stand for 5 minutes then stir the chocolate through until glossy and smooth. Allow to stand for a further 30 minutes at least to thicken before assembling the cake.
- Melt the white chocolate and dip in fresh strawberries half way. Allow to set on baking paper until ready to assemble.
- To assemble take 1 cake and put on serving platter bottom side up. Spread a generous amount of strawberry and orange compote over the cake leaving a 1 cm border all around. Add the cool custard directly on top of the compote leaving the 1cm border as previously.
- Take the other cake and on the bottom side of the cake spread a generous amount of the compote.

- Place the compote side of this cake onto the custard part of the other cake.
- Place the ganache on the centre of the top cake gently pushing with the spoon towards the edges to allow the ganache to gently dribble off the sides.

70. Chocolate Easter Egg Mousse Cake Recipe

Serving: 12 | Prep: 40mins | Cook: 15mins | Ready in: 55mins

Ingredients

- Flourless chocolate sponge
- 70 g egg yolks
- 40 g caster sugar
- 90 g egg whites
- 1 pinch cream of tartar
- 45 g caster sugar *extra
- 45 g Callebaut dark chocolate
- 10 g Callebaut Dutch cocoa
- Chocolate mousse
- 285 ml Bulla pure cream
- 30 g caster sugar
- 60 g water
- 40 g liquid glucose
- 300 g Callebaut milk chocolate chopped
- Topping
- 160 ml Bulla pure cream
- 130 g Callebaut dark chocolate
- 20 g roasted hazelnuts roughly chopped
- 4 chocolate Easter eggs

Direction

- Flourless chocolate sponge: Line an 18cm cake ring or tin with baking paper.
- In a KitchenAid fitted with a whisk attachment, whisk the egg yolks and 40 grams sugar together until light and creamy.
- In a separate bowl, whisk the egg whites and cream of tartar to a medium peak.

- Gradually add the extra 45 grams caster sugar to the egg whites and continue mixing for one minute so the sugar dissolves.
- Melt the chocolate on a double boiler or in the microwave.
- Fold the cocoa powder and melted chocolate through the egg yolk mixture. Using a spatula, gently fold this mixture into the egg whites by hand.
- Place the mixture into the prepared cake tin and bake at 165°C for approximately 15 minutes. When it is ready, the top will bounce back after you gently press on the surface of the sponge. Because the cake is flourless, the top of the cake will collapse unevenly.
- Cool the cake on a cooling rack. Once cool, trim the top with a serrated knife to create an even layer.
- Reline the cake tin or ring with baking paper and place the sponge into the base.
- Chocolate mousse: In the bowl of the KitchenAid, whisk the cream to a semi-whipped consistency so it still collapses but has some body. Set aside in the fridge.
- Boil the sugar, water and glucose in a saucepan until the sugar has dissolved. Pour immediately over the chopped milk chocolate and whisk by hand until combined.
- Fold the mixture through the semi-whipped cream with a spatula. Use the mousse as soon as the mixing is complete. Pour over the chocolate sponge and place in the freezer for three hours or you can store it for up to one week. Cover it in plastic wrap once frozen.
- Topping: Unmould the cake while frozen and place it on your serving plate.
- Boil the cream and pour it over the chocolate and whisk to combine to create a ganache.
- While the ganache is still soft, spread it over the top of the frozen mousse and create some drips on the edges.
- Break the Easter eggs and place them in the centre and sprinkle with roasted hazelnuts.

71. Chocolate Indulgence Overload Recipe

Serving: 20 | Prep: 60mins | Cook: 60mins | Ready in: 120mins

Ingredients

- 4 cups brown sugar
- 2 cups strong black coffee (liquid)
- 500 g butter
- 500 g dark chocolate
- 4 eggs
- 3 cups gluten-free flour
- 1/2 cup gluten-free self-raising flour
- 1/2 cup gluten-free cocoa powder
- White chocolate ganache
- 250 g white chocolate
- 125 ml cream
- Dark chocolate ganache
- 1 kg dark chocolate
- 400 g cream
- Chocolate truffles and decoration
- 500 g milk chocolate
- 200 g cream
- 200 g coconut
- 200 g slivered almonds

Direction

- Make all three ganache components by gently heating the cream in separate saucepans. Remove from heat and stir in chocolate to each cream mixture. Once chocolate is completely combined, set aside for later use.
- Preheat oven to 160C degrees. Line 2 x 20cm round cake pans.
- Combine sugar, coffee, chocolate and butter in another saucepan and gently heat until sugar is dissolved, chocolate and butter is melted and mixture is smooth. Do not over heat. Pour into a bowl.
- Add eggs to mix. Make sure the mix isn't too hot or the eggs will cook.
- Stir in both flours and cocoa powder.
- Pour half of the mix into each prepared cake pan. Smooth surface and bake for 60 minutes.

Check to see if cakes set by inserting a metal skewer. If it comes out clean remove the cake from the oven. If not continue to cook the cake.
- Cool completely. Preferably refrigerate overnight
- To make chocolate truffles - Roll chocolate truffle ganache into 15g balls and roll the balls in coconut. Refrigerate until ready to decorate the cake
- To assemble the cake - Place one cake on a cake board. Beat white chocolate ganache to make it spreadable. Spread over the top of the cake, this is a good time to make a flat surface by adding more ganach to make it level. Top with second cake. Beat dark chocolate ganache to make it spreadable Cover top and sides of cake. Top with chocolate truffles and decorate with slivered almonds.

72. Chocolate Marshmallow Cake Recipe

Serving: 6 | Prep: 30mins | Cook: 60mins | Ready in: 90mins

Ingredients

- 86 g unsalted butter
- 225 g caster sugar
- 1/2 tsp vanilla essence
- 2 egg lightly beaten
- 85 g milk chocolate broken into pieces
- 150 ml buttermilk
- 175 g self-raising flour
- 1/2 tsp bicarbonate of soda
- 1 pinch salt
- 55 g milk chocolate grated *to decorate
- Frosting
- 175 g white marshmallows
- 1 tbs milk
- 2 egg whites
- 2 tbs caster sugar

Direction

- Grease an 850 ml ovenproof pudding basin with butter.
- Cream the butter, sugar and vanilla together until very pale and fluffy, then gradually beat in the eggs.
- Melt the plain chocolate in a heatproof bowl over a saucepan of simmering water.
- When the chocolate has melted, stir in the buttermilk gradually until well combined.
- Remove the pan from heat and cool slightly.
- Sift the flour, bicarbonate of soda and salt into a separate bowl.
- Add the chocolate mixture and the flour mixture alternately to the creamed mixture, a little at a time.
- Spoon the creamed mixture into the prepared basin and smooth the surface.
- Bake in a preheated oven, 160C for 50 minutes, until a skewer inserted into the centre of the cake comes out clean.
- Turn out on to a wire rack to cool.
- Frosting: Put the marshmallows and milk in a small saucepan and heat very gently until the marshmallows have melted.
- Remove the pan from the heat and leave to cool.
- Whisk the egg whites until soft peaks form, then add the sugar and continue whisking, until stiff peaks form.
- Fold the egg white into the cooled marshmallow mixture and leave to stand for 10 minutes.
- When the cake is cool, cover the top and sides with the marshmallow frosting. Sprinkle grated milk chocolate over the top.

73. Chocolate Mousse Cake Recipe

Serving: 12 | Prep: 40mins | Cook: 0S | Ready in: 40mins

Ingredients

- 200 g Aeroplane Sweet Treats choc honeycomb mousse
- 20 cm basic chocolate cake halved
- 500 ml full cream milk cold
- 200 g chocolate malt balls
- 300 ml thickened cream whipped

Direction

- Line a 20 cm springform pan with plastic wrap.
- Place ½ plain chocolate cake into base to create bottom layer.
- Beat milk with Aeroplane Sweet Treats Choc Honeycomb Mousse. Mix until just thick and creamy.
- Fold in half the amount of chocolate malt balls. Pour over cake layer in pan.
- Top the mousse with remaining ½ of chocolate cake.
- Spread with whipped cream and top with halved chocolate malt balls.
- Chill until ready to serve.
- To serve, lift cake out from pan using the plastic wrap as handles, and holding base gently remove cling wrap before placing onto a serving plate.

74. Chocolate Sponge Cake

Serving: 8 | Prep: 20mins | Cook: 25mins | Ready in: 45mins

Ingredients

- 4 egg separated
- 1/2 cup caster sugar
- 2 tsp golden syrup
- 1 tsp bicarbonate of soda
- 1/2 cup cornflour
- 1 tbs plain flour
- 1 1/2 tbs cocoa powder
- 1/2 cup chocolate icing *to decorate
- 1/2 cup desiccated coconut *to decorate
- Filling
- 1 cup whipped cream
- 1 tsp caster sugar

- 1 tsp vanilla extract

Direction

- Preheat oven to 180C or 160C fan forced.
- Grease a 20 cm springform pan.
- Place egg whites in electric mixer bowl and beat until soft peaks form.
- Combine caster sugar and bicarbonate of soda, and gradually add to egg whites while still mixing.
- Add egg yolks and beat together.
- Add golden syrup and beat again, briefly, until combined.
- Sift dry ingredients 3 times and then add to wet mixture. Fold in gently.
- Pour mixture into the prepared springform tin and bake for 20-25 minutes.
- Allow the sponge to cool for 5 minutes before turning onto a cake cooler.
- Cut sponge into two layers and fill with whipped cream sweetened with caster sugar and vanilla extract.
- Ice with chocolate icing and desiccated coconut.

75. Chocolate On Chocolate Cake

Serving: 20 | Prep: 80mins | Cook: 105mins |Ready in: 185mins

Ingredients

- 250 g butter chopped
- 1/2 cup milk
- 180 g dark chocolate chopped
- 1 cup caster sugar
- 1 cup brown sugar
- 3 egg lightly beaten
- 1 cup plain flour sifted
- 1 1/2 cup self-raising flour
- 1/4 cup cocoa powder sifted
- 46 g Cadbury Picnic Chocolate bar, finely chopped
- 1/3 cup caramel spread
- 2 x 46 g Cadbury Picnic chocolate bar, chopped *to decorate
- Milk chocolate ganache
- 2 x 220 g milk chocolate chopped
- 1 cup thickened cream
- Dark chocolate ganache
- 90 g dark chocolate
- 1/4 cup thickened cream

Direction

- Place butter, milk, chocolate, ¾ cup water and sugars in a saucepan over medium heat. Cook, stirring occasionally, for about 10 minutes or until smooth and combined. Set aside to cool completely.
- Preheat oven to 160°C/140°C fan-forced. Grease a 6cm deep, 22cm round cake pan. Line base and side with 2 layers of baking paper.
- Stir egg into chocolate mixture until combined. Add sifted flours and cocoa. Mix well. Pour mixture into prepared pan. Bake for 1 hour 30 minutes or until a skewer inserted into centre of cake comes out clean. Cool completely in pan.
- Make Milk chocolate ganache: Place chocolate and cream in a microwave-safe bowl. Microwave on HIGH (100%), stirring with a metal spoon every 30 seconds, for 2 to 3 minutes, or until smooth. Refrigerate for 30 minutes or until mixture is a thick spreadable consistency.
- Cut cake in half horizontally. Place cake base on a serving plate. Spread with ⅓ of the milk chocolate ganache. Top with finely chopped Picnic bar and dollop with caramel spread. Top with remaining cake half. Spread remaining milk chocolate ganache over top and side of cake.
- Make Dark chocolate ganache: Place chocolate and cream in a microwave-safe bowl. Microwave on HIGH (100%), stirring with a metal spoon every 30 seconds, for 1 to 2 minutes or until smooth. Refrigerate for 20 minutes or until cooled and thickened slightly.

- Spread top of cake with dark chocolate ganache. Decorate with extra chopped Picnic bars. Serve.

Nutrition Information

- Calories: 538.467 calories
- Saturated Fat: 19 grams saturated fat
- Protein: 7 grams protein
- Cholesterol: 69 milligrams cholesterol
- Total Fat: 30 grams fat
- Total Carbohydrate: 60 grams carbohydrates
- Sodium: 239 milligrams sodium

76. Chocolate, Raspberry And Macadamia Cake Recipe

Serving: 8 | Prep: 10mins | Cook: 30mins | Ready in: 40mins

Ingredients

- 1 cup frozen raspberries
- 1/2 cup macadamias roughly chopped
- 1 tsp Flora pro-activ spread *extra for greasing
- 1/2 cup icing sugar for dusting
- 125 g Flora pro-activ spread
- 2/3 cup caster sugar
- 3 eggs
- 1 tsp vanilla essence
- 4 tbs cocoa powder
- 1 1/2 cups self-raising flour
- 1/2 cup Pauls lactose-free Zymil milk

Direction

- Preheat oven to 180C fan forced. Grease a fluted round baking tin with Flora pro-activ.
- In a large bowl, sift together the flour and cocoa powder, then set aside.
- Using an electric mixer, beat together the Flora pro-activ and sugar until creamy, then add in the eggs one at a time, then the vanilla and the milk and continue to mix. Turn the mixer

down to low, then add in the flour and cocoa gently and mix until just combined.
- Sprinkle the macadamias and raspberries into the baking tin and then top with the cake mixture. Bake for 20 to 30 minutes, or until a skewer comes out clean. Cool the cake in the tin for about 10 minutes and then invert the cake onto a rack. To serve, sprinkle with icing sugar.

77. Dark Chocolate Cake Recipe

Serving: 12 | Prep: 30mins | Cook: 40mins | Ready in: 70mins

Ingredients

- 125 g butter softened
- 1 1/4 cup caster sugar
- 2 egg
- 1 tsp vanilla essence
- 1/4 cup cocoa powder
- 2 cup self-raising flour
- 1 tsp bicarbonate of soda
- 1 cup boiling water
- 500 ml whipped cream
- 170 g raspberry jam

Direction

- Preheat oven to 180C, and grease or line 2 round baking tins.
- In a mixing bowl, cream butter and caster sugar.
- Beat eggs in a separate bowl and add vanilla essence.
- Sift cocoa powder, flour and soda over butter mixture. Add eggs. Stir ingredients until mixed.
- Add boiling water slowly so eggs don't cook. Mix well and pour equal amounts into each baking tin.
- Bake for approximately 30 minutes, and wait 15 minutes before removing from tin.

- After cake has cooled, layer one cake with a thin layer of jam and a thick layer of cream and place other cake on top.
- Sift with icing sugar or top with chocolate icing.

78. Decadent Chocolate Mud Cake With Choc Swirled Cream Recipe

Serving: 12 | Prep: 40mins | Cook: 60mins | Ready in: 100mins

Ingredients

- 200 g butter chopped
- 150 g dark chocolate
- 1 3/4 cup caster sugar
- 1 cup milk
- 1 1/2 cup plain flour
- 1/2 cup self-raising flour
- 1 tsp vanilla essence
- 2 egg
- 1 handful white chocolate curls *to decorate
- 1 handful dark chocolate curls *to decorate
- Dark chocolate ganache and chocolate swirled cream
- 600 ml cream
- 225 g dark chocolate

Direction

- Grease three 18cm round cake pans, lining the base and sides with baking paper. Preheat oven to 160°C.
- Combine butter, chocolate, sugar and milk in a saucepan, stirring over low heat, without boiling, until smooth. Transfer mixture to large bowl and let the mixture cool.
- Whisk sifted flours into the mixture, then stir in essence and eggs. The mixture will be a smooth, runny consistency.
- Pour mixture into the cake pans and bake for 50mins.

- Turn cakes onto a wire rack to cool. Trim tops of cakes to level (if required).
- Place the cake base on a serving plate. Spoon half of the chocolate swirled cream over the cake. Repeat with another cake layer and the remaining chocolate cream. Top with the remaining cake layer.
- Spread top with dark chocolate ganache and decorate with white and dark chocolate curls/flakes.
- Dark chocolate ganache: Melt dark chocolate and ½ cup cream in microwave for 1min. Repeat until mixture is smooth. Set aside to cool.
- Chocolate swirled cream: Whisk remaining cream in a bowl until soft peaks form. Fold ¼ cup of cooled dark chocolate ganache through whipped cream to create a swirled effect.

79. Delicious Homemade Chocolate Cake Recipe

Serving: 8 | Prep: 15mins | Cook: 70mins | Ready in: 85mins

Ingredients

- 125 g butter softened
- 3/4 cup caster sugar
- 2 eggs lightly beaten
- 1 1/4 cup self-raising flour sifted
- 1/4 cup cocoa sifted
- 1/2 cup milk

Direction

- Preheat oven to 180C fan-forced. Grease a 5cm deep, 20cm round cake pan. Line bases and sides with baking paper.
- Using an electric beater, beat butter and sugar until light and fluffy. Add eggs one at a time beating after each addition. Stir in flour, cocoa and milk until combined.

- Spread in the prepared pan and bake for 1 hour and 10 mins or until skewer inserted and comes out clean.
- Stand in pan for about 5 mins on a cooling rack until cooled.

80. Double Choc Ripple Cake Log Recipe

Serving: 10 | Prep: 20mins | Cook: 0S | Ready in: 20mins

Ingredients

- 500ml thickened cream
- 1/4 cup cocoa powder
- 1/4 cup icing sugar
- 200g Choc Ripple biscuits
- 25g dark chocolate, to serve
- Fresh raspberries, to serve

Direction

- Whip cream until thick. Add cocoa and icing sugar and continue beating until fully combined.
- Spread a layer of chocolate cream along the middle of a long serving plate. Take one Choc Ripple biscuit and spread chocolate cream on the base. Stand the biscuit upright in the cream. Take a second biscuit, spread the base with cream and sandwich it with the first biscuit.
- Continue layering the biscuits with chocolate cream to form a long log.
- Use remaining cream to completely cover the log. Refrigerate overnight or at least 4 hours to set and to allow the biscuits to soften.
- Grate chocolate over the top and decorate with fresh raspberries.

81. Double Chocolate Cake Recipe

Serving: 0 | Prep: 15mins | Cook: 40mins | Ready in: 55mins

Ingredients

- 125 g butter softened
- 3/4 cup caster sugar
- 2 eggs
- 1 1/4 cups self-raising flour
- 2 tbs custard powder
- 1/3 cup cocoa powder
- 1/2 cup water
- Butter cream
- 125 g butter
- 1 1/3 cups icing sugar sifted
- 1/2 cup cocoa powder
- 2 tbs milk

Direction

- Preheat oven to 180C and grease a deep 23 cm round cake tin.
- Place butter, sugar, eggs, flour, custard powder and cocoa in mixing bowl.
- Add water and mix until well combined.
- Spread evenly in tin and bake for 40 minutes. Turn onto a rack to cool
- Butter cream: Place butter, icing sugar, cocoa and milk in a small bowl.
- Mix until well combined
- Spread over top and sides of the cake.

82. Easiest Mud Cake Recipe

Serving: 12 | Prep: 30mins | Cook: 95mins | Ready in: 125mins

Ingredients

- 1 1/2 cups hot water
- 250 g unsalted butter
- 200 g dark cooking chocolate
- 1/4 cup cocoa powder

- 2 cups caster sugar
- 2 eggs lightly beaten
- 2 tsp vanilla essence
- 1 1/2 cups self-raising flour

Direction

- In a saucepan over low heat melt together, butter, cocoa, chocolate, sugar, vanilla and hot water.
- When cooled add flour and eggs and mix well. The mixture will be very runny.
- Pour into a lined 30 cm cake tin and bake at 150 C for 1 hour and 15 minutes.
- Allow to cool for 5 minutes before turning out.
- When cool sprinkle with icing sugar.
- May be served re-heated in the microwave or cool with cream or ice cream.

83. Easy Chocolate Cake Recipe

Serving: 8 | Prep: 15mins | Cook: 85mins | Ready in: 100mins

Ingredients

- 125 g butter
- 1 1/2 cups sugar
- 1/2 tsp bicarbonate of soda
- 2 tbs cocoa powder heaped
- 1 cup water
- 2 eggs
- 1 1/2 cups self-raising flour

Direction

- Place butter, sugar, bicarbonate of soda, cocoa and water in a saucepan and bring to boil for 5 minutes.
- Allow to cool for 15 minutes and either beat in eggs and flour with beaters. Alternatively, put into a food processor, add eggs and flour and process for a minute or so.
- Pour mixture into a greased and lined 20 cm round tin.

- Bake in the oven at 180C for 55-60 minutes.

84. Eggless Chocolate Cake Recipe

Serving: 6 | Prep: 15mins | Cook: 35mins | Ready in: 50mins

Ingredients

- 1 1/2 cups plain flour
- 1 cup sugar
- 4 tbs cocoa
- 1 tsp bicarbonate of soda
- 1/2 tsp salt
- 1 cup water
- 1/3 cup vegetable oil
- 2 tbs white vinegar
- 2 tsp vanilla extract

Direction

- Combine dry ingredients.
- Combine wet ingredients and stir into flour mixture.
- Pour mixture into a 20cm round tin and bake at 175-180C for 25-35 minutes (pan should be 1/3 to 1/2 full, to accommodate rising).
- Stand for 10 minutes before turning out. Cake will be delicate while still hot.
- Microwave: using a ring or Bundt microwaveable pan, lightly oil the pan.
- Cut a paper ring to line the bottom of the pan. Pour in batter and microwave on high 5-7 minutes on a rotating turntable.
- Stand for 2 minutes in the oven when done. Cool for 10 minutes.

85. Flourless Chocolate Hazelnut Cake Recipe

Serving: 10 | Prep: 30mins | Cook: 40mins | Ready in: 70mins

Ingredients

- 1 cup hazelnuts ground roasted
- 6 egg yolks
- 3 egg whites
- 150 g unsalted butter
- 1 tsp vanilla extract
- 200 g dark chocolate
- 1 1/2 tbs cocoa
- 200 g caster sugar

Direction

- Preheat the oven to 180C, line the base of the spring form tin with baking paper and grease the sides.
- Melt the butter and chocolate in a saucepan on low heat then remove from heat once melted.
- Add the ground hazelnuts, cocoa and sugar in a large bowl, reserving 2 tablespoons of sugar.
- Separate the eggs and add the 6 yolks to the chocolate mix and beat until well combined.
- Beat the egg whites with an electric mixer until foamy then add the reserved sugar and beat until glossy.
- Combine the chocolate mix and the hazelnut mixture in the large bowl then fold in half of the egg whites.
- Repeat with the remaining egg whites.
- Place the mixture in the greased tin and bake for about 40-50 minutes or until a knife comes out clean.

86. Gluten Free Chocolate Cake Recipe

Serving: 10 | Prep: 15mins | Cook: 25mins | Ready in: 40mins

Ingredients

- 1 2/3 cup gluten-free all-purpose flour mix
- 1 2/3 cup sugar
- 1 tsp bicarbonate of soda
- 1/4 tsp salt

- 250 g butter
- 1/3 cup cocoa powder
- 1 cup water
- 2 egg
- 1/2 cup sour cream
- 1 1/2 tsp vanilla essence

Direction

- Preheat oven to 180C. Grease a lamington tin or a 30 cm x 20 cm flat tin, and line the base with baking paper.
- In a large bowl, sift flour, sugar, bicarbonate of soda and salt. Stir with a whisk.
- Mix cocoa and water until smooth.
- In a medium saucepan melt butter. Add cocoa mixture. Bring to boil, stirring to stop it catching on the base. Remove from heat.
- Beat eggs, cream and vanilla.
- Pour chocolate mixture into the dry mixture and beat well. Add egg mix and beat until combined. Batter will be thin. Pour into tin.
- Bake at 180C for 25 minutes for a lamington tin, or slightly longer for smaller tin, until skewer inserted in the centre comes out clean. Do not over bake.
- Stand 5 minutes before removing from tin.

87. Heaven Cake Recipe

Serving: 0 | Prep: 15mins | Cook: 45mins | Ready in: 60mins

Ingredients

- 350g dark chocolate broken into pieces
- 180g butter chopped
- 3/4 cup caster sugar
- 5 eggs separated
- 1/3 cup plain flour
- 1 tbs cocoa powder sifted
- 1 tbs icing sugar sifted

Direction

- Place chocolate, butter and sugar in a heat proof bowl over a saucepan of simmering water. Heat, stirring until mixture is smooth. Set aside to cool slightly.
- Add egg yolks to chocolate mixture one at a time, beating well after each addition. Gently fold in the flour.
- Beat egg whites until stiff peaks form.
- Lightly fold into chocolate mixture.
- Pour into a greased 23cm spring form tin.
- Bake at 180C for 45 minutes or until a wooden skewer pulls clean from centre of cake.
- Allow to cool in tin.
- Dust with cocoa and icing sugar just before serving.
- Serve wedges of cake with sweetened whipped cream and chocolate shavings.

88. Low Calorie One Bowl Chocolate Cake Recipe

Serving: 12 | Prep: 15mins | Cook: 35mins | Ready in: 50mins

Ingredients

- Cake
- 125 g unsalted butter chopped
- 100 g dark chocolate chopped
- 1/2 cup Whole Earth Baking Sweetener Blend
- 2 free-range eggs
- 3/4 cup milk
- 1 tsp vanilla extract
- 1 1/4 cups self-raising flour
- 1/4 cup Dutch cocoa
- 1 dark chocolate curls *to decorate
- Chocolate icing
- 1 tbs Whole Earth Sweetener Baking Blend
- 1 tbs boiling water
- 125 g butter chopped softened
- 2 tbs Dutch cocoa

Direction

- Preheat oven to 180C fan-forced. Grease a 22cm round cake tin and line base and sides with baking paper.
- Put butter and chocolate into a large microwave safe bowl. Microwave on high 100% for 30 second intervals, stirring, until melted and smooth.
- Add Whole Earth Baking Blend, eggs, milk and vanilla, then beat with a whisk until combined. Sift in flour and cocoa and stir with whisk until a smooth batter forms. Pour into prepared tin. Smooth surface and bake for 30-35 minutes or until cooked when tested with a skewer. Set aside for 15 minutes to cool slightly, then remove from tin and transfer to a wire rack to cool completely.
- To make chocolate icing: put Whole Earth Baking Blend and boiling water into a small bowl and stir. Then set aside for 5 minutes until most of the Baking Blend has dissolved.
- Put butter into a large bowl and beat with electric hand beaters for 1 minute or until light and creamy. Add the Baking Blend mixture and cocoa and beat again on low speed until mixed. Then beat on high for 1 minute until smooth.
- Spread icing over the top of the cake. Decorate with chocolate curls.

89. Moist Chocolate Cake

Serving: 8 | Prep: 10mins | Cook: 45mins | Ready in: 55mins

Ingredients

- 2 cup sugar
- 2 egg
- 2/3 cup canola oil
- 1 tsp vanilla extract
- 2 1/3 cup plain flour
- 2/3 cup cocoa powder
- 2 tsp baking powder
- 2 tsp bicarbonate of soda
- 1 tsp salt

- 2 cup boiling water

Direction

- Mix oil, sugar, eggs and vanilla.
- Sift dry ingredients together and fold into wet mix with the 2 cups of boiling water.
- Mix until smooth. Pour into a greased 25 cm square cake tin or 2 x 22 cm round tins.
- Bake at 180C for 40-45 minutes.

90. Moist Chocolate Cake With Salted Caramel Chantilly, Fresh Banana And Custard Recipe

Serving: 12 | Prep: 30mins | Cook: 60mins | Ready in: 90mins

Ingredients

- 1 1/4 cups plain flour
- 2 cups white sugar
- 3/4 cup dark chocolate melted
- 1 1/2 tsp bicarbonate of soda
- 1/4 tsp salt
- 2 eggs
- 1 cup buttermilk
- 1/2 cup butter melted
- 1 tbs vanilla extract
- 1 banana
- 1 tub Pauls double thick vanilla custard *to serve
- Salted Caramel Chantilly
- 1/2 cup white sugar
- 2 tbs water
- 1/4 tsp sea salt flakes
- 2 cups thickened cream

Direction

- Preheat oven to 150C. Grease and flour a 20cm round cake pan (or line with baking paper circles) and set aside.
- Start melting your butter and chocolate together over boiling water or in microwave.

- In a large bowl stir together flour, sugar, bicarbonate of soda, and salt. Add eggs, buttermilk, melted chocolate with butter, and vanilla extract. Beat until smooth (about 3 minutes).
- Pour batter into pan and bake on middle rack of oven for about 60 minutes, until knife inserted in centre comes out clean with just a few moist crumbs attached.
- To make the salted caramel whipped chantilly cream, boil the water and sugar in a large saucepan. When it is dark brown colour add the salt and start pouring the cream slowly and whisk rapidly (be careful: use a pot big enough because the caramel will bubble up double the size).
- Strain it into a bowl to cool down in the fridge, as soon it is really cold you can start whipping your cream until nice and fluffy (be careful not to over whip).
- To assemble the cake, cut the chocolate cake in half horizontally. Put some salted caramel whipped chantilly cream on the outside and some thick vanilla custard in the middle. Cut 1 banana and add it over the cream. Place the top of the cake back on and garnish with chocolate pieces if desired.

91. Nanna's Famous Chocolate Cake Recipe

Serving: 6 | Prep: 25mins | Cook: 35mins | Ready in: 60mins

Ingredients

- 1 cup water
- 1/2 cup rolled oats
- 100 g butter
- 1 cup brown sugar
- 2 tbs brown sugar
- 4 tbs cocoa powder
- 1 tsp vanilla essence
- 2 egg

- 1 cup plain flour
- 1 tsp baking powder
- 1 tsp bicarbonate of soda
- 1 pinch salt

Direction

- Simmer the water and rolled oats for 2-3 minutes.
- Remove from heat and mix in remaining ingredients.
- Pour into a greased cake tin and bake at 200C for 10 minutes. Reduce heat to 180C and bake for another 30 minutes or until cooked.
- Ice with chocolate icing.

92. Our Favourite Chocolate Cake

Serving: 10 | Prep: 30mins | Cook: 80mins | Ready in: 110mins

Ingredients

- 1 3/4 cup plain flour
- 1 1/2 cup white sugar
- 3/4 cup cocoa powder
- 2 tsp bicarbonate of soda
- 1 tsp baking powder
- 1 tsp salt
- 2 egg
- 1 cup ground coffee
- 1 cup milk
- 1/2 cup vegetable oil
- 1 tsp vanilla extract

Direction

- Preheat oven to 160C (or 150C for fan forced). Grease and line a 23 cm round cake pan.
- In large bowl combine flour, sugar, cocoa, baking soda, baking powder and salt. Make a well in the centre.
- Add eggs, coffee, milk, oil and vanilla. Beat for 2 minutes on medium speed. Batter will be thin.

- Pour into prepared pan. Bake for approximately 60 minutes or until toothpick inserted into centre of cake comes out clean.
- Cool for 10 minutes, then remove from pan and finish cooling on a wire rack.

93. Sarah's Chocolate Cake Recipe

Serving: 14 | Prep: 25mins | Cook: 80mins | Ready in: 105mins

Ingredients

- 2 cups plain flour
- 1.125 tsp bicarbonate of soda
- 1/4 tsp baking powder
- 1 tsp salt
- 1 cup boiling water
- 2/3 cup cocoa powder
- 170 g butter brought to room temperature
- 1 1/2 cups caster sugar
- 1 tsp vanilla essence
- 2 eggs
- Frosting
- 250 g dark chocolate chopped
- 250 g butter softened
- 1/2 cup pure icing sugar
- 2/3 cup sour cream
- 1/4 tsp salt
- Ganache
- 200 g dark chocolate
- 100 g butter chopped
- Decoration
- 1/3 cup pomegranate seeds
- 14 cherries

Direction

- Preheat oven to 180C. Grease and line the base and sides of a 20cm x 9cm (deep) round cake pan.
- Chocolate cake: In a large bowl, combine flour, baking soda, baking powder and salt. Set aside.

- Mix hot water and cocoa powder in a heatproof bowl until dissolved. Set aside for 5 minutes to cool.
- Using an electric mixer, beat butter for 30 seconds and then gradually add sugar. Beat for 2 minutes.
- Add eggs one at a time and then beat in the vanilla until fluffy. Gradually add the flour mixture and cocoa mixture in three parts until just blended.
- Pour the mixture into the prepared pan and bake for 1 hour and 20 minutes or until a skewer inserted comes out clean. Cool cake for 20 minutes. Turn cake onto a wire rack, top-side up. Cool completely.
- Frosting: Melt chocolate in a heatproof bowl set over a saucepan of simmering water (don't let the bowl touch the water). Stir occasionally until melted. Cool for 5 minutes. Using an electric mixer, beat butter, sugar and salt until light and fluffy. Gradually beat in chocolate, then sour cream, beating until well combined.
- Cut cake into 3 even layers. Place base on a serving plate. Spread with 1/2 of the frosting. Repeat with the second layer. Refrigerate while preparing the chocolate ganache.
- Chocolate ganache: Melt chocolate in a heatproof bowl over simmering water (again, don't let the bowl touch the water). Gradually add butter and stir until smooth. Set aside for 5 minutes to cool. Drizzle over the cake and decorate with pomegranate seeds and cherries. Serve immediately.

94. Simple Chocolate Cake Recipe

Serving: 10 | Prep: 15mins | Cook: 50mins | Ready in: 65mins

Ingredients

- 1 cup self-raising flour
- 3 tbs cocoa powder
- 250g unsalted butter
- 1/2 cup caster sugar

- 1 tsp vanilla essence
- 2 eggs
- Icing
- 1 cup icing sugar sifted
- 1 tsp cocoa powder sifted
- 1 dash milk
- 2 tsp butter softened

Direction

- In a bowl, combine flour, cocoa, sugar, vanilla essence and melted butter.
- Add eggs and mix together for 1 minute.
- Pour into a lined cake tin and bake for 25 - 35 minutes at 160C.
- If the cake springs back it's cooked. Do not overcook.
- Icing: Mix together icing sugar, cocoa, milk and butter.
- Ice cake once it has cooled.

Chapter 4: Christmas Cake Recipes

***

95. 3 Ingredient Mini Christmas Cakes Recipe

Serving: 10 | Prep: 5mins | Cook: 35mins | Ready in: 40mins

Ingredients

- 1 kg mixed dried fruit
- 3 cups cranberry juice
- 3 cups self-raising flour

Direction

- Combine mixed dried fruit and cranberry juice in a bowl. Stir well and allow to soak for 24 hours. Stir every 6-8 hours.
- Preheat oven to 125C.
- Stir flour into fruit mix and combine well. Add up to another cup of juice here if the fruit has absorbed all the liquid.
- Spoon mixture into patty pans and bake for 25-35 minutes or until a skewer inserted in the middle of the cake comes out clean.

96. Best Christmas Cake Recipe

Serving: 12 | Prep: 35mins | Cook: 175mins |Ready in: 210mins

Ingredients

- 375 g sultanas
- 250 g raisins chopped
- 250 g currants
- 125 g mixed peel
- 125 g glace cherries halved
- 60 g glace pineapple chopped
- 250 g butter
- 1 cup brown sugar firmly packed
- 1/2 cup brandy
- 1/2 cup water
- 2 tsp orange rind grated
- 1 tsp lemon rind grated
- 1 tbs treacle
- 2 eggs lightly beaten
- 1 3/4 cups plain flour
- 1/3 cup self-raising flour
- 1 1/2 tsp bicarbonate of soda

Direction

- Line a deep 23 cm or 20 cm square cake tin with three thicknesses of greaseproof paper, bringing paper 5 cm above the edge of tin.
- Combine fruit, butter, sugar, brandy and water in a pan, stir over heat until butter is melted and sugar dissolved.

- Bring to the boil, reduce heat and simmer covered for 10 minutes.
- Remove from heat, cool to room temperature.
- Stir in orange and lemon rind, treacle and eggs.
- Stir in sifted dry ingredients, spread mixture evenly into tin.
- Bake at 140C for 2-2½ hours. Cover hot cake with foil, cool in tin.

97. Boiled Fruit Cake

Serving: 0 | Prep: 240mins | Cook: 80mins |Ready in: 320mins

Ingredients

- 1 kg mixed fruit
- 1 cup sherry
- 1 cup brown sugar
- 1 cup water
- 250 g butter chopped
- 1 tsp bicarbonate of soda
- 1 tsp vanilla essence
- 1 1/2 cup self-raising flour sifted
- 1/2 cup plain flour sifted
- 4 large egg lightly beaten

Direction

- Place fruit in a large, stainless steel saucepan.
- Add sherry and leave for at least 4 hours, or preferably overnight.
- Line base and sides of a round 23 cm x 9 cm deep cake tin with non-stick baking paper.
- Add sugar, water and butter to the fruit.
- Place over low heat and stir occasionally until butter is melted.
- Add bicarbonate of soda and vanilla essence. Simmer for 1 minute.
- Allow mixture to cool.
- Add the flours, alternating with the eggs, folding with a wooden spoon until well blended. Do not over mix.
- Spoon mixture into prepared tin.

- Bake at 180C (150-160C fan forced) for 1-1¼ hours, or until a skewer inserted into the centre comes out clean.
- Cool in the tin before turning onto a cake rack.

98. Boiled Fruit Cake Recipe

Serving: 10 | Prep: 15mins | Cook: 65mins | Ready in: 80mins

Ingredients

- 1 cup water
- 1 cup sugar
- 375g mixed dried fruit
- 200g butter
- 1 tsp mixed spice
- 1 tsp bicarbonate of soda
- 2 eggs beaten
- 2 cups self-raising flour

Direction

- Boil all ingredients together for 5 minutes (except eggs and flour).
- When cooled, add eggs and flour.
- Pour into a greased cake tin and bake for approximately 1 hour at 160-180C.

99. Bud's Christmas Cake

Serving: 0 | Prep: 360mins | Cook: 180mins | Ready in: 540mins

Ingredients

- 3 cup butter
- 3 cup raw sugar
- 6 cup plain flour
- 1 pinch salt
- 8 cup mixed fruit
- 3 tsp treacle
- 2 cup almonds

- 2 cup walnuts
- 2 cup hazelnuts
- 2 tsp ground cinnamon
- 12 egg
- 2 lemon juiced
- 750 ml brandy

Direction

- Soak mixed fruit and nuts in half the rum or brandy for at least 1 week or more.
- Stir once a day to ensure liquid is well blended. Fruit should swell.
- Preheat oven to 180C.
- Cream butter and sugar. Add eggs one at a time and beat well.
- Sift flour, salt and spices together.
- Add to egg mixture and slowly blend in well.
- Add half of the fruit and nut mix and lemon juice and blend in.
- Fold in remaining fruit and nut mix.
- Place batter in large greased and lined cake tin and bake for 3 hours or until cooked.
- Remove from oven and pour remaining alcohol evenly over hot cake.
- Allow to cool, turn out onto presentation plate and decorate.

100.   Chocolate Royal Christmas Cakes Recipe

Serving: 0 | Prep: 10mins | Cook: 0S | Ready in: 10mins

Ingredients

- 12 Arnott's Chocolate Royals
- 100 g white chocolate
- 12 spearmint leaf lollies
- 12 Cadbury Jaffas

Direction

- Melt white chocolate, then drizzle on top of Chocolate Royals, so that it trickles down the side.

- Alternatively the Chocolate Royals can be dipped into the chocolate.
- Place a Jaffa on top of each, then place half a mint leaf either side.

---

101. Christmas Cake

Serving: 0 | Prep: 120mins | Cook: 210mins | Ready in: 330mins

Ingredients

- 750 g mixed dried fruit
- 150 g dried dates chopped
- 120 g dried apricots chopped
- 1/2 cup Cointreau
- 440 g (crushed) canned pineapple
- 180 g unsalted butter softened
- 1 cup brown sugar
- 3 egg
- 1 1/2 cup plain flour
- 2/3 cup self-raising flour
- 1/2 tsp bicarbonate of soda
- 1 tbs mixed spice
- 1 tbs ground cinnamon
- 1 tbs ground nutmeg
- 1/4 cup blanched almonds
- 100 g glace cherries

Direction

- Combine fruit, dates, apricot and Cointreau in a bowl. Soak for 2 hours, then stir in pineapple.
- Preheat oven to 160C. Line base and sides of a 22 cm round tin with 2 layers of baking paper.
- Cream butter and sugar with an electric mixer.
- Add eggs, 1 at a time, beating after each addition. Mixture will look curdled at this stage.
- Sift dry ingredients and fold in alternately with fruit mixture, in 3 batches, until well combined. Spoon mixture into tin.
- Smooth surface with a wet hand to help prevent large cracks. Tap cake tin on bench a couple of times to remove any air pockets.
- Decorate the top outer edge of the cake with almonds, then a circle of cherries and finish with a centre circle of almonds.
- Bake for 3½ hours, or until an inserted skewer comes out clean. Cover cake with foil mid way through cooking to prevent overbrowning.
- Remove cake from oven and place a sheet of baking paper on top.
- Leave hot cake in tin and wrap with 2 large tea towels, then place in a plastic bag. This will allow steam to moisten the cake. Leave overnight to cool.

---

102. Christmas Cake Balls Recipe

Serving: 0 | Prep: 15mins | Cook: 15mins | Ready in: 30mins

Ingredients

- 800 g dark fruit cake
- 250 g dark chocolate
- 125 g butter
- 2 tbs rum
- 1 orange zested *optional
- Icing
- 250 g dark chocolate
- 40 silver cachous

Direction

- Melt the butter and chocolate in a bowl over hot water.
- Crumble the fruit cake into a large bowl.
- Add the rum and mix it through.
- Stir in melted butter and chocolate mixture until it is combined and pour it into the cake mixture. Mix well until all is combined.
- Line baking trays with greaseproof paper. Roll a teaspoon of the mixture into a ball, place on trays.

- Continue until all the mixture is used up.
- Refrigerate for 1-2 hours to set.
- Make white glace icing or melt chocolate. Ice the balls, allowing the icing/chocolate to trickle down the sides.
- Put a small piece of glace cherry or a silver cachou on top of each one and return to the refrigerator to set.

103. Christmas Gift Cake

Serving: 8 | Prep: 0S | Cook: 130mins | Ready in: 130mins

Ingredients

- 400 g sweetened condensed milk
- 400 g water
- 250 g butter
- 500 g mixed fruit beaten
- 3 egg beaten
- 1/4 cup glace cherries
- 1/4 cup mixed nuts
- 2 1/2 cup plain flour
- 1 tsp bicarbonate of soda
- 1/2 tsp nutmeg
- 1/2 tsp ginger
- 1/2 tsp cinnamon sugar
- 1 tsp instant coffee powder
- 1 pinch salt
- Syrup
- 1/2 cup brandy
- 3 tbs golden syrup

Direction

- Boil the the condensed milk, water, butter and mixed fruit together for 3 minutes. Cool.
- Add remaining ingredients.
- Place mixture into 2 x 15 cm tins lined with baking paper.
- Bake at 125-140C for 1-2 hours.
- Bring the syrup ingredients to the boil. Pour slowly over hot cake.

104. Christmas Stained Glass Cake

Serving: 20 | Prep: 15mins | Cook: 80mins | Ready in: 95mins

Ingredients

- 500 g brazil nut whole
- 12 dates
- 1 cup glace cherries whole
- 3/4 cup plain flour
- 1/2 tsp baking powder
- 1/2 tsp salt
- 1/4 cup caster sugar
- 3 egg
- 1 tsp vanilla essence

Direction

- Grease a loaf tin and line sides and base with greaseproof paper.
- Heat oven to 150C.
- Mix all dry ingredients together and beat eggs until frothy.
- Pour into mixture and add vanilla.
- Stir well until all mixture is combined.
- Spoon into tin and bake for approximately 1 hour.
- Remove from tin and peel off paper.
- Leave to cool and then slice very thinly to serve.
- Store in the fridge, wrapped in foil.

105. Father In Law's Rum Plum Pudding Recipe

Serving: 8 | Prep: 10mins | Cook: 180mins | Ready in: 190mins

Ingredients

- 1 cup self-raising flour

- 3/4 cup brown sugar
- 1 1/2 tbs butter
- 2 eggs
- 500g mixed dried fruit
- 1 tsp mixed spices
- 1/2 cup strong, cold tea
- 1 splash rum

Direction

- Grease and flour a pudding tin, or grease and flour a pudding cloth.
- Fill a saucepan one-third up with water. Put on a medium heat and bring to the boil.
- Meanwhile in a large bowl add the butter, brown sugar and flour and rub together. Mix in the eggs, dried fruit, spices, cold tea and rum. When ready, the mixture should be wet and glossy.
- Pour the mixture into the pudding tin or cloth. If you are using a cloth, tie it with string leaving some room to expand.
- Place the tin or pudding cloth into the saucepan of water, and steam for three hours. You may need to top up the water in the saucepan and do not let it boil dry.
- Turn the pudding onto a plate and serve hot with custard.

106. Fig And Craisin Fruit Cake

Serving: 10 | Prep: 45mins | Cook: 560mins | Ready in: 605mins

Ingredients

- 2 x 170g Craisins dried cranberries
- 350g dried figs, thinly sliced
- 1/2 cup brandy
- 250g butter, softened
- 1 1/2 cup brown sugar
- 4 eggs
- 1 1/2 cup plain flour
- 1/2 cup self-raising flour

- 2 tsp ground ginger
- 1 tsp ground cinnamon
- 1 1/2 cup pistachios
- 2 tbs golden syrup

Direction

- Combine the fruit and brandy in a large bowl and stand overnight.
- Grease and line a deep 23cm square cake pan with brown paper and 2 layers of baking paper.
- Beat butter and sugar with an electric mixer, until just combined. Add eggs, one at a time.
- Stir in fruit mixture and sifted flour and spices. Mix well. Spread mixture into prepared pan and press nuts into top.
- Cook at 150C for one hour.
- Cover cake loosely with foil and cook for 2 more hours.
- When cooked, remove from the oven and cover pan tightly with foil. Allow to cool completely. To serve brush with warmed golden syrup.

107. Gluten Free Thermomix Christmas Cake

Serving: 0 | Prep: 25mins | Cook: 455mins | Ready in: 480mins

Ingredients

- 100 g pitted dates
- 150 g raisins
- 150 g currants
- 100 g dried cranberries
- 100 g mixed peel
- 200 g brown sugar
- 1 orange zest only
- 1/2 tsp salt
- 300 g unsalted butter
- 100 g water
- 90 g brandy
- 300 g gluten-free all-purpose flour mix

- 150 g pecans
- 1 tsp ground cinnamon
- 1/2 tsp ground nutmeg
- 1/2 tsp ground ginger
- 1/4 tsp ground cloves
- 80 g glace cherries
- 5 eggs
- 1/4 cup pure icing sugar for dusting

Direction

- Place dates, raisins, currants, cranberries, mixed peel, sugar, orange zest, salt, butter and water into mixing bowl and cook 10 min / 100 degrees / reverse / speed soft . Transfer into a large bowl.
- Place a separate bowl onto mixing bowl lid and weigh brandy into bowl. Add brandy to fruit mixture, stir to combine and set aside to macerate for 4 hours. Clean and dry mixing bowl.
- Preheat oven to 130°C. Double line a square cake tin (20 cm) with baking paper and set aside.
- Place flour mix, nuts, spices and cherries into mixing bowl and mix 5 sec / reverse / speed 2. Transfer into large bowl with fruit mixture.
- Place eggs into mixing bowl and mix 5 sec/speed 6. Transfer into large bowl with flour and fruit mixture. Stir well until all ingredients are incorporated.
- Transfer into prepared cake tin and smooth top with aid of spatula. Bake for 2½-3 hours (130°C), or until a wooden skewer inserted into the centre of the cake comes out clean. Allow cake to cool in tin for 10 minutes, then turn out onto a wire rack to cool completely. When cake is cool, wrap in aluminium foil until ready to serve (see Tips). Dust with icing sugar or decorate as desired.

108.   Limoncello Christmas Cake Recipe

Serving: 12 | Prep: 30mins | Cook: 2mins | Ready in: 32mins

Ingredients

- 225g butter
- 100g raw sugar
- 125g brown sugar
- 1 tbs molasses
- 4 eggs
- 340g plain flour
- 1 tsp cinnamon
- 1 tsp nutmeg
- 1kg dried mixed fruit
- 100g almonds, chopped
- 1/2 lemon, rind only
- 4 tbs limoncello

Direction

- Pour the limoncello over the dried fruit and chopped almonds and allow it to soak overnight.
- Grease and line a 23cm round tin with baking paper.
- Melt the butter in a small saucepan and then add the sugars, molasses and eggs. Add the spices, flour and the butter mixture to the dried fruit in batches, and stir with a large wooden spoon until stiff and thick. If you think the mixture is too heavy, add a tbs or two of milk.
- Spoon into the cake tin and bake at 150C fan-forced for one hour. The cake should start to be a bit brown on top. Reduce the heat to 140C fan-forced and bake a further hour and a half.
- When cooked, remove from the oven and allow to cool.

109. Macadamia Christmas Cake Recipe

Serving: 0 | Prep: 0S | Cook: 0S | Ready in:

Ingredients

- Christmas cake
- 375 g Sunbeam sultanas
- 375 g Sunbeam mixed fruit
- 1/2 cup rum
- 250 g butter
- 1 cup brown sugar firmly packed
- 4 eggs
- 100 g dark chocolate melted
- 1 cup plain flour
- 2 tsp ground ginger
- 2 tsp ground cinnamon
- 2 cups Sunbeam macadamias halved

Direction

- Combine sultanas, mixed fruit and rum in a large bowl. Cover and allow to stand overnight.
- Preheat oven to 140°C. Line the base and sides of a 20cm deep square cake tin with a double layer of baking paper.
- Beat butter and brown sugar until light and creamy. Add eggs, one at a time, beating well after each addition. Add melted chocolate and beat until combined. Stir butter mixture into soaked fruit.
- Blend 1 cup of Macadamia nuts in a food processor until smooth, to make a meal.
- Sift plain flour, ginger and cinnamon onto fruit mixture, add macadamia meal and nuts and stir until combined.
- Pour into tin and level the top. Bake for 1½ - 1¾ hours or until a skewer inserted in the centre of cake comes out clean.

110. Malteser Christmas Cake Recipe

Serving: 6 | Prep: 15mins | Cook: 50mins | Ready in: 65mins

Ingredients

- 1 1/2 cups brown sugar
- 1 cup milk
- 190 g butter
- 1 1/4 cups self-raising flour
- 3/4 cup plain flour
- 3/4 cup cocoa powder
- 4 eggs
- 300 g dark chocolate melts
- 125 ml thickened cream
- 30 g butter
- 465 g Mars Maltesers
- 200 g white chocolate melts
- 2 Allen's Jaffas

Direction

- Preheat the oven to 180°C. Grease the inside of your pudding steamer with butter.
- In a large bowl put the brown sugar, milk and butter and melt it all together in the microwave.
- Now whisk in the dry ingredients: flours and cocoa. Mix the eggs together in a jug and whisk them in too.
- Whisk until it's all combined. Pour it into your steamer and put it in the oven (no lid) for 40 minutes. Check it after 40 minutes and turn the heat down to 170°C.
- Cook for another 10 minutes or until a skewer comes out clean. Let it cool completely before adding the ganache.
- To make the ganache, melt the dark chocolate, butter and cream together in the microwave. Leave it for about 15 minutes to set and thicken.
- Cut the bumpy top off your pudding cake, so that you can flip it over and decorate it down side up.
- Cover the cake with ganache.

- Before the ganache cools completely, start adding the Maltesers. Begin in the centre, forming one row down the middle of the cake. Work outwards from there in lines across the cake.
- Put the cake in the fridge to chill for at least two hours.
- Once the cake is chilled, melt the white chocolate melts in a bowl in the microwave. Leave them to cool to room temperature before you pour them over the cake (otherwise all the Maltesers will melt.)
- Once the chocolate is just at room temperature (don't wait too long or the chocolate will start to set hard again) pour it over the top of your cake so that it looks like the custard on a Christmas pudding.
- Finish it off with two Jaffas and some any glossy green leaves you can find in your garden. You could also use the holly from a Christmas decoration.

111. Melt And Mix Christmas Cake Recipe

Serving: 0 | Prep: 0S | Cook: 0S | Ready in:

Ingredients

- Cake
- 500 g Sunbeam Gourmet Selection mixed fruit
- 1/2 cup Sunbeam slivered almonds
- 2 cup plain flour
- 1/2 tsp bicarbonate of soda
- 1 cup brown sugar firmly packed
- 1 tsp nutmeg
- 2 tsp ground cinnamon
- 250 g butter melted
- 3 egg lightly beaten
- 1/4 cup brandy

Direction

- Preheat oven 150°C. Double line a 20cm round tin with baking paper.

- Combine all ingredients together and stir until combined. Spoon into prepared tin and bake for 1 hour or until skewer inserted comes out clean.

112. Mini Chocolate Christmas Cakes

Serving: 0 | Prep: 15mins | Cook: 100mins | Ready in: 115mins

Ingredients

- 1/3 cup apple juice
- 375 g mixed dried fruit
- 35 g dried apricots chopped
- 75 g soft butter
- 1/3 cup brown sugar
- 1/2 tsp vanilla essence
- 1 egg room temperature
- 1/2 cup self-raising flour
- 1/2 tsp mixed spice
- 95 g dark choc bits *to decorate
- 180 g white chocolate melts *to decorate
- 1 cup glace cherries

Direction

- Heat apple juice in a heatproof, microwave-safe bowl on high for 1 minute.
- Add the dried fruit and apricot and stir. Cover and set aside for 1 hour, stirring occasionally.
- Preheat oven to 160C. Lightly grease two 12 hole, 30 mL capacity mini muffin pans.
- Using an electric mixer, beat the butter, brown sugar and vanilla until pale and creamy. Add egg. Beat to combine.
- Stir in fruit mixture.
- Sift flour and spice over mixture. Stir until combined. Stir in chocolate bits.
- Spoon mixture into muffin holes to completely fill. Smooth surface and bake for 25-30 minutes, or until a skewer inserted into the centre comes out clean.

- Cool for 10 minutes in pan. Run a knife around the edges to loosen the cakes. Turn out onto a wire rack to cool completely.
- Melt chocolate according to packet directions. Spoon over cakes, allowing some to run down the sides.
- Arrange cherries on top to resemble holly. Refrigerate until set.

113. Mini Christmas Cakes Recipe

Serving: 0 | Prep: 40mins | Cook: 20mins |Ready in: 60mins

Ingredients

- 1/2 cup apple juice
- 375 g mixed fruit
- 1/2 cup dried apricots finely chopped
- 100 g butter
- 1/3 cup brown sugar
- 1/2 cup self-raising flour sifted
- 1 egg
- 100 g slivered almonds
- 1 tsp mixed spice

Direction

- Soak fruit in warmed apple juice for 30 minutes. Add brandy after warming if using a mixture.
- Cream butter and sugar, add egg and then rest of the ingredients. Mix well.
- Grease a mini muffin pan and fill each hole with cake mixture.
- Bake at 160C for about 20 minutes.

114. Mrs Murphy's Christmas Cake Recipe

Serving: 6 | Prep: 30mins | Cook: 200mins |Ready in: 230mins

Ingredients

- 250 g butter
- 250 g brown sugar
- 1 cup milk boiled
- 500 g plain flour
- 1 1/2 kg mixed fruit
- 3 egg beaten
- 1 tbs golden syrup
- 1 tsp bicarbonate of soda dissolved
- 1 tsp vanilla essence
- 1 tsp almond essence
- 1 tsp rum
- 1 tsp brandy
- 1 pinch salt

Direction

- Boil milk, and pour over sugar and butter. Allow to cool.
- Add all other ingredients and mix well.
- Line a 20 cm round tin with brown paper and then greaseproof paper.
- Pour mixture into cake tin.
- Bake at 160C for 3 hours, or 2½ hours for a square tin.

115. Mrs Roberts' Christmas Cake

Serving: 0 | Prep: 10mins | Cook: 270mins |Ready in: 280mins

Ingredients

- 500 g sugar
- 500 g butter
- 500 g sultanas
- 500 g currants

- 500 g raisins
- 560 g plain flour
- 250 g blanched almonds
- 250 g mixed peel
- 1/2 tsp liqueur
- 2 tsp lemon essence

Direction

- Line a greased tin with 3 thicknesses of paper and heat oven to 120C.
- Cream butter and sugar and add soda.
- Add eggs one at a time, beating well between each addition, adding a little of the flour if it curdles.
- Mix the spices, essence and ratafia into the flour, then add fruits and a little flour alternately until all combined.
- Bake for approximately 4-4½ hrs.

116. Mum's Boiled Fruit Cake Recipe

Serving: 10 | Prep: 15mins | Cook: 125mins | Ready in: 140mins

Ingredients

- 450 g canned pineapple crushed
- 375 g mixed dried fruit
- 125 g raisins
- 1 cup sugar
- 125 g butter
- 1 tsp bicarbonate of soda
- 1 tsp mixed spice
- 1 tsp nutmeg
- 1 cup self-raising flour
- 2 eggs
- 1 cup plain flour
- 60 g pecans chopped optional

Direction

- Combine the first 8 ingredients in a saucepan. Bring to the boil and simmer for approximately 5 minutes. Cool.
- To the cooled mixture, add the self-raising flour and 1 egg. Mix well. Add the plain flour and the other egg.
- Mix in the pecans.
- Place mixture into a well greased and floured 20cm x 20cm cake tin.
- Bake for approximately 2 hours at 150C.

117. Mum's Christmas Cake

Serving: 8 | Prep: 0S | Cook: 70mins | Ready in: 70mins

Ingredients

- 375 g mixed dried fruit
- 1 cup sugar
- 3 tbs rum
- 4 tbs butter
- 1 cup water
- 1 tsp bicarbonate of soda
- 2 cup self-raising flour
- 1/2 cup plain flour
- 1/2 cup mixed nuts chopped
- 1/2 cup glace cherries whole
- 1/4 cup crystalized ginger roughly chopped
- 1/4 tsp ground ginger
- 1/4 tsp ground cinnamon
- 1/4 tsp mixed spice
- 1/4 tsp nutmeg
- 2 egg

Direction

- Place first 6 ingredients together in a large saucepan and boil for 10 minutes.
- Allow to cool slightly, then add the remaining ingredients and mix well.
- Pour mixture into a greased and papered lined cake tin.
- Bake at 180C for about 1 hour.
- Check by inserting a skewer through the centre to ensure cooked through, as cooking

time will vary depending on the size of the cake tin.

118.   Mum's Easy Boiled Fruit Cake Recipe

Serving: 0 | Prep: 10mins | Cook: 80mins | Ready in: 90mins

Ingredients

- 1 cup sugar
- 1 cup water
- 3 cup mixed dried fruit stems trimmed washed
- 1 cup self-raising flour
- 1 cup plain flour
- 1 tsp nutmeg
- 1 tsp bicarbonate of soda
- 200 g butter
- 2 egg beaten

Direction

- Pre-heat oven to 200C.
- Place sugar, water, fruit, nutmeg, soda and butter into a large saucepan over low heat and stir until boiling. Allow to cool for 5 minutes.
- Add beaten eggs. Sift the flours and add to the mix and stir well with a wooden spoon.
- Put ingredients in a greased and lined 20 cm round cake tin.
- Bake for 1-1¼ hours or until skewer comes out clean.

119.   Never Fail Christmas Cake

Serving: 10 | Prep: 30mins | Cook: 100mins | Ready in: 130mins

Ingredients

- 1 cup water
- 1 kg mixed fruit
- 250 g butter
- 1 tbs white vinegar
- 2 tbs mixed spice
- 1 tsp bicarbonate of soda
- 395 g condensed milk
- 1 tsp lemon essence
- 1 tsp almond essence
- 1 tsp vanilla essence
- 2 cup plain flour
- 1 tsp baking powder
- 1 tbs lemon rind optional
- 1 tbs brandy

Direction

- Bring to the boil water, butter, mixed fruit, vinegar and mixed spice.
- Turn off the heat and add baking soda, condensed milk, and flavouring.
- When the mixture is cool, add the flour, baking powder lemon rind and brandy or sherry.
- Bake in a prepared cake tin at 140C, checking after 1½ hours.
- If using a fan forced oven, check after 1 hour.

120.   No Bake Christmas Cakes

Serving: 30 | Prep: 360mins | Cook: 0S | Ready in: 360mins

Ingredients

- 800 g fruit cake
- 1/2 cup sherry
- 40 g slivered almonds toasted
- 50 g dried cranberries
- 50 g dried blueberries
- 150 g milk chocolate
- 100 g white chocolate
- 2 tbs cachous

Direction

- Crumble fruit cake and mix with cranberries, blueberries and alcohol. Leave to marinate for up to two weeks, stirring occasionally.
- Add almonds and, using clean wet, hands, form mixture into walnut size balls. These can be placed in paper patty holders.
- Melt milk chocolate and spread on top of cakes. Melt white chocolate and dribble over milk chocolate to represent snow.
- Before white chocolate sets sprinkle with decorations.

---

121. Rich Christmas Cake Recipe

Serving: 12 | Prep: 20mins | Cook: 210mins | Ready in: 230mins

Ingredients

- 1 1/2 kg mixed dried fruit
- 250 g glace cherries red and green
- 100 g mixed peel
- 1 tbs orange rind grated
- 1 tbs lemon rind grated
- 1/2 cup brandy
- 500 g butter
- 1 1/2 cups CSR dark brown sugar
- 8 eggs
- 2 bananas mashed
- 1 tsp vanilla essence
- 4 cups plain flour sifted
- 1 cup self-raising flour sifted
- 1 tbs CSR soft icing mixture for dusting

Direction

- Place the mixed fruit, cherries, mixed peel, orange rind, lemon rind and brandy or rum in a large bowl and mix well. Cover and leave overnight.
- Cream butter and sugar until it is light and fluffy, add the eggs one at a time, beating well

after each addition, and then add the bananas and vanilla essence. Stir in the fruit mixture, mix well and add the flour. Mix until well combined.
- Place in a deep 25cm cake tin, which had been lined with two layers of brown paper and one layer of grease proof paper. Bake at 150°C for approximately 3.5 hrs, or until a skewer inserted into the middle of the cake comes out clean.
- Dust with soft ccing mixture.

---

122. Rocky Road Christmas Pudding Recipe

Serving: 0 | Prep: 15mins | Cook: 0S | Ready in: 15mins

Ingredients

- 290g pkt dark chocolate melts
- 100g white marshmallows
- 1 cup shredded coconut
- 1 cup unsalted peanuts
- 150g glace cherries
- 50g white chocolate melts
- 3 spearmint leaf lollies

Direction

- Line a small 3-cup capacity pudding bowl with a few layers of plastic wrap, leaving some overhanging.
- Melt dark chocolate in 30-second bursts in the microwave, stirring in between, until melted and smooth. Pour into a large bowl and add marshmallows, coconut, peanuts and glace cherries, reserving one cherry to garnish.
- Gently stir to combine and pour into prepared pudding dish. Cover with overhanging plastic wrap. Refrigerate for an hour to set.
- Melt white chocolate in 30-second bursts in the microwave, stirring in between, until melted and smooth. Removing pudding from the fridge and gently pull on the plastic wrap to release. Turn out onto a serving dish. Drizzle

over with white chocolate and garnish with reserved cherry and spearmint leaves. When white chocolate has set, slice and serve.

123.   Slow Cooker Christmas Cake Recipe

Serving: 0 | Prep: 10mins | Cook: 300mins | Ready in: 310mins

Ingredients

- 1kg mixed dried fruit
- 395g tin condensed milk
- 1 cup milk
- 1 cup Baileys Irish Cream
- 1 orange, zested and juiced
- 2 cups plain flour
- 2 tsp ground cinnamon
- 1/2 tsp ground nutmeg
- 1/2 tsp allspice

Direction

- Place dried fruit in a bowl with condensed milk, milk, Baileys and orange zest and juice. Stir well, cover and leave to soak overnight in the fridge.
- Remove from fridge and bring to room temperature. Stir well. Combine flour with spices, then fold through dried fruit mixture.
- Line base and sides of a slow cooker with 2 layers of baking paper, greasing the top layer with a little oil or butter. Pour in batter and smooth over the top. Place a tea towel over the top of the slow cooker just under the lid. Cook for 4 hours on low, until a skewer inserted into the centre comes out clean. Remove from slow cooker and allow to cool.

124.   Sultana Cake

Serving: 12 | Prep: 30mins | Cook: 75mins | Ready in: 105mins

Ingredients

- 225g butter
- 1 cup sugar
- 1 tbs cornflour
- 1/2 cup water
- 3 egg
- 1 1/2 cup plain flour
- 1 tsp baking powder
- 1 tsp vanilla essence
- 2 1/4 cup sultanas
- 3/4 cup water

Direction

- Preheat oven to 180C (160C fan forced).
- Boil the sultanas in the water until all moisture has been absorbed. Set aside to cool.
- Cream butter and sugar until light and creamy.
- Add eggs, one at a time, beating well after each addition.
- Hand mix through the vanilla essence and cornflour mixed with half cup water.
- Sift the flour and baking powder together then fold into the mix. If the mix should appear to curdle or separate, just keep stirring. It will come back together.
- Fold through the sultanas.
- Pour mixture into a greased and lined 20cm square or 22cm round cake pan.
- Bake for 1 to 1¼ hours or until cooked through.
- Leave cake in pan for 20 minutes before turning out onto a cooling rack.

125.   Super Moist Boiled Christmas Fruit Cake Recipe

Serving: 0 | Prep: 20mins | Cook: 70mins | Ready in: 90mins

Ingredients

- 500 g mixed dried fruit
- 125 g butter
- 1 1/2 cups water
- 1 cup brown sugar
- 1 tsp bicarbonate of soda
- 1 tsp allspice
- 2 eggs beaten
- 1 cup self-raising flour
- 1 cup plain flour
- 3 tbs sherry *optional
- 1/2 cup almonds

Direction

- Place the first 5 ingredients into a large saucepan and boil for 5 minutes. Cool mixture.
- Add eggs, flour, nuts, spices and sherry. Mix well.
- Bake in a springform tin lined with baking paper and cook in a 170C oven for 70 - 90 minutes. Cool cake in the tin before removing and storing in an airtight container.

126.   Unbaked Christmas Fudge Cake

Serving: 12 | Prep: 15mins | Cook: 0S | Ready in: 15mins

Ingredients

- 250g ginger biscuits, crushed
- 1/2 cup walnuts, chopped
- 1/4 cup sherry
- 1/4 cup golden syrup
- 1/2 cup icing sugar
- 1/2 cup marmalade
- 125g butter, melted
- 1/2 tsp cinnamon sugar
- 1/2 tsp ground cloves
- 3/4 cup mixed peel
- 1/2 cup glace cherries, chopped
- 1/2 cup prunes, chopped
- 1 1/2 cup sultanas

Direction

- Place biscuits and nuts into large bowl.
- Combine sherry, golden syrup, icing sugar, marmalade, butter and spices. Pour this mix over crushed biscuits and mix well.
- Add dried fruit and mix together.
- Spoon into a lined loaf tin, cover and chill for 24 hours before cutting. Store in fridge.

Chapter 5: Christmas Fruit Cake Recipes

***

127.   3 Ingredient Fruit Cake Recipe

Serving: 8 | Prep: 360mins | Cook: 90mins | Ready in: 450mins

Ingredients

- 375 g mixed fruit
- 600 ml chocolate flavoured milk
- 2 cup self-raising flour

Direction

- Soak the fruit in the chocolate milk overnight.
- Stir in flour.
- Bake at 160C for approximately 1½ hours, or until skewer inserted comes out clean.

128. Amazing Fruit Cake Recipe

Serving: 4 | Prep: 5mins | Cook: 90mins | Ready in: 95mins

Ingredients

- 1 kg mixed fruit dried
- 600 ml chocolate flavoured milk
- 2 cups self-raising flour

Direction

- Place fruit in a bowl and cover with flavoured milk. Mix and refrigerate overnight.
- Add the self-raising flour and mix well.
- Grease and line a cake tin with baking paper.
- Pour mixture into cake tin and cook for 1½ hours in a preheated 180C oven.

129. Boiled Caramelised Apple Fruit Cake Recipe

Serving: 16 | Prep: 15mins | Cook: 75mins | Ready in: 90mins

Ingredients

- 75g butter, melted
- 1/3 cup brown sugar
- 200g dried apple slices
- 400g tin condensed milk
- 400g tin pie apple
- 375g mixed dried fruit
- 125g butter
- 1 tsp cinnamon
- 1 tsp bicarb soda
- 2 eggs
- 1 1/2 cups self-raising flour

Direction

- Preheat oven to 160C. Grease and line a 22cm cake tin. Combine melted butter and brown sugar, and pour in prepared tin.
- Arrange 8 -9 dried apple slices over the caramel in the base of the tin. Set aside.
- Chop the remaining dried apple. Add to a medium saucepan with the condensed milk, pie apple, dried fruit, 125g butter and cinnamon. Cook over gentle heat for 5 minutes, stirring continuously to ensure it doesn't stick on the bottom. Turn off the heat and stir through bicarb soda. Set aside to cool.
- Beat eggs in a large bowl. Add cooled fruit mixture and stir to combine. Fold through flour.
- Pour batter into the prepared tin over caramel and apple circles. Bake for 40 minutes, then remove from the oven and cover with a piece of foil. Return to the oven and bake for a further 40 minutes until a skewer inserted into the centre comes out clean. Slide a knife between the tin and the cake to loosen, then up-end onto a plate. Peel off baking paper, dust with icing sugar and serve.

130. Boiled Cherry Fruit Cake Recipe

Serving: 10 | Prep: 10mins | Cook: 105mins | Ready in: 115mins

Ingredients

- 200g butter, chopped
- 375g pkt mixed dried fruit
- 200g glace cherries, plus extra to serve
- 1 cup brown sugar
- 1/4 cup dry sherry
- 1 cup self-raising flour
- 1 cup plain flour
- 2 tsp mixed spice
- 1/2 tsp bicarbonate of soda
- 3 eggs, lightly whisked
- Icing sugar, to dust

Direction

- Place the butter, mixed fruit, cherries, brown sugar, sherry and 1 cup water in a saucepan over medium heat. Bring to the boil. Reduce heat to low and simmer for 10 minutes. Set aside to cool.
- Preheat oven to 160C/140C fan forced. Line the base and side of a round 20cm cake pan with baking paper
- Add the flours, mixed spice, bicarbonate of soda and eggs to the fruit mix and stir until well combined. Pour into the prepared pan. Bake for 55 mins or until a skewer inserted into the cake comes out clean. Set aside to cool in the pan.
- Dust with icing sugar and top with extra cherries to serve.

---

131. Boiled Pineapple Fruit Cake Recipe

Serving: 20 | Prep: 15mins | Cook: 95mins | Ready in: 110mins

Ingredients

- 500 g mixed dried fruit
- 440 g (crushed) canned pineapple
- 1 cup sugar
- 125 g butter chopped
- 1 tsp mixed spice
- 1/2 tsp ground cinnamon
- 1 tsp bicarbonate of soda
- 2 eggs beaten
- 1 cup self-raising flour
- 1 cup plain flour

Direction

- Place fruit, crushed pineapple including juice, butter, sugar and spices in a saucepan. Boil for 5 minutes.
- Add bicarbonate of soda. Turn off heat and allow to cool.

- Add eggs and flour.
- Preheat oven 160C. Pour into a prepared cake tin and bake for 40 minutes or until the top is golden.
- Remove from oven, cover with foil and bake for a further 50 minutes.

---

132. Condensed Milk Fruit Cake Recipe

Serving: 8 | Prep: 25mins | Cook: 130mins | Ready in: 155mins

Ingredients

- 1125g mixed fruit
- 250g butter, chopped
- 1 tsp bicarbonate of soda
- 1 cup water
- 395g condensed milk
- 1 tbs white vinegar
- 2 tbs sherry
- 1 tsp vanilla essence
- 2 cups plain flour, sifted
- 1 tsp baking powder
- 1/2 tsp salt
- 1/2 tsp ground cloves
- 1/4 cup glace cherries *to decorate
- 1/4 cup almonds *to decorate

Direction

- Put mixed fruit, butter, bicarb soda and water in a pan and bring to the boil. Allow to cool.
- Add condensed milk, vinegar, sherry or brandy and vanilla essence.
- Sift flour, baking powder, salt and ground cloves, and gradually add to fruit mixture.
- Put into a greased, paper-lined tin and bake at 150C for 2 hours. Check with a skewer and adjust cooking time if necessary.
- Put a cherry in each corner and place almonds to make a flower effect.
- Brush with sherry or brandy to glaze.

133. Easy Christmas Fruit Cake Recipe

Serving: 10 | Prep: 60mins | Cook: 180mins | Ready in: 240mins

Ingredients

- 250 g butter
- 1 kg mixed dried fruit
- 200 g brown sugar firmly packed
- 125 ml brandy
- 125 ml water
- 1/2 tsp bicarbonate of soda
- 2 tsp orange rind grated
- 1 tsp lemon rind grated
- 1 tbs treacle
- 5 eggs lightly beaten medium
- 250 g plain flour
- 50 g self-raising flour
- 2 tbs glace cherries optional *to decorate
- 2 tbs blanched almonds optional *to decorate

Direction

- Grease a deep 23 cm round cake tin, line base and sides with 3 layers of baking paper to 5 cm above edge of tin.
- In a large saucepan, place butter, fruit, sugar, brandy and water.
- Bring to boil, stirring, then simmer covered for 10 minutes.
- Stir in soda, cover and allow to cool.
- Stir rinds, treacle, eggs and flours into cooled mixture. Spread evenly into prepared tin.
- Decorate with the cherries and almonds.
- Bake at 140C for about 2¾ hours, checking after 2 hours.
- Cover hot cake tightly with foil, cool in tin.

134. Easy Fruit Cake Recipe

Serving: 6 | Prep: 5mins | Cook: 60mins | Ready in: 65mins

Ingredients

- 200 g self-raising flour
- 120 g soft butter
- 160 g caster sugar
- 3 eggs
- 1/2 cup milk
- 1 tsp vanilla extract
- 1/2 tsp baking powder
- 1 cup sultanas
- 1/2 cup cherries

Direction

- Preheat oven to 180C.
- Mix dry ingredients together. Add fruit and then wet ingredients.
- Pour into a greased loaf tin and bake for 45-60 minutes.

135. Easy Mango Fruit Cake Recipe

Serving: 10 | Prep: 10mins | Cook: 50mins | Ready in: 60mins

Ingredients

- 375g mixed fruit
- 425g canned mango in syrup
- 1/2 tsp bicarbonate of soda
- 1 cup self-raising flour
- 1 egg
- 1/2 cup walnuts chopped,

Direction

- Place fruit, mango and bicarbonate of soda into a saucepan.
- Boil for 5 minutes. Allow to cool.
- Add flour, egg and walnuts and mix well.

- Pour into a ring tin.
- Bake at 170C fan-forced for 40 - 45 minutes.

136.   Golden Fruit Cake Recipe

Serving: 0 | Prep: 0S | Cook: 180mins | Ready in:
180mins

Ingredients

- Fruit cake
- 1 kg Sunbeam mixed fruit
- 125 g Sunbeam raisins
- 125 g Sunbeam currants
- 1 cup Sunbeam slivered almonds
- 1 cup brandy
- 1/2 cup (crushed) canned pineapple drained
- 1 granny smith apple grated small
- 250 g Western Star salted butter softened
- 1/2 cup caster sugar
- 2/3 cup brown sugar firmly packed
- 4 egg
- 2 cup plain flour
- 1/2 cup self-raising flour
- 1/2 tsp bicarbonate of soda
- 2 tsp mixed spice
- 120 g Sunbeam blanched almonds *to decorate

Direction

- Preheat oven to 150°C. Combine fruit and ½ cup of brandy in a large bowl. Cover and store in a cool, dark place for 5-7 days, stirring each day.
- Grease a 22cm round deep cake tin. Line with three layers of brown paper, extending papers 5cm above rim.
- Stir slivered almonds, pineapple and grated apple into fruit mixture.
- Beat butter and sugars together until creamy. Add eggs, one at a time, beating until combined. Add creamed mixture to fruit mixture, mix well. Stir in sifted dry ingredients. Spread evenly into pan. Tap pan several times on bench to settle mixture.

- Decorate with blanched almonds. Bake for 3-3½ hours or until a skewer inserted in centre comes out clean. Deeply prick over the top of the cake with a fine skewer. Spoon extra brandy over cake. Leave hot cake in tin and wrap in foil, then a thick tea towel to cool overnight.

137.   Golden Passionfruit Cake Recipe

Serving: 8 | Prep: 10mins | Cook: 40mins | Ready in:
50mins

Ingredients

- 125 g butter
- 3/4 cup caster sugar
- 2 eggs
- 2 cups self-raising flour
- 1/2 cup milk
- 4 passionfruit pulp
- Icing
- 1 tbs soft butter
- 1 1/2 cups icing sugar
- 2 passionfruit pulp

Direction

- Preheat oven to 180C.
- Cream butter and sugar.
- Add eggs and mix.
- Add sifted flour alternating with milk.
- Add passionfruit pulp and mix well.
- Pour into paper-lined or greased cake tin.
- Cook for approximately 40 minutes or until skewer inserted into cake comes out clean.
- Icing: Mix butter with icing sugar until well combined.
- Add passionfruit pulp and mix well.
- When cake is completely cooled, split it in half lengthways. Ice lower half with ⅓ of the icing.
- Place the top back on and ice with the remaining icing.

138. Gourmet Fruit Cake

Serving: 10 | Prep: 30mins | Cook: 140mins | Ready in: 170mins

Ingredients

- 1 1/2 cup mixed nuts roughly chopped
- 4 cup mixed dried fruit
- 3/4 cup dried apricots
- 1/2 cup brandy
- 1 cup glace cherries chopped
- 3/4 cup plain flour
- 3/4 cup sugar
- 1/2 tsp baking powder
- 3 egg
- 1 tsp vanilla essence

Direction

- Soak the dried fruit in the brandy in a large bowl until soft.
- Add the nuts and cherries.
- Sift dry ingredients together 2 to 3 times and add to the fruit.
- Add beaten eggs and vanilla, and mix well.
- Pour into a greased and lined ring tin.
- Bake in a slow oven for 1½-2 hours.
- Glaze top with warm apricot jam for a shiny finish (optional).
- Slice thinly to serve.

139. Mango Fruit Cake Recipe

Serving: 8 | Prep: 15mins | Cook: 60mins | Ready in: 75mins

Ingredients

- 425 g canned mango in syrup
- 500 g mixed dried fruit
- 1/2 cup water
- 1 1/2 tsp bicarbonate of soda
- 1 1/2 cup self-raising flour
- 2 egg lightly beaten

Direction

- Grease a 15 cm x 25 cm loaf pan and line base and sides with baking paper.
- Combine the undrained mango slices, mixed dried fruit and water in a large pan.
- Bring to boil and simmer, uncovered, for 1 minute. Allow to cool.
- Stir in eggs and combined sifted bicarbonate of soda and flour.
- Mix well and pour mixture into prepared pan.
- Cook in a moderately slow oven, about 160C for 1 hour or until cooked.
- Cool cake in pan.

140. Moist Boiled Fruit Cake

Serving: 10 | Prep: 25mins | Cook: 120mins | Ready in: 145mins

Ingredients

- 1 cup mixed fruit
- 1 cup sugar
- 1 cup water
- 125 g butter
- 2 cup plain flour
- 1 tsp mixed spice
- 1 tsp bicarbonate of soda
- 1 pinch salt
- 1 egg
- 1 cup apple cooked

Direction

- Preheat oven to 180C (170C fan forced).
- Grease cake tin well and cover bottom with baking paper or greaseproof paper.
- Place sugar, water, mixed fruit and butter into a saucepan and bring to the boil.
- Allow to boil, slightly, for 3 minutes.
- Remove from stove and allow to cool.

- Sift flour, mixed spice, bicarbonate of soda and salt.
- Add to fruit mixture.
- Make a well in the middle of mixture.
- Add egg and stewed apple. Combine well.
- Pour mixture into cake tin and place on middle shelf of oven.
- Bake for 1 to 1¼ hours. Test cake with skewer to ensure it is cooked through.
- Allow to cool for 5-10 minutes before moving from cake tin, onto a cake rack.

141. Pineapple Fruit Cake Recipe

Serving: 8 | Prep: 10mins | Cook: 80mins | Ready in: 90mins

Ingredients

- 500 g mixed dried fruit
- 450 g (crushed) canned pineapple reserve liquid
- 2 tsp mixed spice
- 1 tsp ground ginger
- 1/2 tsp bicarbonate of soda
- 2 eggs beaten
- 1 cup plain flour
- 1 cup self-raising flour
- 1 tbs sweet sherry
- 125 g butter
- 1 cup sugar

Direction

- Preheat a fan-forced oven to 170C degrees. Grease a 22cm round cake pan.
- In a saucepan, mix sugar, butter, dried fruit, pineapple and syrup, mixed spice and ginger. Bring to the boil. Let boil for one minute.
- Take off heat and add bicarb soda, stir. Allow to cool to room temperature.
- Add flours and beaten eggs and mix with a spoon.

- Pour into a greased cake pan. Bake for 1 hour. Test with a toothpick, if it comes out clean, it's done.
- Drizzle warm cake with sherry.

142. Pumpkin Fruit Cake

Serving: 10 | Prep: 30mins | Cook: 105mins | Ready in: 135mins

Ingredients

- 225 g butter
- 1 1/2 cup caster sugar
- 2 egg
- 1 1/2 cup mixed dried fruit
- 1 cup pumpkin mash warmed
- 1 1/2 cup plain flour
- 1 1/2 cup self-raising flour

Direction

- Preheat oven to 150C.
- Beat butter and sugar together, then add eggs one at a time while beating.
- Mix in mashed pumpkin carefully. Add fruit.
- Sift flours together and fold in.
- Bake in a greased, lined 20 cm x 20 cm tin for 1½ hours.

Chapter 6: Birthday Cake Recipes

***

143.   AFL Football Birthday Cake Recipe

Serving: 12 | Prep: 90mins | Cook: 220mins | Ready in: 310mins

Ingredients

- 500g unsalted butter
- 500g dark chocolate, chopped
- 4 cups caster sugar
- 2 1/2 cups milk
- 6 eggs, lightly beaten
- 1 cup milk
- 2 cups self-raising flour
- 2 cups plain flour
- 2/3 cup cocoa powder
- Buttercream
- 125g butter, softened
- 1 1/2 cups icing sugar mixture
- 1 tbs milk
- Decorations
- 700g ready to roll red fondant icing
- 100g ready to roll black fondant icing
- 100g ready to roll white fondant icing

Direction

- Preheat the oven to 160C/140C fan-forced . Grease and flour a Dolly Varden cake tin; line base with baking paper.
- Combine half the butter, chocolate, sugar and milk in a large saucepan and stir over low heat until smooth. Remove from heat. Transfer to a large bowl and cool 15 minutes.
- Whisk half the eggs into the chocolate mixture. Then whisk in half the sifted flours and half the cocoa until the mixture is smooth.
- Pour mixture into prepared tin. Bake for 1¾ hours or until a skewer inserted into the centre comes out almost clean (a small amount of sticky cake mixture is fine). Completely cool cake in the tin, then turn out onto a plate. Cover with plastic wrap.
- Repeat steps 1-4 with remaining cake ingredients to make a second Dolly Varden mud cake.

- To make buttercream, using electric beaters, beat butter in a bowl until very pale. Gradually add icing sugar, in batches, beating well between batches. Add the milk and beat to combine.
- Trim tops off cooled cakes so they fit together like a football, join halves with a little of the buttercream. Trim a slice off the base so the cake sits flat. Trim cake all over to ensure a smooth surface. Make ends of football slightly pointier by joining on a little piece of extra cake (from the trimmings) with some of the buttercream. Place cake on cake board, securing with a little buttercream.
- Spread remaining buttercream all over the football to coat. Knead the red fondant on a surface dusted with icing sugar until smooth. Roll icing out to about 3mm thick on an icing sugar dusted surface, large enough to cover the cake. Gently lift onto the cake and using your hands and smooth all over, gently easing the icing in and under the cake trying not to pleat the icing. Trim off any excess icing and smooth all over with your hands.
- Roll out the black icing to about 5mm thick on an icing sugar dusted surface, cut out letters and numbers using cutters or with a sharp knife, and attach to the cake with a little water. Roll the white icing into a thin sausage, flatten slightly and cut into 3cm lengths. Make small holes in top of cake for the shoelaces to fit into, using the end of a paintbrush. Moisten holes lightly and insert a piece of shoelace. Using a fork, mark the football into sections and around the laces to represent the stitching.

144.   ANZAC Day Cake Recipe

Serving: 8 | Prep: 15mins | Cook: 30mins | Ready in: 45mins

Ingredients

- 125 g unsalted butter
- 250 g golden syrup

- 6 eggs
- 120 g self-raising flour
- 120 g rolled oats
- 150 g desiccated coconut
- 80 g icing sugar
- 1/4 cup caster sugar
- 1/4 cup rum

Direction

- Preheat oven to 170C then grease cake tin and dust lightly with caster sugar.
- Melt butter and golden syrup over low heat, set aside to cool slightly, then beat in eggs.
- Combine flour, oats, icing sugar and coconut in a bowl, then stir in butter mixture.
- Spoon into prepared tin and bake for 20-25 minutes, test with cake skewer to make sure it's cooked.
- Combine caster sugar and rum, then bring to the boil and simmer for 5 minutes.
- Pour over cake and serve with whipped cream.

---

145.   All In One Chocolate Cake Recipe

Serving: 10 | Prep: 15mins | Cook: 45mins | Ready in: 60mins

Ingredients

- 1 cup self-raising flour sifted
- 3 tbs cocoa powder heaped sifted
- 1 cup caster sugar
- 3 tbs butter large
- 1/3 cup milk
- 2 eggs

Direction

- Place all ingredients in a mixer bowl and mix on medium speed for approximately 3-4 minutes.

- Pour mixture into a greased and floured cake tin.
- Bake at 180C for approximately 40-45 minutes.

---

146.   Australia Day Lamington Ice Cream Cake Recipe

Serving: 8 | Prep: 15mins | Cook: 5mins | Ready in: 20mins

Ingredients

- 225 g double unfilled sponge cake
- 1 1/2 Litres vanilla ice cream
- 125 g fresh raspberries
- 125 g dark chocolate chopped
- 1 tbs coconut oil
- 1/4 cup shredded coconut

Direction

- Lay 2 large sheets of plastic wrap on top of each other and use to line a 1.75L (7-cup) loaf pan, allowing the sides to overhang. Line with a sheet of baking paper, extending over the 2 long sides.
- Break up the sponge cake into a food processor and process briefly to form coarse crumbs. Spoon 500ml of the ice cream into a large mixing bowl and add half the crumbs. Allow ice cream to soften slightly then use a metal spoon to mix in the crumbs until evenly combined (the ice cream should be just soft but not melted). Spoon into the pan and smooth the surface, pressing down firmly to make an even layer. Freeze for 2 hours or until firm.
- Spoon another 500ml of ice cream into a mixing bowl and mash with a large metal spoon until softened. Spread over the first layer in the pan, smoothing the surface. Return to the freezer. Puree the raspberries in a food processor and pour over the ice cream. Freeze for 2 hours or until firm.

- Use the remaining ice cream and crumbs to make another layer (see step 2). Spread into the pan. Fold the paper and overhanging plastic over the surface and freeze for another 2 hours, or overnight, until very firm.
- Melt the chocolate and coconut oil in the microwave until just warm and melted, but not hot. Stir until combined and smooth, then transfer to a jug and cool to room temperature.
- Invert the loaf pan onto a chilled serving platter and remove the plastic and paper. Slowly pour the chocolate mixture over the loaf, allowing it to drizzle down the sides a little. Working quickly before it sets, sprinkle the top with coconut. Return to the freezer until serving time.

147.   Baileys Cake

Serving: 12 | Prep: 10mins | Cook: 50mins | Ready in: 60mins

Ingredients

- 125g butter
- 1 cup sugar
- 2 eggs
- 1 cup Irish cream-based liqueur
- 2 cups plain flour
- 4 tsp baking powder
- 1 tbs icing sugar to decorate

Direction

- Melt butter in a saucepan large enough to mix all the ingredients.
- Remove from heat and add sugar and eggs. Mix to combine, then stir in Baileys.
- Sift flour and baking powder into mixture and fold in.
- Line the bottom of a 20cm cake pan with baking paper and then pour in the mixture.
- Bake at 180C for 45 minutes, or until cake springs back when lightly touched.

- Cool in the pan for 5 minutes before turning out onto a cooling rack.
- Sift a small amount of icing sugar on top and serve warm or cold.

148.   Baileys Cheesecake Recipe

Serving: 12 | Prep: 20mins | Cook: 5mins | Ready in: 25mins

Ingredients

- Base
- 185 g digestive biscuits
- 100 g butter melted
- 2 tbs caster sugar *optional
- Filling
- 3 tsp gelatine powder
- 2 tbs water
- 500 g cream cheese
- 15 ml Baileys Irish cream liqueur
- 300 g sweetened condensed milk
- 300 ml thickened cream whipped
- 100 g milk chocolate grated *to decorate

Direction

- Base: Crush biscuits and mix with melted butter.
- Press evenly into the base of a springform tin and refrigerate while preparing filling.
- Filling: Sprinkle gelatine over water in a small heatproof bowl. Microwave for 30 seconds and stir until gelatine dissolves. Cool for 5 minutes.
- Beat cream cheese, Irish cream and condensed milk together until smooth.
- Beat cream in small bowl until soft peaks form.
- Stir in warm gelatine mixture into cream cheese mixture.
- Fold in whipped cream and grated chocolate.
- Pour into springform pan and refrigerate for 4-5 hours to set or overnight for a firmer cheesecake.

- Garnish with grated chocolate and whipped cream, if desired.

149. Best Chocolate Cake Recipe

Serving: 10 | Prep: 30mins | Cook: 80mins | Ready in: 110mins

Ingredients

- 2 cup sugar
- 1 3/4 cup plain flour
- 3/4 cup cocoa powder
- 2 egg
- 1 1/2 tsp bicarbonate of soda
- 1 tsp salt
- 1 1/2 tsp baking powder
- 1/3 cup canola oil
- 1 cup milk
- 2 tsp vanilla essence
- 1 tbs instant coffee powder
- 1 cup boiling water
- Frosting
- 100 g dark chocolate
- 125 g butter
- 1 1/2 cup icing sugar
- 1 tsp vanilla essence
- 1 egg yolks

Direction

- Using electric beaters, mix together all ingredients except the coffee and boiling water.
- Mix the coffee with the boiling water and gradually add and beat until smooth. Mixture will be runny.
- Pour cake batter into a lined 25 cm round or square cake tin.
- Bake at 180C for 1 hour or until skewer inserted comes out clean.
- Allow to cool and ice with chocolate ganache or frosting.
- Frosting: Melt chocolate and cool slightly.

- Cream butter, icing sugar and vanilla together. Add egg yolk and melted chocolate, and beat until fluffy.

150. Best Chocolate Mud Cake Recipe

Serving: 10 | Prep: 10mins | Cook: 55mins | Ready in: 65mins

Ingredients

- 350g dark chocolate good quality
- 225g unsalted butter
- 600ml water
- 3 eggs
- 400g caster sugar
- 400g self-raising flour

Direction

- Preheat oven to 170C. Line base and sides of a pan with baking paper.
- Add chocolate, butter and water to a saucepan over low heat. Stir until chocolate is melted and mixture is smooth. Remove from heat and cool slightly.
- Lightly beat eggs in a large bowl and gradually add cooled chocolate mix.
- Add sifted flour and sugar, and continue to beat until smooth.
- Pour mix into prepared tin and bake for 45 minutes, or until cooked when tested with a clean skewer.

151. Cheesecake Log

Serving: 10 | Prep: 15mins | Cook: 0S | Ready in: 15mins

Ingredients

- 1 lemon zested juiced
- 1/2 cup condensed milk

- 1/4 cup milk
- 250g butternut snap biscuits
- 3/4 cup cream
- 125g cream cheese

Direction

- Finely grate ½ teaspoon rind from the lemon. Squeeze to extract two tablespoons of juice.
- Soften cream cheese and beat with the lemon rind until creamy.
- Add condensed milk and lemon juice, and beat until smooth and combined. Chill for two hours until well thickened.
- Pour milk into a shallow bowl and remove cream cheese mix from fridge.
- Dip one side of biscuit into the milk, then spread with approximately one tablespoon of cream cheese mix and sandwich together with another milk-dipped biscuit.
- Stand sandwiched biscuits on a serving plate and continue adding dipped and spread biscuits until all mix and biscuits are used.
- Chill until firm.
- Beat cream and spread generously over biscuit log, then sprinkle lightly with cinnamon or nutmeg or grated chocolate.
- Refrigerate for minimum two hours, or until biscuits have softened.
- Cut into diagonal slices to serve.

152. Cherry Ripe Cheesecake Recipe

Serving: 0 | Prep: 40mins | Cook: 15mins | Ready in: 55mins

Ingredients

- 200 g butternut snap biscuits
- 1/3 cup desiccated coconut
- 80 g butter melted
- 250 g cream cheese
- 1/3 cup fresh lemon juice
- 395 g condensed milk

- 3 tsp gelatine powder
- 1/4 cup hot water
- 300 ml thickened cream
- 110 g Cherry Ripe chocolate bar chopped

Direction

- Preheat oven to 180 C.
- Lightly grease a round cake pan and line with baking paper, leaving some paper sticking out.
- Place biscuits in a food processor and process until fine.
- Transfer to a bowl and stir in coconut and butter.
- Press into the base of the pan and bake for 10-12 minutes. Allow to cool.
- Beat cream cheese, lemon juice and condensed milk until smooth and combined.
- Fold in the gelatine mixture.
- Beat the cream in a separate bowl until soft peaks form, then fold in the Cherry Ripe.
- Combine both mixtures and pour onto chilled biscuit base. Chill until set.
- Remove cheesecake from pan by gently pulling at paper and place on a serving plate.

153. Chocolate Cheesecake Recipe

Serving: 6 | Prep: 360mins | Cook: 10mins | Ready in: 370mins

Ingredients

- 250 g cream cheese room temperature
- 395 g condensed milk
- 1 cup thickened cream
- 100 g butter melted
- 250 g Arnott's milk coffee biscuits
- 200 g Lindt chocolate
- 200 g Lindt 70% cocoa dark chocolate
- 1/4 cup dark rum

Direction

- In a food processor, add biscuits and process until fine.
- Add melted butter through funnel of processor whilst running.
- Press into the bottom of a lightly greased and lined spring form cake tin.
- Bake at 180C for approximately 10 minutes. Set aside.
- Melt dark chocolate in a glass measuring cup or bowl in the microwave for about 40 seconds.
- Add the milk chocolate and microwave a further minute, stir and return for another 10-20 seconds if it isn't fully melted, until smooth. Do not overheat. Cool slightly.
- Place cream cheese and condensed milk in a large mixer bowl and beat until combined.
- Increase mixer speed to high and whilst blending, add thickened cream and alcohol (or coffee). Slowly add melted chocolate whilst mixing and incorporate well. Beat until mixture is smooth and lightened in colour.
- Pour into base and refrigerate for at least 4-6 hours before serving.

154.   Chocolate Mud Cake Recipe

Serving: 8 | Prep: 40mins | Cook: 105mins | Ready in: 145mins

Ingredients

- 250g butter chopped
- 200g dark chocolate
- 2 cups caster sugar
- 1 1/3 cups water
- 1 tsp instant coffee granules
- 3/4 cup plain flour
- 3/4 cup self-raising flour
- 1/4 cup cocoa powder
- 3 eggs lightly beaten

Direction

- In a large saucepan, add the first 5 ingredients.
- Melt together over a low heat until sugar is dissolved and butter and chocolate are melted. Allow to cool for 10 minutes.
- Sift plain flour, self raising flour and cocoa into a large mixing bowl.
- Add the cooled liquid and beat gently.
- Add the eggs and mix gently.
- Pour mixture into a greased cake tin and bake at 150C for 1¾ hours.

155.   Cream Cake

Serving: 12 | Prep: 30mins | Cook: 60mins | Ready in: 90mins

Ingredients

- 4 egg
- 2 cup caster sugar
- 2 cup cream
- 3 cup self-raising flour
- 1 1/2 tsp vanilla extract optional *to taste

Direction

- Preheat oven to 180C (160C fan-forced).
- Grease a 20 cm round cake tin and also 1 bar tin or loaf tin.
- Beat together eggs and sugar until light and fluffy.
- Add cream, flour and vanilla or lemon, fold together until mixed, pour into prepared tins.
- Bake round tin for approximately 50 minutes and the bar or loaf tin will for approximately 40 minutes.

156.   Creamy White Chocolate Cheesecake Recipe

Serving: 12 | Prep: 20mins | Cook: 15mins | Ready in: 35mins

Ingredients

- 185 g chocolate biscuits
- 100 g butter melted
- Filling
- 3 tsp gelatine powder
- 2 tbs water
- 500 g cream cheese
- 400 g sweetened condensed milk
- 300 ml cream
- 150 g white chocolate

Direction

- Base: Crush biscuits in a food processor or with rolling pin and then mix with melted butter.
- Press evenly into the base of a springform tin and refrigerate while preparing filling.
- Filling: Melt chocolate in a double boiler or microwave.
- Sprinkle gelatine over the water in small heatproof jug, stand in small saucepan of simmering water and stir until gelatine dissolves. Cool for 5 minutes.
- Beat cheese and condensed milk with electric mixer until smooth.
- Beat cream in small bowl with electric mixer until soft peaks form.
- Stir warm gelatine mixture into cheese mixture.
- Fold in cream and melted chocolate.
- Pour into spring form tin and refrigerate for 4-5 hours to set.

157.　　Custard Cake Recipe

Serving: 10 | Prep: 15mins | Cook: 70mins | Ready in: 85mins

Ingredients

- 2 cups self-raising flour
- 250 g butter room temperature
- 2 tsp vanilla essence

- 2 cups caster sugar
- 4 eggs
- 3/4 cup custard powder
- 1 cup milk

Direction

- Preheat a fan-forced oven to 160C.
- Put all the ingredients in a large mixing bowl. Mix with electric mixer until just combined.
- Pour into lined 23cm deep square tin. Cook 1 hour.
- Check cake with skewer. Sometimes it takes another 5-10 minutes to cook in the middle.

158.　　Easy Caramello Cheesecake Recipe

Serving: 12 | Prep: 25mins | Cook: 0S | Ready in: 25mins

Ingredients

- 375g Arnott's Choc Ripple Biscuits
- 220g butter, melted
- 3 tsp gelatine
- 500g cream cheese, at room temperature
- 1/2 cup brown sugar
- 1 tsp vanilla essence
- 300ml thickened cream, whipped
- 380g tin Nestle Top 'n' Fill Caramel
- Caramello Koalas, to serve
- Caramello bars, to serve

Direction

- Prepare a 24cm springform cake tin by greasing lightly with butter and lining the base and sides with baking paper. In a food processor, blitz biscuits into a fine crumb. Add butter and blitz until just combined. Pour into prepared tin and use a large spoon or small glass to press into a thin tart shell, lining the base and up the sides. Refrigerate for 30 minutes.

- Using an electric mixer, beat cream cheese with sugar and vanilla until smooth.
- Place 2 tbs boiling water in a small bowl and sprinkle over gelatine. Whisk with a fork until gelatine is completely dissolved. Add to cream cheese with whipped cream, and beat for a further minute to combine. Pour into biscuit base, smooth over the top, then return to fridge for at least an hour, or overnight, to set.
- Just prior to serving, release cheesecake from the springform tin and carefully transfer to a serving plate, removing baking paper lining. Place Top 'n' Fill Caramel in a bowl and whisk well. Pour over cheesecake. Decorate with Caramello Koalas and chopped Caramello bars.

159. Fantastic Lemon Cheesecake Recipe

Serving: 12 | Prep: 30mins | Cook: 260mins | Ready in: 290mins

Ingredients

- 250g Arnott's Marie biscuits, crushed
- 125g butter, melted
- Filling
- 85g lemon jelly crystals
- 1 tsp gelatine powder
- 1 cup boiling water
- 375ml CARNATION Light & Creamy Evaporated Milk
- 250g cream cheese, cubed
- 2/3 cup sugar
- 2 lemons, juiced
- 1 lemon, zest only

Direction

- Mix together melted butter and biscuits.
- Line a large springform pan with the crumb mix, including the sides.
- Refrigerate until set.

- Combine the lemon jelly, gelatine and boiling water together and mix well. Refrigerate to cool.
- Beat cream cheese and sugar together and blend until smooth.
- Add lemon juice, lemon rind and the lemon jelly mixture. Mix well.
- In a separate bowl, beat the tin of carnation milk until thick and stiff.
- Add the cream cheese and lemon mixture into it and combine well.
- Pour the mixture into the prepared biscuit base and refrigerate to set.

160. Ferrero Rocher Cheesecake Recipe

Serving: 8 | Prep: 30mins | Cook: 240mins | Ready in: 270mins

Ingredients

- 250 g plain chocolate biscuits
- 150 g butter melted
- Filling
- 3 tsp gelatine powder
- 1/4 cup boiling water
- 500 g cream cheese softened
- 2 tbs sour cream
- 16 Ferrero Rocher chocolates chopped
- 300 g thickened cream whipped
- 1/2 cup caster sugar
- Decoration
- 50 g dark chocolate melted

Direction

- Base: Blend plain chocolate biscuits until finely crushed.
- Add melted butter and process until just combined.
- Press biscuit mixture into the base of a 20cm springform pan and up then up the sides.
- Cover and refrigerate, then prepare the filling.

- Filling: Sprinkle gelatine over water in a small heatproof jug.
- Stand the jug in a small pan of simmering water and stir until gelatine dissolves. Cool slightly.
- Beat cream cheese, sugar and sour cream in a bowl with an electric mixer until smooth.
- Stir in gelatine mixture, then chopped up Ferrero Rochers.
- Fold in whipped cream and then pour over the chilled crumb base.
- Decoration: Drizzle melted chocolate in parallel lines 1 cm apart across the cheesecake.
- Drag skewer back and forth through the mixture to create a marbled effect.
- Refrigerate for approximately 3 hours, or until set.

161. Flourless Orange Cake Recipe

Serving: 8 | Prep: 15mins | Cook: 175mins | Ready in: 190mins

Ingredients

- 2 oranges large
- 5 eggs large
- 250 g raw sugar
- 250 g ground almonds
- 1 tsp baking powder
- 2 tsp orange liqueur optional
- 1/2 cup icing sugar *to decorate

Direction

- Place oranges in saucepan and boil for two hours, topping up water as necessary.
- Allow to cool, then cut into pieces, place in a blender and blend until smooth (pips and peel can be included).
- Preheat oven to 200C and line a 20cm round cake tin.
- Beat eggs and sugar together.

- Mix in baking powder, stir in the pureed oranges and gently fold in almond meal.
- Mix in orange liqueur if using, then pour mixture into tin.
- Bake for 55 minutes, or until knife inserted in centre comes out clean. Allow cake to cool in pan before removing.
- Dust with icing sugar prior to serving.

162. Frosty Fruits Cheesecake Recipe

Serving: 12 | Prep: 30mins | Cook: 2mins | Ready in: 32mins

Ingredients

- 250g Arnott's Arrowroot biscuits, crushed
- 100g butter, melted
- 150g pineapple, peeled, diced
- 1 passionfruit pulp removed
- Filling
- 3 tsp gelatine powder
- 2 tbs water
- 500g cream cheese softened
- 1/2 cup caster sugar
- 1 tsp vanilla extract
- 300ml thickened cream
- Frosty Fruits Jelly
- 6 Frosty Fruits icy poles
- 2 1/2 tsp gelatine powder
- 2 tbs water

Direction

- To make the base, lightly grease a 22cm round springform cake pan. Combine crushed biscuits and melted butter in a bowl. Stir to combine. Press over base of pan. Refrigerate for 30 minutes or until firm.
- To make the filling, sprinkle gelatine over water in a heatproof cup. Stand cup in a pan of simmering water, until dissolved and then cool slightly. Using electric beaters, beat cream cheese and sugar until smooth. Beat in vanilla

and cream until light and fluffy and then beat in the gelatine mixture. Spread mixture into pan and smooth the surface. Refrigerate for 3 hours or until just set.

- To make the Frosty Fruits jelly, remove sticks from icy poles. Place in a microwave-safe bowl. Melt in the microwave on HIGH (100%) for 1 minute or until completed melted. Sprinkle gelatine over water in a heatproof cup. Stand cup in a pan of simmering water, until dissolved. Whisk gelatine mixture into melted Frosty Fruit mixture until combined. Pour jelly over filling. Refrigerate for 3 hours or until set. Serve topped with pineapple and drizzled with passionfruit pulp.

163. Gluten Free Carrot Cake Recipe

Serving: 12 | Prep: 20mins | Cook: 55mins | Ready in: 75mins

Ingredients

- 3/4 cup canola oil
- 1 tsp vanilla essence
- 1 1/2 cups carrot grated
- 1/2 cup walnuts chopped
- 1 1/2 tsp gluten-free baking powder
- 3/4 cup sugar
- 2 eggs
- 1/2 cup sultanas
- 1 cup gluten-free self-raising flour
- 1/2 tsp ground cinnamon
- Icing
- 2 tbs light cream cheese
- 1/2 tsp vanilla essence
- 2 tsp margarine
- 3/4 cup gluten-free icing sugar

Direction

- Place oil, sugar and vanilla into a bowl. Beat with an electric mixer until well combined.

- Add eggs and continue to beat until light and creamy.
- Stir through carrot, sultanas and walnuts.
- Sift flour, baking powder and cinnamon into mixture and mix well.
- Spoon mixture into a lightly greased and lined 21 cm ring tin. Bake in a moderate oven for 50-55 minutes or until a skewer inserted into the cake comes out clean.
- Stand for 5 minutes before turning out onto a wire rack to cool.
- To make the icing, beat cream cheese, margarine and extra vanilla together in a bowl. Add icing sugar and mix well.
- Spread icing over cake.

164. Golden Gaytime Frozen Cheesecake Recipe

Serving: 12 | Prep: 30mins | Cook: 5mins | Ready in: 35mins

Ingredients

- 200g butternut snap biscuits crushed
- 100g butter melted
- 2 Golden Gaytime ice creams
- Filling
- 500g cream cheese softened
- 3/4 cup brown sugar
- 1 tsp vanilla extract
- 300ml thickened cream
- Chocolate Sauce
- 1/3 cup thickened cream
- 100g dark chocolate chopped

Direction

- Lightly grease a 22cm round springform cake pan. Combine crushed biscuits and melted butter in a bowl. Stir to combine. Press over base of pan. Refrigerate for 30 minutes or until firm.
- Using electric beaters, beat cream cheese and sugar until smooth. Beat in vanilla and cream

until light and fluffy. Spread mixture into pan and smooth the surface. Freeze overnight or until just firm.

- To make the chocolate sauce, combine cream and chocolate in a small saucepan over low heat. Stir for 2-3 minutes or until mixture is smooth. Cool for 30 minutes or until thickened slightly.
- Remove frozen cheesecake from pan and place on a serving plate. Drizzle cheesecake with chocolate sauce. Remove sticks from Golden Gaytimes and cut into chunks. Pile Gaytime chunks in the centre of the cheesecake. Serve immediately.

165. Healthy Apple Cake Recipe

Serving: 12 | Prep: 15mins | Cook: 45mins | Ready in: 60mins

Ingredients

- 2 cups wholemeal self-raising flour, sifted
- 4 green apples, diced, peeled
- 1 cup pecans, chopped
- 1/2 cup macadamia oil
- 3/4 cup Capilano* Light & Smooth Honey
- 2 eggs
- 1 tsp nutmeg
- 1 tsp ground cinnamon

Direction

- Preheat oven to 180C and grease a 20cm round cake tin.
- In a bowl, mix together the oil, honey and eggs, and beat well.
- Fold in sifted flour, nutmeg and cinnamon.
- Stir apples and pecans gently through the batter and pour into the prepared cake tin.
- Bake for approximately 45 minutes, or until a wooden skewer is pulled clean from centre of cake.
- Turn out onto a wire rack and cool.

166. Honeycomb Cheesecake Recipe

Serving: 10 | Prep: 360mins | Cook: 5mins | Ready in: 365mins

Ingredients

- 250g plain biscuits
- 155g butter melted
- 1/2 cup whipped cream
- 100g chocolate honeycomb bar chopped *to decorate
- Filling
- 2 tsp gelatine powder
- 1/4 cup water
- 200g milk chocolate chopped
- 375g cream cheese room temperature
- 1/2 cup caster sugar
- 300ml thickened cream
- 50g chocolate honeycomb bar chopped

Direction

- Grease a 24cm round springform pan and line the base with baking paper.
- Process biscuits until crushed. Add butter and process until combined.
- Press mixture over the base and up sides of prepared pan. Refrigerate, then prepare filling.
- To make the filling, sprinkle gelatine over water in a small heatproof jug. Stand jug in a pan of simmering water.
- Stir until dissolved. Remove and cool.
- Place chocolate in a heatproof bowl. Sit bowl over pan of simmering water. Stir until melted.
- Remove and cool for 10 minutes.
- Beat cream cheese and sugar in small bowl with electric mixer until smooth.
- With mixer on low speed, beat in cream, then chocolate and gelatine mixture until smooth. Fold in chopped chocolate bar.

- Pour filling over biscuit base. Cover and refrigerate overnight until set.
- To serve, remove the pan. Transfer cheesecake to a serving plate. Decorate with whipped cream and crumbled chocolate honeycomb bars.

167.   Jelly Cheesecake Recipe

Serving: 8 | Prep: 15mins | Cook: 0S | Ready in: 15mins

Ingredients

- 500 g cream cheese
- 80 g butter melted
- 2 x 85 g jelly crystals
- 400 ml water
- 125 g biscuits

Direction

- Dissolve the lemon jelly crystals in ½ cup boiling water. Whisk the jelly with cream cheese until smooth.
- Combine the crushed biscuits and butter. Press into the base of a pan.
- Pour the cream cheese filling over the biscuits, and then spread evenly to cover the biscuit base. Refrigerate.
- Prepare second packet of jelly according to the packet instructions. Allow to cool, then gently pour over the cream cheese mixture.
- Set in fridge for roughly 4 hours or until firm.

168.   Lamington Sponge Cake

Serving: 8 | Prep: 20mins | Cook: 25mins | Ready in: 45mins

Ingredients

- melted butter, to grease
- 3/4 cup plain flour
- 4 eggs at room temperature
- 2/3 cup caster sugar
- 60g butter melted
- 1 ½ cups desiccated coconut
- 1/3 cup strawberry jam warmed
- 300ml thickened cream whipped
- Chocolate icing
- 2 cups icing sugar
- 1/4 cup cocoa
- 1/4 cup milk
- 25g butter chopped

Direction

- Preheat oven to 180C/160C fan-forced. Brush a 20cm (base measurement) cake pan with melted butter to grease. Line the base and sides with a little of the flour.
- Using electric beaters, beat the eggs and sugar in a large bowl for 8-10 minutes or until thick, pale and creamy. Sift half the flour over the egg mixture. Use a large metal spoon to fold until just combined. Repeat with remaining flour mixture. Working quickly, fold in the melted butter until combined.
- Spoon cake mixture into prepared pan and smooth the surface. Bake for 20 minutes or until golden and the cake springs back when lightly tapped. Turn immediately, top-side up, onto a baking-paper-covered wire rack to cool.
- To make the chocolate icing, sift the icing sugar and cocoa powder into a heatproof bowl. Stir in the milk and add the butter. Set bowl over a saucepan of simmering water. Stir until melted and smooth. Cool for 10 minutes. Refrigerate for 20 minutes or until icing is slightly thickened.
- Place the cake on a wire rack set over a tray. Spoon half the icing over the cake to coat. Refrigerate cake for 30 minutes. Spoon remaining icing over cake. Sprinkle with coconut. Refrigerate for 30 minutes or until icing is set.
- Using a serrated knife, cut cake in half. Sandwich cake with the jam and whipped cream. Serve.

169.   Lemon Coconut Cake Recipe

Serving: 12 | Prep: 15mins | Cook: 40mins | Ready in: 55mins

Ingredients

- 1 1/2 cups self-raising flour
- 1/2 cup desiccated coconut
- 1 tbs lemon rind grated
- 1 cup caster sugar
- 125 g butter melted
- 2 eggs
- 1 cup milk

Direction

- Preheat the oven to 180C. Grease a 20 cm deep round cake tin.
- Combine all ingredients into a bowl, mixing well with wooden spoon until batter is smooth.
- Pour the mixture into cake tin and bake 40 minutes.

170.   Lemon Custard Magic Cake Recipe

Serving: 12 | Prep: 20mins | Cook: 55mins | Ready in: 75mins

Ingredients

- 4 eggs separated
- 1 cup icing sugar mixture
- 1 tbs lemon rind, finely grated
- 1/4 cup lemon juice
- 3/4 cup plain flour
- 125 g butter cooled melted
- 400 ml milk slightly warmed
- 2 tbs caster sugar
- 1 pinch icing sugar mixture *extra for dusting

Direction

- Preheat the oven to 180C/160C fan-forced. Grease a 20cm square cake pan and line with baking paper, allowing it to overhang on all sides.
- Using electric beaters, beat egg yolks and icing sugar in a large bowl until pale and thick. Beat in lemon rind and juice until combined. Beat in flour until combined. Pour in butter and beat until combined. Gradually add milk and beat until well combined.
- Using electric beaters, beat egg whites in a bowl until soft peaks form. Gradually beat in caster sugar until dissolved.
- Fold a third of the egg white into the flour mixture. Repeat in two more batches until just combined (you may have a few lumps). Pour into prepared pan.
- Bake for 50-55 minutes or until the cake is set, but wobbles slightly. Set aside in the pan to cool completely. Carefully cut into slices and serve dusted with extra icing sugar.

171.   Malteser Layer Cake Recipe

Serving: 12 | Prep: 20mins | Cook: 0S | Ready in: 20mins

Ingredients

- 2 x 600g chocolate mud cakes
- 400g tub chocolate frosting
- 600g Maltesers chocolates

Direction

- Place one mud cake on a serving platter and top with some of the chocolate frosting. Place second cake icing side down on top of the chocolate frosting, stacking the cakes. Spread remaining frosting over the entire top and sides of the two cakes.

- Beginning in the centre and working in a circle, arrange Maltesers over the top and sides of the cake, pressing into the icing.

172.   Mango Cheesecake Recipe

Serving: 12 | Prep: 25mins | Cook: 390mins | Ready in: 415mins

Ingredients

- 1/4 cup cold water
- 1 tbs gelatine powder
- 125 g biscuits
- 75 g butter melted
- 500 g cream cheese softened
- 2/3 cup caster sugar
- 500 g mango diced
- 300 ml thickened cream
- 1 mango sliced *to serve

Direction

- Grease a 22cm-round (base) springform cake pan. Line side with baking paper, extending paper 1cm above edge of pan.
- Place water in a small heatproof jug. Sprinkle over gelatine. Microwave on HIGH (100%) for 20 to 30 seconds or until gelatine is dissolved, stirring halfway through cooking. Set aside to cool.
- Meanwhile, process biscuits until fine crumbs. Add butter. Process until combined. Press biscuit mixture over base of prepared pan. Refrigerate while preparing filling.
- Wipe processor clean. Process cream cheese, sugar and half the diced mango until smooth and combined. Add cream. Process for 30 seconds or until combined. With motor running, gradually add cooled gelatine mixture, processing until combined. Transfer to a bowl. Fold in remaining diced mango. Pour over prepared base in pan. Refrigerate overnight or until set.

- Serve chilled cheesecake topped with sliced mango.

173.   Mango And Salted Caramel Ice Cream Cake Recipe

Serving: 8 | Prep: 20mins | Cook: 15mins | Ready in: 35mins

Ingredients

- 5 Calypso mangoes
- 1 1/4 cups self-raising flour
- 80 g butter chilled chopped
- 1/2 cup brown sugar
- 1 cup honey roasted macadamias roughly chopped
- 3 L vanilla ice cream
- Quick salted caramel
- 1/2 cup thickened cream
- 2 packets Werther's Original Chewy Toffees unwrapped
- 2 tsp sea salt flakes crushed

Direction

- Preheat oven to 180C fan-forced. Combine the flour and butter in a food processor. Process until the mixture resembles fine breadcrumbs. Add sugar and ½ cup of the macadamia nuts, process until crumble forms clumps. Spread out on a baking tray and bake for 15 minutes or until golden. Cool.
- Quick salted caramel: Pour the cream into a small saucepan, add the caramels. Stir over medium-high heat for 3-4 minutes until cream comes to the boil. Remove from the heat and stir until caramels have melted and sauce is smooth. Stir in the salt. Set aside to cool.
- Line the base and sides of a 4cm deep, 20cm x 30cm (base) baking dish with baking paper, allowing a 2cm overhang at both long sides. Scatter the crumble over the base of the pan to cover.

- Peel 3 of the mangoes. Chop the fruit. Swirl chopped mango, remaining macadamia nuts and ¾ cup salted caramel through the ice cream. Spoon over the crumble base. Smooth the surface. Cover and freeze overnight.
- Peel and chop the remaining 2 mangoes, spoon over the ice cream. Cut into pieces and serve drizzled with remaining salted caramel.

---

174. Mars Bar Cheesecake Recipe

Serving: 12 | Prep: 60mins | Cook: 420mins | Ready in: 480mins

Ingredients

- 250g chocolate biscuits
- 125g butter, melted
- 1 tbs vanilla sugar
- Butterscotch Sauce
- 1 tbs brown sugar
- 20g butter
- 2 tbs cream
- Chocolate Sauce
- 60g milk chocolate, finely chopped
- 2 tbs cream
- Filling
- 1/4 cup water boiling
- 3 tsp gelatine powder
- 500g cream cheese, softened
- 1/2 cup caster sugar
- 200ml thickened cream
- 3 Mars Bars, finely chopped

Direction

- Base: Process biscuits until mixture resembles fine breadcrumbs. Mix in butter and vanilla sugar until just combined.
- Press mixture evenly over base and up ½ the side of spring-form tin. Place on tray and refrigerate about 30 minutes or until firm.
- Butterscotch Sauce: Combine brown sugar, butter and cream in small saucepan. Stir over

low heat, without boiling, until sugar dissolves. Set aside to cool and thicken.
- Chocolate Sauce: Combine chocolate and cream in another small saucepan, stir until chocolate melts. Set aside to cool and thicken.
- Filling: Sprinkle gelatine 1 teaspoon at a time over the boiling water in a heatproof jug and stir until gelatine dissolves. Cool for several minutes.
- Beat cream cheese in a medium bowl with electric mixer until smooth. Add caster sugar and beat until soft peaks form. Beat in cream until soft peaks form. Beat in gelatine mixture until combined. Stir through the chopped Mars Bars.
- Spoon half of the cream cheese mixture into crumb crust and drizzle the butterscotch and chocolate sauce over cream cheese mixture. Pull skewer backwards and forwards through mixture to create a rippled effect.
- Repeat with remaining cream cheese mixture and sauces. Cover cheesecake, refrigerate for several hours or overnight until set.
- Garnish with extra Mars Bars for effect and drizzle with any remaining sauces.

---

175. No Bake Caramel Cheesecake Recipe

Serving: 8 | Prep: 15mins | Cook: 0S | Ready in: 15mins

Ingredients

- 250 g butternut snap biscuits crushed
- 125 g butter melted
- Filling
- 2 x 250 g cream cheese
- 380 g NESTLE Top n Fill Caramel
- 3 tsp gelatine powder

Direction

- Base: Combine biscuit crumbs and butter.
- Press into the base of springform pan.
- Refrigerate to set.

- Filling: Mix using an electric mixer, the cream cheese and Top 'n' Fill Caramel.
- Dissolve gelatine in 1 tablespoon of water, stir with fork or whisk until fully dissolved.
- Add to cream cheese mixture and beat until well combined.
- Pour into prepared biscuit base and refrigerate to set.

176. No Bake Cheesecake Recipe

Serving: 12 | Prep: 25mins | Cook: 360mins | Ready in: 385mins

Ingredients

- 250 g sweet plain biscuits
- 125 g unsalted butter, melted
- 375 g cream cheese softened
- 1 lemon zested
- 2 tsp vanilla essence
- 1/3 cup lemon juice
- 400 g NESTLE Sweetened Condensed Milk

Direction

- Process biscuits until finely crushed. Add butter and mix well.
- Press half of the biscuit mixture into the base of a greased and lined 20 cm springform tin.
- Use a glass or spoon to push the remainder of the mixture around the sides of the tin.
- Refrigerate for 15 minutes.
- Beat the cream cheese until smooth and creamy.
- Add lemon zest and vanilla and beat well.
- Gradually add the condensed milk and lemon juice, and continue to beat until smooth.
- Pour into the prepared tin and refrigerate overnight.

177. No Bake Lemon Cheesecake Recipe

Serving: 10 | Prep: 30mins | Cook: 0S | Ready in: 30mins

Ingredients

- 250 g Arnott's Nice biscuits
- 125 g butter melted
- 500 g cream cheese
- 1/3 cup lemon juice *to taste
- 1 cup cream whipped
- 1 cup NESTLE Sweetened Condensed Milk
- 2 tsp white vinegar
- 1 cup cream whipped *extra

Direction

- Crush biscuits finely, then mix with the melted butter.
- Line a 20cm cake tin, then add the biscuit crumb, pressing down to create the base, then place in the fridge to set.
- In a large mixing bowl, sieve the cream cheese.
- Add condensed milk, lemon juice and vinegar and beat until creamy. Fold in whipped cream.
- Pour on top of the crumb crust base and refrigerate overnight.
- Top with extra whipped cream and sprinkle with nutmeg.

178. No Bake Lindt Ball Cheesecake Recipe

Serving: 10 | Prep: 20mins | Cook: 6mins | Ready in: 26mins

Ingredients

- 250 g plain sweet biscuits
- 150 g unsalted butter melted
- 250 g Lindt Lindor Strawberries & Cream balls
- 125 g Lindt Lindor Strawberries & Cream balls *to serve *extra
- 2 tbs warm water

- 1 tsp gelatine powder
- 500 g cream cheese brought to room temperature chopped into pieces
- 100 g caster sugar
- 300 g sour cream
- 200 g white chocolate cooled melted
- 1 packet Lindt Lindor Mango & Cream balls *to serve
- 1 punnet fresh strawberries *to serve
- 1 mango fresh thinly sliced *to serve

Direction

- Line the base of a 7cm-deep, 20cm springform pan with baking paper. Lightly grease the side. Process the biscuits in a food processor until fine crumbs form. Add the butter and pulse to combine. Transfer the mixture to the prepared pan and press firmly into the base and up the side. Place in the fridge until required.
- Place the strawberry Lindor balls in a heatproof bowl. Place over a pan of simmering water (don't let the bowl touch the water), stirring occasionally, for 5 minutes or until melted.
- Place the warm water in a small microwave-safe bowl. Sprinkle over the gelatine and stir until well combined. Microwave for 30 seconds, then use a fork to dissolve the gelatine. Set aside to cool slightly.
- Use electric beaters to beat the cream cheese and sugar until smooth. Add the sour cream and beat to combine. Add the white chocolate and gelatine mixture. Beat to combine.
- Pour half the cream cheese mixture into the pan. Pour half the melted strawberry mixture over the top and use a flat-bladed knife to swirl into the cream cheese mixture. Add the remaining cream cheese mixture and remaining melted strawberry mixture and swirl again. Smooth the surface. Place in the fridge for 4 hours or overnight to set.
- Remove the cheesecake from the pan. Decorate with the mango balls, extra strawberry balls and fresh strawberries and mango.

Serving: 6 | Prep: 25mins | Cook: 70mins | Ready in: 95mins

Ingredients

- 170 g plain flour
- 1 1/2 tsp baking powder
- 1 pinch salt
- 115 g butter
- 115 g caster sugar
- 1 orange rind grated
- 2 egg room temperature
- 2 tbs milk
- Syrup
- 115 g caster sugar
- 250 ml fresh orange juice
- 3 slices orange

Direction

- Preheat oven to 180C. Line and grease 20 cm cake tin.
- Sift flour, salt and baking powder into a bowl.
- With electric mixer, cream butter or margarine until soft. Add sugar and orange rind and continue beating until light and fluffy.
- Beat in eggs one at a time. Fold in flour mixture in 3 batches then add the milk.
- Spoon into tin and bake for about 30 minutes or until cake pulls away from sides.
- Remove from oven but leave in tin.
- Syrup: Dissolve sugar in orange juice over low heat. Add orange slices and simmer 10 minutes.
- Remove slices and drain,let syrup cool.
- Pierce cake all over with skewer and pour syrup over hot cake.
- Turn out onto serving plate when completely cool.

180. Paleo Chocolate Ganache Cake Recipe

Serving: 8 | Prep: 20mins | Cook: 60mins | Ready in: 80mins

Ingredients

- 1 cup coconut sugar
- 1 cup almond meal
- 1/3 cup boiling water
- 1/3 cup raw cacao powder
- 150 g butter
- 100 g raw dark chocolate
- 4 eggs separated
- Ganache
- 100 g raw dark chocolate
- 1 cup coconut cream

Direction

- Preheat oven to 170 degrees celsius. Line a 22cm cake pan with baking paper.
- Mix the raw cacao powder and hot water in a large mixing bowl until smooth.
- In a double boiler, melt the chocolate and butter together. Remove from heat.
- In a large mixing bowl, combine the the melted chocolate with the coconut sugar, almond meal and egg yolks. Stir until well combined.
- Using an electric mixer, beat the egg whites until soft peaks form. Fold egg whites in to the chocolate mix carefully until just mixed through.
- Transfer the batter in to the prepared pan and bake for 1 hour. Allow the cake to cool in the tin for 15 minutes before turning out onto a wire rack to cool.
- To make the ganache, combine the raw chocolate and coconut cream in a small saucepan on low heat, stirring until smooth.
- To serve, drizzle the cake with chocolate ganache and add shredded coconut or raspberries.

181. Passionfruit Sponge Cake Recipe

Serving: 8 | Prep: 0S | Cook: 20mins | Ready in: 20mins

Ingredients

- 20 g butter melted
- 2 tbs plain flour
- 4 eggs separated
- 1/2 cup caster sugar
- 1 cup cornflour
- 1 tbs custard powder
- 1 tsp cream of tartar
- 1/2 tsp bicarbonate of soda
- 1 1/2 cups pure icing sugar
- 2 passionfruit halved pulp removed
- 1 cup thickened cream

Direction

- Preheat oven to 200°C. Brush two 20cm round sandwich pans with melted butter. Dust each pan with 1 tablespoon of plain flour and line bases with baking paper.
- Using an electric mixer, beat egg whites until stiff peaks form. Add caster sugar and beat for 3 minutes, or until sugar dissolves and meringue is thick and glossy. Add egg yolks and beat until just combined. Sift cornflour, custard powder, cream of tartar and bicarbonate of soda over egg mixture. Using a large metal spoon, fold in cornflour mixture. Spoon mixture among prepared pans.
- Bake for 20 minutes, or until golden and cakes spring back when lightly touched. Line 2 wire racks with baking paper. Turn cakes onto prepared racks to cool.
- Sift icing sugar into a bowl. Add passionfruit pulp, 1 tablespoon at a time, and stir until icing is smooth. Stand for 10 minutes, or until thickened slightly.
- Whisk cream until soft peaks form. Place 1 cake, top side down, on a cake stand or serving plate. Spoon over whipped cream.

- Top with remaining cake and spread with passionfruit icing.

182. Peach Cheesecake With Peach Syrup Recipe

Serving: 8 | Prep: 25mins | Cook: 0S | Ready in: 25mins

Ingredients

- Crust
- 250 g butternut snap biscuits
- 80 g unsalted butter melted
- Cheesecake
- 3 tsp gelatine powder
- 500 g cream cheese
- 1/2 cup sugar
- 1 tsp vanilla bean paste
- 250 ml thickened cream whipped
- 4 yellow peaches cored cored peeled
- 1 dollop whipped cream *to serve
- 1 sprinkle white chocolate curls *to serve
- 2 peaches sliced *to decorate *extra
- Sugar syrup
- 1/2 cup sugar
- 1/2 cup water boiled dissolved

Direction

- Crust: Grease and line a 20cm spring form cake tin. In a food processor, place biscuits and pulse until fine crumbs. Add butter and pulse again to combine. Tip into prepared tin and press firmly into the base. Chill in the fridge until needed.
- Cheesecake: Place a small heat proof jug in a small saucepan of lightly simmering water.
- Add 2 tablespoons of water, then sprinkle the gelatine into the jug. Stir to dissolve set aside to cool 5 mins.
- Meanwhile, place cream cheese, vanilla and sugar into a stand mixer. Beat until smooth. Add the cooled gelatine mix and beat to combine.
- Gently fold in whipped cream.

- Pour into prepared pan on top of the biscuit base. Cover and refrigerate until set Minimum 4 hours to overnight.
- In a medium bowl, puree or mash 2 peaches, add sugar syrup then set aside to infuse.
- Place in a sieve over a bowl to strain, set drained syrup aside.
- To assemble, remove cheesecake from the fridge, use the peaches to decorate, drizzle with the syrup.

183. Peanut Butter Rocky Road Cheesecake Recipe

Serving: 10 | Prep: 30mins | Cook: 0S | Ready in: 30mins

Ingredients

- 16 Oreo biscuits crushed
- 80g butter melted
- 750g Philadelphia cream cheese softened
- 1 cup soft brown sugar
- 1 cup Kraft crunchy peanut butter
- 3 tsp gelatine dissolved
- 1 1/2 cups thickened cream lightly whipped
- 50g mini pretzels
- 1 cup Pascall marshmallows halved
- 1/2 cup glace cherries halved
- 1/2 cup roasted peanuts halved
- 125g Cadbury milk chocolate melts melted

Direction

- Combine the Oreo crumbs and butter, then press into the base of a greased and lined 22cm springform pan. Chill.
- Mix the gelatine with 1/4 cup of boiling water. Beat the cream cheese and brown sugar with an electric mixer until smooth. Stir in the gelatine, then the peanut butter. Fold through the whipped cream.
- Spoon mixture over the prepared base. Decorate with mini pretzels, marshmallows, glace cherries and peanuts. Refrigerate for 3 hours or until set.

- Drizzle with chocolate just prior to serving.

184. Peppermint Crisp Cheesecake Recipe

Serving: 8 | Prep: 30mins | Cook: 205mins | Ready in: 235mins

Ingredients

- 170g Arnott's Nice biscuits crushed
- 85g butter melted
- 250g cream cheese
- 395g condensed milk
- 1/3 cup lemon juice
- 1 tsp gelatine powder dissolved
- 1 tbs hot water
- 1 Nestle* Peppermint Crisp chocolate bars grated
- 2 drops peppermint essence

Direction

- Add melted butter to crushed biscuits.
- Press into foil lined tart plate.
- Place in fridge to set.
- Mix all other ingredients together and pour into chilled biscuit base.
- Decorate with grated chocolate.

185. Peppermint Crunch Ice Cream Cake Recipe

Serving: 8 | Prep: 360mins | Cook: 0S | Ready in: 360mins

Ingredients

- 200 g Oreo biscuits
- 2 L vanilla ice cream
- 4 x 35 g Peppermint Crisp chocolate bars
- 1 tbs water

Direction

- Line a springform tin with enough foil to extend over the sides.
- Pulse Oreos in a blender until finely crumbed.
- Transfer Oreos to a bowl and add 1 tablespoon of water, just enough to keep the crumbs together.
- Press the mixture into the prepared tin.
- Place the ice cream in a bowl to soften slightly before mixing through the roughly chopped Peppermint Crisp bars.
- Spread the ice cream over the Oreo base, cover with foil and freeze overnight.
- When set, remove foil and serve.

186. Plain Cake Recipe

Serving: 6 | Prep: 15mins | Cook: 55mins | Ready in: 70mins

Ingredients

- 2 cups self-raising flour
- 3/4 cup sugar
- 1 tsp vanilla essence
- 125 g butter
- 2 eggs
- 2/3 cup milk

Direction

- Preheat oven to 180C.
- Place all ingredients into a medium bowl and mix for approximately 2 minutes, or until combined.
- Pour mixture into a prepared cake tin and bake for 30 minutes.
- If using as muffin mixture, pour into muffin tins and bake for 20 minutes or until cooked.

187.   Queens Cake Recipe

Serving: 10 | Prep: 20mins | Cook: 60mins | Ready in: 80mins

Ingredients

- 80 g butter
- 1 cup sugar
- 1 egg
- 1 tsp vanilla essence
- 1 cup dates chopped
- 1 cup boiling water
- 1 tsp bicarbonate of soda
- 1 1/2 cup plain flour
- 1 tsp baking powder
- 1/2 tsp salt
- 1/2 cup walnuts chopped
- Lemon icing
- 1 cup icing sugar
- 15 g butter
- 1 tbs lemon juice

Direction

- Place dates, boiling water and bicarbonate of soda in a saucepan.
- Stir over low heat until dates are soft and pulpy. Allow to cool.
- Cream butter, sugar and vanilla. Add eggs and beat well.
- Stir in date mixture and walnuts.
- Fold in the flour, salt and baking powder.
- Pour mixture into a greased 25 x 25cm cake tin and bake at 180C for 40-50 minutes or until cooked .
- Cool cake on a wire rack. Ice with lemon icing.
- For the lemon icing, stir icing sugar in top of double saucepan. Stir in softened butter and lemon juice over gentle simmering water until mixture is of good spreading consistency.
- Remove from heat and spread over cake.

188.   Rainbow Surprise Party Cake Recipe

Serving: 0 | Prep: 60mins | Cook: 30mins | Ready in: 90mins

Ingredients

- 4 cups plain flour sifted
- 2 cups caster sugar
- 1 tsp salt
- 2 tsp bicarbonate of soda
- 2 cups milk
- 1/2 cup white vinegar
- 4 eggs
- 2 tsp vanilla extract
- 400 g butter melted
- 2 tsp red liquid food colouring
- 2 tsp blue liquid food colouring
- 2 tsp yellow liquid food colouring
- 2 tsp green liquid food colouring
- 1 tubs Betty Crocker vanilla icing
- 4 tbs hundreds and thousands
- 1/2 cup Nestle Smarties
- 1/2 cup chocolate freckles

Direction

- Preheat oven to 180°C. Grease and line 4 x 20cm cake tins.
- Put the flour, sugar, bicarb soda and salt, and whisk to combine.
- Combine the milk and vinegar in a jug and wait for the milk to curdle or bubble. Add the curdled milk to the dry ingredients with the eggs, vanilla and melted butter. Whisk (or beat on slow) until the batter is smooth.
- Divide the batter evenly between four bowls. Add a few drops of food colouring to each bowl to create your rainbow.
- Transfer each coloured batter portion to one of your cake tins. Bake for 30 minutes, or until a skewer comes out clean.
- Use a scone cutter to cut a circle out of the centre of three of the cakes. (One cake will have to be the lid, so don't cut a circle out of it!)

- To assemble the cake, start with one section with the cut out, spread the top with icing then add the next section with cut out and spread that with icing. Add the third section with cut out and spread it with icing. Now, stop, don't add the lid yet because you need to fill the centre of the cake first.
- Fill the centre of the cake with Smarties and Freckles.
- Place the final layer on, the layer without the cut-out section and then ice the outside of the cake.
- To put the sprinkles on top of the cake, use one of the cake tin sides (with the bottom removed) as a collar. Place it on top of the cake and then add the sprinkles to the top of the cake. Press them down gently with a spoon to get them to stick.

189. Red Velvet Cake Recipe

Serving: 12 | Prep: 20mins | Cook: 30mins | Ready in: 50mins

Ingredients

- 2 1/2 cups plain flour sifted
- 1 tsp baking powder
- 1 tsp salt
- 2 tbs cocoa powder
- 50 ml red liquid food colouring
- 120g unsalted butter, room temperature
- 1 1/2 cups sugar
- 2 eggs room temperature
- 1 tsp vanilla extract
- 1 cup buttermilk room temperature
- 1 tsp white wine vinegar
- 1 tsp bicarbonate of soda
- Cream cheese icing
- 450 g cream cheese softened
- 120 g unsalted butter softened
- 1 tsp vanilla extract
- 2 1/2 cups icing sugar
- 1 pinch salt

Direction

- Cake: Preheat oven to 180C. Butter and flour two 23cm round cake pans, or three 20cm round cake pans.
- Sift together the flour, baking powder and salt into a medium bowl. Set aside.
- In a small bowl, mix food colouring and cocoa powder to form a thin, smooth paste. Set aside.
- In a large bowl, using a hand mixer or stand mixer, beat butter and sugar together until light and fluffy, about 3 minutes.
- Beat in eggs, one at a time, then beat in vanilla and the red cocoa paste, scraping down the bowl frequently with a spatula. Add one third of the flour mixture to the butter mixture, beat well, then beat in half of the buttermilk.
- Beat in another third of flour mixture, then second half of buttermilk. End with the last third of the flour mixture, beat until well combined, making sure to scrape down the bowl with a spatula.
- In a small bowl, mix vinegar and baking soda. Add it to the cake batter and stir well to combine.
- Working quickly, divide batter evenly between the cake pans and bake at 180C for 25-30 minutes, or until a skewer inserted into the centre comes out clean.
- Cool the cakes in their pans on a wire rack for 10 minutes. To remove the cakes from the pan, place a wire rack on top of the cake pan and invert, then gently lift the pan. Allow cakes to cool completely before icing.
- Cream cheese icing: With an electric mixer, blend together cream cheese and butter until smooth.
- Reduce speed to low, and blend in icing sugar, salt and vanilla extract. Increase speed to high, and beat until light and fluffy.

190. Rhubarb Cake Recipe

Serving: 8 | Prep: 15mins | Cook: 75mins | Ready in: 90mins

Ingredients

- 1 1/2 cups sugar
- 1/2 cup butter
- 1 egg
- 2 cups plain flour
- 1 tsp vanilla essence
- 1 tsp bicarbonate of soda
- 1 cup sour milk
- 2 cups rhubarb chopped
- 1/2 tsp salt
- Topping
- 1/2 cup brown sugar
- 1 tbs butter softened

Direction

- Place all ingredients, except rhubarb in bowl, beat until well combined.
- Add rhubarb and fold into mixture.
- Put into a greased and lined square tin.
- To make the topping mix ingredients together and sprinkle evenly over cake.
- Bake at 180C for approximately 1 hour.

191. Rocky Road Cheesecake Recipe

Serving: 10 | Prep: 50mins | Cook: 0S | Ready in: 50mins

Ingredients

- 2 cups biscuit crumbs crumbed
- 500 g cream cheese softened
- 1/2 cup desiccated coconut
- 1/4 cup caster sugar
- 1/4 cup peanut butter
- 80 g butter melted
- 200 g chocolate buttons
- 1/2 cup cream
- 2 tbs gelatine powder cooled dissolved
- 1/4 cup boiling water
- 2 cups marshmallows halved
- 1 cup Turkish delight chopped

Direction

- Combine biscuit crumbs, coconut, peanut butter and butter in a small bowl.
- Line a springform cake pan with baking paper and press mixture into the base and chill for 15 minutes.
- Place cream cheese and sugar in a bowl, beat well until mixed. Dissolve gelatine in the boiling water and let cool.
- Add chocolate melts, cream and gelatine to the mixture and combine well.
- Stir in marshmallows and turkish delight and lightly mix.
- Pour mixture over the biscuit base and chill for 3 hours or until set.

192. Sprinkled Rainbow Cake Recipe

Serving: 12 | Prep: 150mins | Cook: 15mins | Ready in: 165mins

Ingredients

- 330 g raw sugar
- 250 g butter softened
- 4 eggs
- 15 g vanilla essence
- 480 g self-raising flour
- 260 ml Pauls lactose-free Zymil full cream milk
- 6 bottles liquid food colouring
- Icing
- 340 g cream cheese softened
- 1 1/2 cups butter softened
- 6 cups icing sugar
- 1 tbs vanilla essence
- 2 tbs hundreds and thousands

Direction

- Preheat oven to 180 C.
- Generously grease and flour 6 x 9-inch cake pans.
- Mix eggs, vanilla extract and milk in a large mixing bowl until combined.
- Mix in the flour, gradually, until combined.
- Divide the batter into six bowls (about 1 cup of batter per bowl). Add food coloring to each bowl to create a vibrant red, orange, yellow, green, blue, and chocolate.
- Pour each coloured batter into the prepared pans and spread out into an even layer (layers will be thin). Bake for 10-15 minutes.
- Remove and allow to cool on cake racks.
- Meanwhile, make the cream cheese icing by creaming together cream cheese and butter. Mix in icing sugar and vanilla.
- Place the chocolate layer down first and a layer of icing. Repeat with the blue layer, green layer, yellow layer, orange layer and finally the red layer.
- Place a thin coat of the icing on the cake to create a crumb coat. This will make the cake even all around and seal any loose crumbs. Serve!

193.   Sticky Date Cake Recipe

Serving: 12 | Prep: 20mins | Cook: 120mins | Ready in: 140mins

Ingredients

- 4 cups dried dates pitted
- 4 cups cold water
- 2 tsp bicarbonate of soda
- 175g unsalted butter room temperature
- 2 cups brown sugar firmly packed
- 2 tsp vanilla extract
- 6 eggs
- 3 cups self-raising flour sifted

Direction

- Preheat oven to 160C (or 140C fan-forced).
- Grease a 24 cm round cake pan and line base with 2 layers of baking paper, leaving 5cm hanging over the sides.
- Combine dates and water in a large saucepan. Bring to boil.
- Remove from heat and stir in bicarbonate of soda. Allow to stand and cool for 15-25 minutes.
- Transfer this mixture to food processor in two batches. Process each until mixture is smooth and transfer to large bowl.
- Beat butter, sugar and extract in an extra large bowl with an electric mixer on high until well combined.
- Add eggs, one at a time, beating well after each addition.
- Fold in flour and then fold in date mixture until well combined. Mixture will be runny.
- Pour mixture into prepared pan and bake for about 2-2½ hours.
- Check after about 1 hour and 50 minutes with a skewer.
- Cover loosely with foil during cooking if over-browning occurs.
- Stand cake in pan for 10 minutes before turning onto a wire rack.

194.   Strawberry Cake Recipe

Serving: 8 | Prep: 20mins | Cook: 45mins | Ready in: 65mins

Ingredients

- 125 g butter
- 1/2 cup caster sugar
- 2 eggs
- 1 tsp vanilla essence
- 2 cups self-raising flour sifted
- 1/2 cup milk
- 1 cup fresh strawberries mashed
- 1 tsp strawberry essence optional *to taste
- Strawberry icing

- 3 fresh strawberries mashed medium
- 1 1/2 cups pure icing sugar

Direction

- Cake: Preheat oven to 180C (160C fan-forced).
- Lightly grease and line a 20cm cake pan.
- Beat the butter and sugar until light and fluffy.
- Add the eggs and vanilla, and beat until smooth.
- Fold in the flour and milk, mixing well.
- Add strawberries to the mix and fold together, add strawberry essence.
- Spoon mixture into the cake pan.
- Bake for 40-45 minutes, or until a skewer inserted comes out clean. Allow to cool.
- Strawberry icing: Add icing sugar to strawberries, mix until combined.
- Spread onto cold cake and serve.

195.   Strawberry Cheesecake Recipe

Serving: 8 | Prep: 30mins | Cook: 0S | Ready in: 30mins

Ingredients

- 250 g Arnott's Marie biscuits crushed
- 125 g butter melted
- Filling
- 85 g jelly crystals
- 2 tsp gelatine powder
- 1 cup boiling water
- 175 ml CARNATION Light & Creamy Evaporated Milk
- 250 g cream cheese
- 2/3 cup sugar
- 1/2 cup fresh strawberries pureed
- 1 punnet fresh strawberries *to decorate

Direction

- Mix biscuit crumbs and butter.
- Line the base and sides of a large cheesecake pan with crumb mixture. Refrigerate until set.

- Combine jelly crystals, gelatine and boiling water and mix well. Place in fridge.
- Beat cream cheese and sugar until smooth. Add strawberry puree and strawberry jelly mixture. Mix well.
- In a clean bowl, beat milk until thick. Add jelly mixture and cream cheese, and combine well.
- Pour mixture into biscuit base and place in fridge to set.
- When firm, gently top with fresh strawberries.

196.   Strawberry Jelly Cake With Strawberry Cream Cheese Frosting Recipe

Serving: 12 | Prep: 15mins | Cook: 45mins | Ready in: 60mins

Ingredients

- 600 g cake mix
- 85 g strawberry jelly
- 1 punnet fresh strawberries
- 4 eggs
- 120 ml vegetable oil
- Frosting
- 50 g butter
- 250 g cream cheese
- 2 tsp strawberry essence
- 250 g icing sugar mixture
- 250 g pure icing sugar

Direction

- Preheat oven to 180C. Grease and flour a medium-large size cake pan.
- In a large bowl, combine cake mix and jelly crystals.
- Purée the strawberries and add to eggs, oil and water.
- Beat at medium speed until smooth. Pour mixture into prepared pan.
- Bake for 45 minutes or until a skewer inserted into the middle of a cake comes out clean.

- Let cool for 10 minutes and remove from pan.
- Frosting: Beat butter and cream cheese at medium speed until smooth. Mix in strawberry extract and icing sugar.
- Spread frosting over the top of the cooled cake and garnish with strawberries or sugared lollies.
- Alternatively cut the cake horizontally into 3 layers and spread a layer of icing between each layer and finish with frosting and decorations on top.

- Pour half the filling over biscuit base and cover with half of the strawberry puree.
- Using a fork, gently swirl puree through filling.
- Repeat with remaining filling and puree, and swirl with a fork.
- Cover, then refrigerate for several hours, or until set.
- Serve decorated with extra whipped cream and strawberries.

197. Strawberry Ripple Cheesecake Recipe

Serving: 8 | Prep: 180mins | Cook: 0S | Ready in: 180mins

Ingredients

- 250 g chocolate biscuits crushed
- 125 g butter melted
- 250 g fresh strawberries pureed
- 250 g fresh strawberries *to decorate *extra
- 1 cup whipped cream *to decorate
- Filling
- 3 tsp gelatine powder
- 1/3 cup water
- 250 g lite cream cheese
- 200 g low-fat strawberry yoghurt
- 1/2 cup caster sugar
- 300 g thickened cream whipped

Direction

- Combine biscuits and melted butter, then press into base and sides of a 22cm springform tin.
- Sprinkle gelatine over water in a cup.
- Stand cup in a pan of simmering water, until dissolved and then cool slightly.
- Beat cream cheese, yoghurt and sugar in a bowl until smooth.
- Gently fold in cream and gelatine.

198. Three Minute Jelly Cake Recipe

Serving: 0 | Prep: 10mins | Cook: 40mins | Ready in: 50mins

Ingredients

- 125 g butter softened
- 1/2 packet jelly crystals
- 1/2 cup sugar
- 1 3/4 cups self-raising flour
- 2 eggs
- 1/3 cup milk

Direction

- Combine all ingredients in a mixing bowl and stir until just blended.
- Beat for 3 minutes, using a wooden spoon, or a electric mixer on medium speed.
- Bake at 180C in a greased loaf tin for 35-40 minutes, or 2 x 18 cm sandwich tins for 25 minutes.
- When cool, turn out of tins onto a wire rack.
- Ice as desired when cold.

199.   Tim Tam Cheesecake Recipe

Serving: 12 | Prep: 30mins | Cook: 410mins | Ready in: 440mins

Ingredients

- 350 g Arnott's Tim Tams
- 80 g butter melted
- 375 g cream cheese cubed softened
- 1/2 cup caster sugar
- 1 tsp vanilla essence
- 1 cup thickened cream
- 3 tsp gelatine powder
- 1/4 cup boiling water
- 200 g white chocolate cooled melted

Direction

- Place 250 g of the Tim Tams in a blender and process into fine crumbs.
- Add the butter and process to combine. Press the mixture into spring-form baking pan and refrigerate 30 minutes.
- Beat the cream cheese, sugar and vanilla with an electric mixer until smooth, then beat in the cream.
- Mix the gelatine with the boiling water. Stir in the gelatine mixture, dissolved in 1/4 cup of boing water and white chocolate.
- Chop the remaining biscuits and stir into the cream cheese mixture then pour over the Tim Tam base.
- Cover and refrigerate until set.

200.   Toblerone Cheesecake Slice Recipe

Serving: 8 | Prep: 20mins | Cook: 0S | Ready in: 20mins

Ingredients

- 1 cup chocolate biscuits
- 1/3 cup butter melted

- 1/4 cup ground almonds
- 500g cream cheese
- 200g Toblerone chocolate bar melted
- 1/2 cup thickened cream
- 1/2 cup caster sugar

Direction

- Combined biscuit crumbs, butter and almonds, and press into the base of a lightly greased slice tin or spring form pan. Chill.
- Beat cream cheese for 2 minutes or until smooth. Add sugar, melted Toblerone chocolate and cream, continue beating until well combined.
- Pour onto the prepared base and refrigerate for 2-3 hours until set, or overnight.
- Serve topped with chocolate shavings.

201.   Tropical Cheesecake Log Recipe

Serving: 8 | Prep: 40mins | Cook: 0S | Ready in: 40mins

Ingredients

- 3 mangoes
- 250 g cream cheese room temperature
- 1/4 cup caster sugar
- 600 ml thickened cream
- 1/2 tsp vanilla essence
- 250 g Arnott's Granita biscuits
- 1/2 cup unsweetened orange juice
- 2 passionfruit
- 1 punnet fresh raspberries

Direction

- Slice cheeks from one mango and spoon out flesh into a food processor. Blitz to form a puree. Set aside. Reserve remaining two mangoes for garnish.
- Wipe out bowl of food processor. Add cream cheese, caster sugar and 1/2 cup of cream, and

blitz until smooth and well combined. Remove to a bowl and fold through mango puree.

- In a separate bowl, whisk remaining cream with vanilla essence until thick.
- Spread a long, thick rectangle of whipped cream onto your serving platter. Dip a Granita biscuit in orange juice then spread with cream cheese mixture. Stand upright at one end of whipped cream. Repeat with remaining biscuits, sandwiching them together with the cream cheese filling to form a log. Cover the log with remaining whipped cream, then place in the fridge to set for 2 hours or overnight.
- When you are ready to serve, remove cheeks from remaining mangoes and use a large metal spoon to scoop out the flesh. Slice lengthwise into thin slithers. Drape over the top of the log and dot with raspberries. Drizzle over passionfruit pulp and serve.

---

202.   Turkish Delight Fridge Cake Recipe

Serving: 12 | Prep: 15mins | Cook: 20mins | Ready in: 35mins

Ingredients

- 400 g dark chocolate coarsely chopped good quality
- 1 cup thick cream
- 2 tbs Cointreau
- 250 g Arnott's Marie biscuits coarsely chopped
- 6 x 55 g Fry's Turkish Delight bars quartered
- 170 g Ocean Spray Craisins dried cranberries
- 1/2 cup icing sugar mixture for dusting
- 1 tbs double cream *to serve

Direction

- Line the base of a 20 cm springform pan with baking paper.
- Place chocolate and cream in a saucepan over low heat. Stir for 5 minutes or until chocolate melts and mixture is smooth.

- Remove from heat. Stir in Cointreau and set aside for 5 minutes to cool.
- Combine the biscuits, Turkish delight and craisins in a large bowl. Add the chocolate mixture and stir until well combined.
- Press firmly into the prepared pan. Place in the fridge for 6 hours or until firm.
- Dust the cake with icing sugar and cut into slices. Divide among serving plates and serve with cream.

---

203.   Upside Down Banana Chocolate Cake Recipe

Serving: 8 | Prep: 15mins | Cook: 65mins | Ready in: 80mins

Ingredients

- 225g butter softened
- 3 Cavendish bananas large ripe peeled halved lengthways
- 1 cup brown sugar firmly packed
- 3 eggs
- 200g dark chocolate melted
- 1 1/2 cups self-raising flour
- 2 tbs cup milk
- 1/2 cup thickened cream whipped to serve
- Fudge sauce
- 1/2 cup thickened cream
- 200g dark chocolate chopped

Direction

- Preheat oven to 170C. Grease and line base and side of a 22cm (base) springform cake pan.
- Melt 25g of the butter in a large frying pan over medium-high heat until foaming. Add the banana slices, cut side down. Cook for 1 minute until light golden, turn and cook further 30 seconds. Cool for 5 minutes then arrange bananas, cut side down over the base of the prepared pan.
- Combine sugar and remaining butter in food processor. Process until combined. Add eggs

one at a time, process until combined. Add melted chocolate and process, scraping down sides as required. Transfer to a bowl, fold in the combined sifted flour and cocoa, then the milk.

- Spoon cake batter over the bananas and smooth the surface.
- Bake for 50-60 minutes or until a skewer inserted into the centre comes out clean. Stand for 30 minutes in pan. Turn onto a plate.
- For the sauce, combine the cream and chocolate in a small saucepan over medium-low heat. Cook, stirring with a metal spoon until melted and smooth. Drizzle some of the warm sauce over the cake. Cut into pieces and serve with cream and remaining sauce.

204.   Violet Crumble Cheesecake Recipe

Serving: 8 | Prep: 20mins | Cook: 0S | Ready in: 20mins

Ingredients

- Base
- 250g Arnott's Nice biscuits
- 1/3 cup butter melted
- Filling
- 500g cream cheese
- 1/2 cup caster sugar
- 50g Nestle Violet Crumble chocolate honeycomb bar crushed
- 1/2 cup thickened cream

Direction

- Mix biscuits crumbs and butter in blender, and then press into a 20cm springform pan and refrigerate.
- Beat cream cheese with an electric mixer for 2 minutes or until smooth. Add sugar and cream and mix.
- Fold crushed Violet Crumble into mixture and refrigerate until set.

205.   White Chocolate Malteser Cheesecake Recipe

Serving: 12 | Prep: 20mins | Cook: 0S | Ready in: 20mins

Ingredients

- 300 g chocolate biscuits
- 12 dates
- 1/2 cup coconut oil
- 180 g walnuts
- Filling
- 500 g cream cheese
- 3/4 cup caster sugar
- 200 ml thickened cream
- 400 g white chocolate
- 3 tsp gelatine powder
- 1/4 cup boiling water
- 250 g Maltesers

Direction

- Base: Process biscuits and walnuts until the mixture resembles breadcrumbs.
- Add the dates and butter/coconut oil. Process until well combined.
- Grease a springform pan. Firmly press mixture into the bottom of the pan and work up the sides. Cover and refrigerate.
- Filling: While the cream cheese softens, chop the Maltesers in half and set aside.
- Beat cream cheese and sugar with an electric mixer on medium speed until combined. Add the cream and mix until creamy.
- Combine gelatine with boiling water in a jug or mug. Add to the cream cheese mixture. Mix on medium speed until well combined.
- Melt white chocolate in a heatproof bowl over a small saucepan of boiling water. Do not allow the bowl to touch the water.
- Pour the melted chocolate and Maltesers into the bowl with the cream cheese mixture and mix until combined.
- Pour mixture over base. Add any extra maltesers for decoration if desired.

- Refrigerate for 5 hours or overnight.

206. White Chocolate Mud Cake Recipe

Serving: 12 | Prep: 20mins | Cook: 120mins | Ready in: 140mins

Ingredients

- 250g butter
- 250g Nestle* white chocolate
- 200ml water
- 1 1/2 cups caster sugar
- 1 3/4 cups plain flour
- 1 cup self-raising flour
- 2 eggs lightly beaten
- 1/2 cup sour cream
- 1 tsp vanilla essence
- Icing
- 125g butter
- 125g Nestle* white chocolate melted
- 3/4 cup icing sugar

Direction

- Preheat oven to 150C.
- Cake: Heat butter, sugar, chocolate and water in a saucepan and stir over low heat until well combined.
- Sift both flours together and blend into chocolate mixture.
- Stir in eggs, sour cream and vanilla.
- Pour the mixture into a deep 20cm pan and cook for approximately 1-2 hours depending on your oven.
- Icing: Cream together the butter and icing sugar, then add melted chocolate.
- Spread icing over the cake.

207. White Chocolate And Frosted Cherry Cheesecake Recipe

Serving: 10 | Prep: 30mins | Cook: 8mins | Ready in: 38mins

Ingredients

- 250 g plain chocolate biscuits
- 100 g butter melted
- 1 1/2 cups thickened cream
- 2 tsp gelatine
- 500 g cream cheese cubed softened
- 3/4 cup CSR caster sugar
- 200 g white chocolate buttons
- Frosted Cherries
- 1/2 cup CSR caster sugar
- 2 tbs water
- 200 g cherries fresh
- 2 tbs caster sugar *extra for dusting

Direction

- Place biscuits into a bowl of a food processor and pulse until fine crumbs have formed. Add melted butter, continue mixing until well combined. Press mixture into the base of a greased and lined 22 cm spring-form pan. Refrigerate until firm.
- Combine ½ cup of the cream with chocolate buttons in a glass bowl and place over a saucepan of gently simmering water. Allow chocolate to melt, stirring until smooth. Dissolve the gelatine in ¼ cup boiling water, set aside.
- Using electric beaters, whip remaining cream to soft peaks, set aside. Place cream cheese and sugar in the bowl of an electric mixer and beat until smooth. Add in the chocolate mixture and dissolved gelatine, mixing until smooth.
- Fold whipped cream into the cream cheese mixture until well combined. Spoon over prepared base and chill for 2-3 hours until set.
- For the cherries: place sugar and water in a saucepan and stir over low heat until sugar has dissolved. Continue to simmer a further

several minutes until slightly reduced. Cool. Dip half of the cherries in sugar syrup and then into the sugar. Place on a cooling rack to set.

- Just prior to serving, remove cheesecake from pan and decorate with the frosted and fresh cherries.

208. White Chocolate And Mango Cheesecake Recipe

Serving: 8 | Prep: 30mins | Cook: 0S | Ready in: 30mins

Ingredients

- 200 g gingernut biscuits
- 100 g unsalted butter melted
- 50 g crystalized ginger optional
- Filling
- 250 g cream cheese brought to room temperature
- 200 ml condensed milk
- 150 g white chocolate melted
- 150 ml cream
- 3 1/2 tsp gelatine powder
- 125 ml boiling water
- Topping
- 2 mangoes medium
- 4 tbs caster sugar
- 2 tsp gelatine powder
- 100 ml boiling water

Direction

- Base: Blitz the biscuits in a food processor until they've been reduced to fine crumbs.
- Add the ginger, if using, and blitz until completely incorporated into the crumbs. With the machine switched on, pour the melted butter in until all combined.
- Press the crumbs into the base of a lined 24cm springform tin and refrigerate until firm.
- Filling: Add gelatine to the water and stir with a fork until all dissolved. Put aside to cool.

- Combine the cream cheese and condensed milk and beat until smooth and creamy. Stir in the melted chocolate and then pour in the cream.
- Pour in the cooled water and gelatine and stir until combined.
- Pour into the tin and put it into the fridge for at least an hour and a half to firm up.
- Topping: Puree the mango flesh. Add the sugar and blitz again. There should be approximately 350ml of puree.
- Combine water and gelatine.
- Combine with mango puree and pour carefully over top of the cheesecake.
- Refrigerate for 3 hours.
- Serve with some fresh mango, lychees and passionfruit, if desired.

209. White Chocolate And Raspberry Cheesecake Recipe

Serving: 8 | Prep: 20mins | Cook: 5mins | Ready in: 25mins

Ingredients

- 185 g sweet plain biscuits crushed
- 90g butter, melted
- 500g cream cheese, softened
- 395g Nestle* sweetened condensed milk
- 100g Nestle Plaistowe white chocolate
- 1 tbs gelatine powder
- 1/4 cup hot water
- 3/4 cup cream
- 150g fresh raspberries, pureed

Direction

- Sprinkle gelatine over hot water, stir to dissolve and allow to cool.
- Combine biscuits and butter, then press into the base of a 23cm springform pan and refrigerate until firm.
- Beat cream cheese and sweetened condensed milk until smooth, then beat in cream.

- Melt white cooking chocolate, and allow to cool.
- Beat cooled chocolate and gelatine into cream cheese mixture and spoon evenly over crumb base.
- Swirl raspberry puree through the cheesecake mixture.
- If desired, melt more white chocolate and drizzle over top. Refrigerate before serving.

Chapter 7: Sponge Cake Recipes

***

210.	Apple Sponge

Serving: 8 | Prep: 15mins | Cook: 20mins | Ready in: 35mins

Ingredients

- 425g canned apples
- 1 tbs caster sugar
- 2 tbs water
- 3 tsp caster sugar
- Sponge Topping
- 2 eggs
- 1/3 cup caster sugar
- 1/3 cup cornflour
- 1/4 cup self-raising flour

Direction

- Simmer apples, sugar and water in a covered saucepan for about 5 minutes, or until apples are tender. Keep hot while preparing sponge topping.
- Beat eggs in small bowl with electric mixer until thick and creamy, add sugar gradually and beat until dissolved. Lightly fold in sifted flours.
- Pour hot apples and liquid into ovenproof dish. Quickly spread sponge topping over apples, sprinkle with extra sugar.
- Bake at 180C for approximately 20 minutes or until sponge feels firm to the touch and is lightly browned.
- Serve with cream or ice-cream.

211.	Berry Custard Cake Recipe

Serving: 8 | Prep: 30mins | Cook: 70mins | Ready in: 100mins

Ingredients

- 1 cup plain flour
- 100g butter melted
- 1 egg
- 1/2 cup caster sugar
- 1 1/2 tsp baking powder
- 1 tsp vanilla essence
- 3 cup mixed berries fresh
- Custard Topping
- 2 cup sour cream
- 1/2 cup caster sugar
- 1 1/2 tbs custard powder
- 2 egg yolks
- 1 tsp vanilla essence

Direction

- Preheat oven to 180C.
- Prepare a large pan (23cm springform or equivalent) by either greasing and flouring, or using baking paper.
- To make the sponge base, mix together the sifted flour, butter, egg, caster sugar, baking powder and vanilla. Pour into the tin.
- Evenly spread the berries over the sponge base.

- To make the custard topping, beat all the ingredients together and pour over the top of the berries.
- Bake for 50 - 60 minutes. Top should look firm when cooked.
- Serve hot or cold.

212. Best Sponge Cake

Serving: 8 | Prep: 15mins | Cook: 20mins | Ready in: 35mins

Ingredients

- 4 egg fresh room temperature
- 3/4 cup caster sugar
- 1/2 tsp vanilla essence
- 2 tsp plain flour
- 1/2 tsp bicarbonate of soda
- 1 tsp cream of tartar
- 1/2 cup cornflour

Direction

- Preheat oven to 160C fan-forced. Grease and line 2 x 20 cm cake pans.
- Beat eggs and sugar on highest speed for 7 minutes.
- Add plain flour, bicarbonate of soda and cream of tartar a 1 cup measuring cup, fill up with cornflour, sift together several times.
- Add vanilla into egg mixture.
- On lowest speed of mixer, mix in sifted flours for 1 minute or until just combined.
- Divide mixture between tins and bake for 20 minutes or until cake springs back when touched and is coming away slightly from sides of pan.
- Fill and decorate as desired.

213. Custard Sponge Recipe

Serving: 0 | Prep: 10mins | Cook: 25mins | Ready in: 35mins

Ingredients

- 4 eggs room temperature separated
- 3/4 cup caster sugar
- 1 pinch salt
- 3/4 cup cornflour
- 1 tbs custard powder
- 1/2 tsp bicarbonate of soda
- 1 tsp cream of tartar

Direction

- Preheat oven to 200C.
- Grease 2 x 20 cm tins or a larger baking tin.
- Beat egg whites and salt together until firm.
- Gradually add the caster sugar. Beat well until sugar has dissolved.
- Add beaten egg yolks, and beat for 2 minutes.
- Fold in sifted dry ingredients and pour into baking tins.
- Reduce oven temperature to 190C and bake for 20-25 minutes on the centre shelf.
- Dredge cooled cake with icing sugar or cover with whipped cream and crumbled Flake.

214. Dextrose Sponge Cake Recipe

Serving: 8 | Prep: 0S | Cook: 0S | Ready in:

Ingredients

- 3 tbs plain flour
- 2/3 cup cornflour
- 2/3 cup dextrose
- 2 tbs water
- 4 eggs large
- 1 tsp vanilla essence
- 1 tsp cream of tartar
- 1/2 tsp bicarbonate of soda

- 1 sprinkle cornflour for dusting
- Vanilla buttercream
- 1/2 cup dextrose
- 1 1/2 tbs water
- 90 g butter softened
- 1/2 tsp vanilla extract
- 1 1/2 tbs full fat milk powder
- Decoration
- 250 g fresh strawberries
- 2/3 cup thickened cream
- 1 tbs dextrose
- 1/2 tsp vanilla essence
- 1 tbs coconut flakes

Direction

- Preheat oven to 170°C, non-fan forced. Grease and line two 20cm round cake tins with baking paper. Dust base and sides lightly with extra cornflour.
- In a small bowl, combine plain flour and cornflour, stirring together. In a small saucepan, combine dextrose and water. Stir on med/high heat and bring to the boil. Boil for 1 minute, then remove from heat and set aside.
- Separate egg whites from yolks, placing whites in a large bowl, and keeping yolks aside in small bowl. Add vanilla, cream of tartar and bicarb soda to the large bowl with egg whites.
- Using electric beaters on high, beat until fluffy – 2 to 3 minutes.
- Gradually add dextrose syrup, (while it's still hot) in a steady stream, beating constantly.
- Beat on high 3 – 4 minutes, until mixture is voluminous and stiff. Beating on medium/low speed, add egg yolks, one at a time, beating after each addition.
- Sift combined flours into egg mix in two lots, stirring lightly, but thoroughly after each addition. Make sure all of the flour is incorporated and no flour pockets remain.
- Divide batter between the two cake tins, spreading out evenly to the sides with a spatula. Bake 16 – 18 minutes at 170°C (non-fan forced.) Cakes should be golden brown and springy to the touch.

- Using a blunt palette knife, run around the edges before removing the cakes from tins. Leave to cool on a wire rack.
- For vanilla buttercream: 1. Combine dextrose and water in a small saucepan. Stir over a medium heat to dissolve. 2. Bring to the boil and stir whilst boiling for 1 minute. 3. Remove from heat and set over a bowl of cool water. 4. In a small bowl, beat butter and vanilla until creamy. Once syrup has cooled completely gradually pour into butter mix whilst beating. 5. Add milk powder and beat until smooth.
- For decoration: Whip thickened cream with dextrose and vanilla until soft peaks form. Fill cakes with cream, sliced strawberries and top with vanilla buttercream and a scattering of coconut flakes. Store cake in an airtight container in the fridge up to 4 days.

---

215.   Easy Banana Sponge Recipe

Serving: 6 | Prep: 10mins | Cook: 25mins | Ready in: 35mins

Ingredients

- 125 g butter
- 3/4 cup sugar
- 2 bananas mashed
- 2 eggs
- 2 tbs milk
- 1 tsp bicarbonate of soda
- 1 cup plain flour
- 1 tsp baking powder

Direction

- Preheat oven to 180C.
- Line and grease two 20 cm round pans.
- Mix butter and sugar together.
- Stir in the mashed bananas, and then the eggs.
- Heat the milk for 30 seconds in microwave, then stir in the baking soda and mix into the batter.

- Sift flour and baking powder, then stir into the mixture.
- Place half the mix into each pan.
- Bake for 20 minutes.
- Allow to cool, then ice or dust with icing sugar.

216.   Egg Yolk Sponge

Serving: 0 | Prep: 15mins | Cook: 0S |Ready in: 15mins

Ingredients

- 3 egg large yolks
- 2/3 cup caster sugar
- 1 heaped teaspoon baking powder
- 2 tablespoons coconut (optional)
- 2 tablespoons milk
- 1 tablespoon butter
- 1/3 cup hot water
- 2/3 cup plain flour
- 2 tablespoons cornflour
- 1-2 teaspoons vanilla essence

Direction

- Grease 2 deep sponge tins.
- Melt butter with milk in the microwave for approximately 2 minutes.
- Beat the egg yolks with an electric beater until thick.
- Add the hot water and beat again.
- Add caster sugar gradually, beating continually.
- Sift flour, cornflour and baking powder with a pinch of salt. Fold in coconut if using.
- Gently stir in warm milk and butter.
- Bake at 180C for 20-30 minutes.

217.   Grilled Peach And White Chocolate Bombe Alaska Recipe

Serving: 2 | Prep: 180mins | Cook: 20mins |Ready in: 200mins

Ingredients

- 1 white peach
- 1/2 litre vanilla ice cream
- 1/2 cup white chocolate chips
- Sponge cake
- 1/2 cup plain flour
- 1 pinch baking powder
- 2 eggs
- 1/4 cup caster sugar
- 25g melted butter
- Swiss meringue
- 4 egg whites
- 1 pinch cream of tartar
- 1 cup caster sugar

Direction

- Preheat your oven to 180C and line a 9-inch baking tin with baking paper and set aside.
- Sift 1/3 cup plain flour and 1/4 tsp baking powder into a small bowl, then re-sift.
- Place 25g butter in a small microwave-safe bowl and microwave for 50 seconds or until just melted.
- Place 4 eggs and 1/4 cup caster sugar in a small mixing bowl and mix on high speed with electric beaters until light in colour and almost quadrupled in size.
- Sift half the flour mixture into your eggs and fold together gently with a spatula. Sift in the rest of your flour and fold through until well combined.
- Add the melted butter to your mixture and gently mix through.
- Pour your batter out into your pre-prepared baking tray and place in the oven to bake for 15 minutes or until the top is golden and an inserted skewer is removed clean. Set aside to cool.

- To make the ice cream, scoop vanilla ice cream into a large bowl lined with cling wrap.
- Add in 1/2 cup of white chocolate chips and mix thoroughly.
- Once mixed, press the ice cream into the bowl so it fills all air pockets and scoop a small amount of ice-cream out of the centre (where your half a peach will go). Place the bowl in the freezer for 1-2 hours or until your icecream has re-frozen.
- Meanwhile, cut your peaches in half, pit them and remove the skin. Place face-down on a lightly oiled griddle pan over medium heat. Cook for 4-5 minutes or until grill marks appear of the peach, then flip them and cook for 4-5 minutes on the other side. Set aside.
- To make the Swiss meringue, place 4 eggs whites, 1 cup of caster sugar and a pinch of cream of tartar into a large glass or metal mixing bowl and place over a double boiler. (a medium sized saucepan containing a few inches of boiling water). Whisk by hand until all the sugar has dissolved.
- Move your mixing bowl off the double boiler and whisk with electric beaters until your mixture is thick, glossy and holds stiff peaks. This should take around 10 minutes or more depending on the power of your beaters.
- Retrieve your ice cream cases from the freezer and set on the benchtop for 5 minutes to soften slightly.
- Gently remove your ice-cream mould from the bowl, press half a peach into the hole in the centre of the dome, them flip it (peach side down) onto your pre-prepared sponge cake.
- Using a sharp knife and your ice-cream mould as a guide, cut your sponge cake down to size so as it doesn't stick out past your ice-cream dome.
- Transfer your Bombe Alaska onto a spare plate or baking tray, and pipe or rusticly 'paint' your meringue mixture onto the outside of your ice-cream. Ensure you cover all the ice-cream and the sponge cake at the bottom, but you can make your layer as thick or as thin as you'd like, and any shape your desire!

- Transfer your Bombe Alaska onto your serving plate and gently toast your meringue with a blow torch. Serve right away.

---

218. Lamington Cake With Milo Icing Recipe

Serving: 8 | Prep: 30mins | Cook: 20mins | Ready in: 50mins

Ingredients

- 225 g butter brought to room temperature
- 225 g caster sugar
- 4 eggs
- 225 g self-raising flour
- 1 tsp baking powder
- Filling
- 200 ml thickened cream
- 200 g strawberry jam
- Milo icing
- 2 tbs Milo
- 2 tbs cocoa powder
- 2 tbs boiling water
- 1/4 cup coconut *to decorate

Direction

- Preheat the oven to 180C and grease 2 x deep, 20cm round cake tins.
- Beat butter and sugar together with an electric mixer until pale. Add the eggs one at a time, beating well after each addition. Add in the flour and baking powder and beat until just combined.
- Divide the mixture between prepared tins and bake for 15-20 mins until lightly golden brown. Cool on a wire rack before assembling.
- To make the icing - Put all the dry ingredients into a small bowl and stir together. Add in the boiling water a little bit at a time, stirring well, until the mixture becomes a spreadable consistency. Set aside to cool while you start the assembly.

- Whip the thickened cream until light and fluffy using electric beaters.
- Using a serrated knife, carefully slice each cake horizontally so you have 4 cakes. Place the first layer of cake on your cake stand and spread 2 tablespoons of jam evenly across the top, followed by 2 tablespoons of whipped cream. I find it easiest to use a butter knife to spread the jam, followed by an offset spatula for the cream. Put the next layer of cake on, and continue spreading the jam and cream between each layers. When the top layer has been placed, spread the cooled Milo icing over the top of the cake (it may drip over the sides, don't worry!) and finish with a sprinkle of coconut.

219. Lee's Sponge Recipe

Serving: 8 | Prep: 15mins | Cook: 20mins | Ready in: 35mins

Ingredients

- 4 eggs room temperature
- 1/2 cup sugar
- 3/4 cup cornflour
- 1 tbs plain flour
- 1/2 tsp bicarbonate of soda
- 1 tsp cream of tartar

Direction

- Preheat oven to 190C. Line and grease a 25cm round or square cake tin.
- Beat eggs for 10 minutes. Slowly add sugar, then beat for another 10 minutes.
- Sift flours, soda and cream of tartar 3 times. Gently fold into eggs and sugar with either a metal spoon or spatula.
- Pour into tin and place in the upper half of oven.
- Bake for 15-20 minutes. Turn sponge a quarter turn each 5 minutes.

- Cake is cooked when the top springs back when touched.
- Cool on wire rack, wrapped in a clean tea towel.
- Fill and ice as desired.

220. Lemon Coconut Cake

Serving: 10 | Prep: 15mins | Cook: 40mins | Ready in: 55mins

Ingredients

- 1 1/2 cup self-raising flour
- 1/2 cup desiccated coconut
- 1 tbs lemon rind grated
- 1 cup caster sugar
- 125 g unsalted butter melted
- 2 egg
- 1 cup milk
- Icing
- 1 1/2 cup icing sugar
- 1 cup desiccated coconut
- 1/2 tsp lemon rind grated
- 1/4 cup lemon juice

Direction

- Preheat oven to 180C and grease and line a deep 20 cm round cake tin.
- Combine the flour, coconut, lemon rind, sugar, butter, eggs and milk in a large bowl.
- Mix well with a wooden spoon until mixture is smooth. It will be runny.
- Pour the mixture into prepared tin and bake for 40 minutes or until skewer comes out clean when inserted into the centre of the cake.
- Leave the cake to cool slightly before turning out onto a wire rack. Leave to cool.
- Combine all the icing ingredients together in a bowl and spread over the top of the cake when completely cool.

221. Never Fail Cake

Serving: 0 | Prep: 30mins | Cook: 45mins |Ready in: 75mins

Ingredients

- 250 g unsalted butter chopped
- 2 cup sugar
- 4 egg
- 1/2 tsp vanilla essence
- 3 cup self-raising flour
- 1 1/2 cup milk
- 1 pinch salt

Direction

- Using electric beaters, beat the butter and sugar for 20 minutes until light and creamy.
- Add the eggs one at a time, beating well between each addition, then beat in the vanilla essence.
- Stir in 1 cup of flour, then ½ cup of the milk.
- Repeat until all the flour and milk is used, making sure there are no lumps in the batter.
- Transfer to the prepared dish.
- Bake at 160C for about 45 minutes, until the cake springs back when gently touched in the middle and comes away from the edges of the pan.
- Cool in the tin for 5 minutes, then release the sides and cool completely on a wire rack before icing.

222. No Fail Sponge Recipe

Serving: 0 | Prep: 15mins | Cook: 20mins |Ready in: 35mins

Ingredients

- 5 eggs separated
- 1 tsp glycerine
- 3/4 cup caster sugar
- 1 cup cornflour sifted
- 1 tsp bicarbonate of soda sifted
- 1 tsp cream of tartar
- 1 pinch vanilla essence *to taste

Direction

- Separate white from yolks. Beat whites until stiff.
- Add yolks and glycerine and mix.
- Gradually add caster sugar and beat for 3 minutes on medium speed. Add vanilla if required.
- Sift dry ingredients several times. Fold into the mixture.
- Pour into 2 greased, lined tins.
- Bake at 180C for 15-20 minutes.

223. Pink Layer Cake

Serving: 8 | Prep: 25mins | Cook: 45mins |Ready in: 70mins

Ingredients

- 375 g plain flour sifted
- 1 1/2 tsp baking powder
- 400 g CSR caster sugar
- 250 g butter melted
- 4 extra-large egg lightly beaten
- 375 ml milk
- 1/2 tsp vanilla paste
- 4 drops pink gel food colouring
- Buttercream
- 200 g soft butter room temperature
- 530 g CSR soft icing sugar mixture sifted
- 4 fresh strawberries mashed
- 1/2 cup fresh strawberries *to decorate

Direction

- Preheat oven to 160°C (140°C fan forced). Lightly grease and line the bases of two 19cm springform cake pans with baking paper.
- Sift flour and baking powder into a large mixing bowl, add caster sugar, butter, eggs,

108

milk, vanilla and mix with electric mixer for 2 minutes on medium speed or until smooth and well combined. Add pink food colour and mix until colour is well incorporated.

- Pour into the two prepared pans and bake for 40 - 45 minutes or until a skewer inserted comes out clean. Cool in pans for 10 minutes before turning out onto wire racks to cool completely. Carefully slice each cake in half horizontally to create 4 layers.
- For butter cream – beat butter in a medium sized bowl with an electric mixer for 5 minutes until pale and creamy. Add icing sugar, beat for a further 10 minutes or until light and fluffy. Remove 1 cup of icing mixture and fold through mashed strawberries to create fruity butter cream.
- Place one layer of cake onto a serving platter and use a palette knife to spread 1/3 cup of strawberry buttercream. Repeat with remaining cake layers. Spread remaining white buttercream over sides and top of the cake. Decorate with strawberries.

---

224. Poached Pear And Pomegranate Sponge Cake Recipe

Serving: 0 | Prep: 40mins | Cook: 60mins | Ready in: 100mins

Ingredients

- 4 eggs room temperature separated
- 2/3 cup caster sugar
- 2/3 cup self-raising flour
- 1/3 cup cornflour
- 1 tsp cream of tartar
- 1 tsp vanilla essence
- Cream
- 300 ml thickened cream
- 1/2 pomegranate juiced *to decorate
- 3/4 cup icing sugar
- Pears

- 3 pears
- 1/2 cup water
- 2 tsp white sugar
- Glaze
- 1/4 cup chardonnay
- 2 tsp white sugar

Direction

- Preheat your oven to 160C.
- Grease and line the base of a 20cm diameter non-stick spring form tin. Don't grease the edges, this may go against every baking instinct you have, but to get the maximum rise from your cake, it needs to be able to grip the sides a little.
- Separate your eggs, place your yolks in one mixing bowl, the whites in another and 1/3 a cup of sugar in with each.
- Beat your egg whites on high speed with an electric mixer until it holds soft peaks and is of a meringue texture (smooth, glossy, and thick).
- Beat your egg yolks on high speed with an electric mixer until egg yolks have doubled in size.
- Into a separate bowl, sift together your self-raising flour, cornflour, and cream of tartar.
- Pour egg yolks into your whites and sift your dry ingredients for a second time into the bowl on top.
- Fold together gently with a spatula until well combined.
- Pour mixture into pre-prepared tin. Avoid filling your cake tin more than half way, or you risk it spilling over in the oven.
- Place in your preheated oven for 25 minutes, or until a skewer inserted into the centre of your cake is removed clean.
- Place cake in the refrigerator to cool.
- Cut your pears into roughly 1cm x 1cm cubes, skin on or off, it's up to you (I've left it on.)
- Place 1/2 cup water and 1tbs caster sugar into a small saucepan, and place over a low heat.
- Toss your pears through the liquid and allow to simmer until the pears are soft and the

liquid has thickened slightly, roughly 10 - 15 minutes. Set aside to cool.

- Once your cake has cooled completely, you can start working on your whipped cream icing.
- Place the seeds of half a pomegranate into a food processor and blitz until it forms a thick paste (the seed centres will remain whole).
- Place a sieve over a medium sized mixing bowl, and place your pomegranate paste into the sieve. Set aside, allowing the pomegranate juice to drip into the bowl.
- Retrieve your bowl from underneath your sieve, and add 300ml cream and 1/2 a cup of icing sugar, and beat together on high with electric beaters until cream hold stiff peaks. Set aside.
- Place 1/4 cup of chardonnay and 2 tsp sugar into a saucepan over a low heat.
- Allow to simmer softly until the sugar has dissolved into the chardonnay (roughly 5 minutes.) Remove from the heat and set aside.
- Retrieve your cake from the fridge, carefully slice the top 1cm off your cake.
- Pour your chardonnay over your separated cake top and set aside for a moment to soak in.
- Cut chardonnay sponge into 1cm x 1cm cubes.
- Apply a layer of pomegranate cream on top of the bottom slice of cake (save some for decoration on top).
- Arrange sponge cubes and pears on top of your cream, pipe small dots of cream on top and sprinkle with whole pomegranate seeds.

---

225.   Raspberry Meringue Trifle Recipe

Serving: 8 | Prep: 15mins | Cook: 15mins | Ready in: 30mins

Ingredients

- 300 g frozen raspberries
- 1 cup caster sugar

- 1 sponge cake
- 1/2 cup port
- 500 ml vanilla ice cream
- Meringue topping
- 2 egg whites
- 1/2 cup sugar

Direction

- Trifle: Place the berries and sugar in a small saucepan over low heat.
- Bring to the boil and simmer for 2 minutes, or until slightly syrupy. Set aside to cool.
- Slice sponge to fit an ovenproof/freezer-safe dish. Dip the slices of sponge into the port.
- Cover the base of the dish with the sponge, top with berries and ice cream.
- Freeze until ready to serve.
- Meringue topping: Preheat a griller until hot.
- Whisk the egg whites until soft peaks form. Gradually add the sugar and whisk until smooth and glossy.
- Remove dish from freezer and top with meringue.
- Grill the meringue for 1-2 minutes until golden brown.

---

226.   Sex On The Beach Peach Trifle

Serving: 8 | Prep: 180mins | Cook: 60mins | Ready in: 240mins

Ingredients

- 4 eggs
- 1/2 cup caster sugar
- 70g plain flour
- 12g cornflour
- 1/2 tsp baking powder
- Cranberry Sauce
- Jelly
- 2 white peaches, cubed
- 2 cups water, plus extra
- 1/4 cup sugar

- 85g packet of Aeroplane Jelly
- 100ml vodka
- Custard
- 800ml thickened cream
- 12 egg yolks
- 3 tbsp cornflour
- 2 cups grapefruit juice
- cup caster sugar
- Marinated peaches
- 4 white peaches
- 1/2 cup peach schnapps
- 2/3 cup white sugar
- Peach toppers
- 2 white peaches
- white sugar
- Cream
- 600ml thickened cream
- 1/2 tsp vanilla essence
- 110g icing sugar

Direction

- Preheat your oven to 180C. Prepare a 9-inch (23cm) diameter cake tin. Set aside.
- Separate your eggs, place your yolks in one mixing bowl, the whites in another.
- Beat your egg whites on high speed with an electric mixer, pouring in half of your caster sugar as you go, until it holds soft peaks and is of a meringue texture (smooth, glossy, and thick).
- Clean and dry or change your beaters, and beat your egg yolks on high speed, gradually pouring the second half of your caster sugar as you go, until egg yolks have roughly doubled in size.
- Pour egg yolks into your whites and using a soft silicone spatula, fold them together gently.
- Into a separate bowl, sift together your self-raising flour, cornflour, and cream of tartar. Then sift them a second time into the mixing bowl with your eggs.
- Add vanilla essence, and fold wet and dry ingredients together gently until well combined. Ensure you scrape the bottom of the mixing bowl to pick any last small pockets of flour.
- Pour mixture into the prepared tin and place on the centre rack in the oven for 25 minutes, or until a skewer inserted into the centre of the cake is removed clean.
- Allow cake to cool in the tin for 20-25 minutes. Run a knife around the edge of your cake to release it from the tin, and gently transfer it onto a cooling rack. Place in the fridge to cool. Once cooled, cut up into roughly 1-inch by 1-inch cubes and set aside.
- To make the custard, separate your 12 egg yolks into a bowl, whisk lightly with a fork and set aside.
- Meanwhile, add your full cream milk and cornflour to a saucepan and place over medium heat.
- Whisk your milk mixture continuously, ensuring you scrape the bottom occasionally to avoid the cornflour sticking and burning.
- Once the mixture has started to bubble lightly at the edges, remove from heat, add your egg yolks and whisk together.
- Return your saucepan to the heat and continue to whisk until the mixture comes together and thickens dramatically. Set aside to cool.
- Place 2 cups grapefruit juice and 1 cup caster sugar in a medium saucepan and place over a medium heat.
- Allow the mixture to simmer for 30 minutes to an hour or until you can draw a solid line through the residual 'syrup' on your spatula.
- Set aside to cool slightly, pour your syrup into your custard and whisk thoroughly to combine. Set aside to cool completely.
- To make the jelly, cut 2 white peaches into roughly 2cm square cubes and place in a large saucepan with 2 cups of water and 1/4 cup sugar. Bring to the boil, reduce for a simmer and leave it bubbling away for half an hour.
- Remove your saucepan from the cooktop, set aside to cool slightly, just below boiling, and pour the liquid into a measuring cup through a strainer to remove peach chunks. You require 350ml of water to make this jelly, so to ensure you have the correct amount of liquid you must either remove some if you have

more or add boiling water to equal 350ml if you have less.

- Add the contents of an 85g packet of jelly into your peach liquid and whisk until all granules are dissolved.
- Add 100ml of vodka to the jelly, mix thoroughly and pour your jelly into your trifle bowl. Set in the fridge for 4 hours to set.
- Once your jelly has set quarter 4 white peaches and place into a deep bowl. Add 1/2 cup peach schnapps and 2/3 cup white sugar to the bowl, toss together with tongs, cover with cling wrap and set aside to soak for half an hour.
- Once your peaches have marinated, you can start assembling. Gently pour your custard into the trifle bowl atop your jelly and gently spread it out evenly with a spatula.
- Retrieve your sponge cake cubes and arrange randomly atop your custard.
- Heat your cranberry sauce in the microwave for 20-30 seconds in 10 seconds sections until it's runny, then drizzle a generous amount over your sponge cake cubes.
- Drain the liquid from your marinated peaches and arrange the slices atop your drizzled sponge cubes. Set aside while you prepare the finishing touches.
- Place 600ml thickened cream, 110g icing sugar and 1/2 tsp vanilla essence into a large mixing bowl.
- Using electric beaters on high speed, whip the cream until it forms stiff peaks.
- Gently scrape the cream into your trifle bowl atop your peach slices and using a spatula, gently press it down into the peaches as you level the layer.
- Cover your trifle bowl with cling wrap and place in the fridge until you're ready to serve.
- Just before serving your trifle, quarter 2 white peaches, roll each slice in a bowl of white sugar and arrange neatly atop your trifle.

227.　　　Sponge Cake

Serving: 0 | Prep: 10mins | Cook: 25mins | Ready in: 35mins

Ingredients

- 1/2 cup caster sugar
- 1/2 tsp bicarbonate of soda
- 1/2 tsp cream of tartar
- 3/4 cup cornflour
- 1 tbs custard powder
- 4 egg fresh

Direction

- Sift bi-carbonate of soda, cream of tartar, cornflour and custard powder together 4 times.
- Beat sugar and eggs in an electric mixer on high for 5 minutes.
- Fold dry ingredients into egg mixture and beat on slow.
- Grease 2 x 18 cm cake pans with butter and line the bottoms with baking paper.
- Pour cake mixture into two tins, banging each tin on the bench to remove any air bubbles.
- Bake at 190C for 20-25 minutes.

228.　　　Sponge Cake Recipe

Serving: 8 | Prep: 15mins | Cook: 30mins | Ready in: 45mins

Ingredients

- 1 cup cornflour
- 3/4 cup sugar
- 2 tsp plain flour
- 1 tsp cream of tartar
- 1/2 tsp bicarbonate of soda
- 4 eggs large separated
- 1 pinch salt

Direction

- Sift cornflour, plain flour, cream of tartar and bicarbonate of soda three times.
- Beat egg whites and salt until stiff. Gradually add sugar and beat until quite stiff.
- Add egg yolks and beat until thick.
- Fold in the flour mixture.
- Pour mixture evenly into two greased and lined round pans.
- Bake for 20-30 minutes at 180C.

229.   Strawberry Trifle Recipe

Serving: 8 | Prep: 15mins | Cook: 0S | Ready in: 15mins

Ingredients

- 250g jam sponge roll
- 1 tbs sherry optional
- 170g strawberry jelly crystals
- 600ml milk
- 85g instant strawberry pudding mix
- 300ml thickened cream
- 250g fresh strawberries
- 425g canned peaches drained
- 1 Cadbury Flake chocolate bar shaved

Direction

- Set 1 of the jellies in a shallow dish or cake tin following packet instructions.
- Slice jam roll into 2cm pieces and place over base of glass bowl. Sprinkle with sherry.
- Make up second lot of jelly and pour over cake. Refrigerate until set.
- Dice first set jelly and layer over cake. Follow with a layer of peaches.
- Combine milk and pudding mix in a bowl and whisk until mixture is thick.
- Spread pudding mix over peaches. Chill.
- Beat cream until soft peaks form and spread over pudding mix.
- Decorate top with fresh strawberries and crumbled Flake bar.
- Chill in refrigerator until ready to serve.

230.   Strawberry And Cream Sponge Cake

Serving: 0 | Prep: 15mins | Cook: 30mins | Ready in: 45mins

Ingredients

- 6 eggs separated
- 6 tbs caster sugar
- 5 tbs gluten-free self-raising flour
- 1 tbs soy flour
- 1 tsp gluten-free baking powder
- 600 ml thickened cream whipped
- 400 g fresh strawberries sliced

Direction

- Preheat oven 180C. Grease and line a 24 cm round cake tin.
- Sift flour and baking powder in a bowl, set aside.
- Beat egg whites until stiff. Add sugar one tablespoon at a time beating well after each addition.
- Turn speed to low and add egg yolks one at a time until blended through.
- Gently fold in flour in 2 lots. Bake for 30 minutes or until skewer comes out clean.
- Leave in tray until cooled a little. Cool completely before filling and decorating with whipped cream and strawberries.

231.   Traditional Sicillian Cassata Ricotta Cake Recipe

Serving: 12 | Prep: 60mins | Cook: 40mins | Ready in: 100mins

Ingredients

- 2/3 cup sugar
- 1 tsp lemon rind

- 6 egg
- 1 cup plain flour
- Marzipan dough
- 1 cup almond meal
- 1 cup caster sugar
- 1 egg whites lightly beaten
- Liqueur syrup
- 1/4 cup caster sugar
- 1/4 cup water
- 2 1/2 tbs Grand Marnier
- Ricotta mixture
- 1 cup caster sugar
- 400 g ricotta drained
- 1 tsp vanilla extract
- 1/2 tsp ground cinnamon
- 2 tbs candied orange peel chopped into pieces
- Candied orange peel
- 1/2 cup caster sugar
- 1/2 cup water
- 1 orange
- Thick glaze
- 1 cup icing sugar
- 2 tbs lemon juice
- Decoration
- 2 tbs whole candied fruit halved thinly sliced

Direction

- Preheat oven to 180C°. Grease and flour a 23cm springform cake pan and set it aside.
- To make a basic sponge cake - Combine caster sugar, lemon zest and eggs in a large bowl and beat with electric beaters on high speed with until pale and light (for approximately 5 minutes). Add flour and fold to combine.
- Pour the mixture into the prepared cake tin and smooth the top. Bake for approximately 40 minutes. Ensure that a toothpick or skewer inserted in centre of cake comes out clean.
- Transfer cake pan to a wire rack and let the cake cool completely. Remove the cake from the cake pan and set aside.
- Line bottom and sides of a 23cm springform cake pan with plastic wrap and set aside.
- Once cooled, cut the sponge cake into a circle 2cm smaller than the size (diameter) of your cake pan. Then slice the sponge in half across

the centre to make 2 full sized circular discs. Set aside.

- To make the marzipan dough - In a food processor combine almond meal with caster sugar and process until finely ground. With food processor running, slowly add enough egg white to form a smooth marzipan dough.
- Transfer marzipan dough to a work surface dusted with a little of the icing sugar and knead until smooth. Using a rolling pin, roll marzipan until 1cm thick and a circle sized 10cm diameter larger than your cake tin.
- In the centre of the large marzipan dough circle, cut another circle of marzipan dough to the size of your cake pan for the top of the cake. Place this smaller circle in the bottom of the cake pan. Use the remaining strips of marzipan dough to neatly line the sides of the cake tin - flattening where they overlap to form one continuous ring. Set aside.
- To make the liqueur syrup - heat caster sugar and water in a saucepan over medium-high heat. Cook until sugar dissolves, then stir in the liqueur. Set aside.
- To make candied orange - cut orange peel into thin strips with all pith removed. Place sugar and water in a small saucepan with thin orange skin strips over medium heat. Bring to the boil and let it boil for about 1 minute. Lift out the orange skin strips and lay them on a plate.Continue cooking the water and sugar until it forms a syrup. Return the orange skin strips to the syrup until syrup reduces further (about 30 seconds).
- To make the ricotta mixture - in a large bowl, combine caster sugar with the ricotta, vanilla extract, and cinnamon until smooth. Add 1 tbs of the candied orange peel (chopped up in small pieces). Set aside.
- To assemble the cake place one disc of the sponge cake on top of the disc of marzipan dough on the bottom of the cake tin and trim to fit. Then sprinkle with 5 tbs of the liqueur syrup. Place ricotta mixture on top of cake layer and spread evenly to the extents of the cake tin. Cover top of ricotta mixture with remaining sponge cake disc and trim to fit.

Then sprinkle with 5 tbs of the liqueur syrup. Trim excess almond marzipan from the sides and then wrap the cake pan in plastic wrap and refrigerate until chilled (approximately 2 hours).

- To make the thick glaze - Combine icing sugar and lemon juice in a medium bowl.
- Prior to serving - Invert the cake tin onto a serving dish and peel off plastic wrap. Pour glaze over cake to cover evenly. Decorate with candied fruits. Refrigerate cake until set – a further 2 hours or overnight.

---

232. Walnut Cream Slice Recipe

Serving: 0 | Prep: 5mins | Cook: 20mins | Ready in: 25mins

Ingredients

- 150 g butter
- 1/4 cup sweetened condensed milk
- 1/4 cup sugar
- 1 1/4 cups plain flour
- 1 tsp baking powder
- 2 tbs walnuts chopped
- 3 drops vanilla essence
- Icing
- 3/4 cup icing sugar
- 50 g butter
- 1 tsp sweetened condensed milk

Direction

- Melt the butter, condensed milk and sugar together in a saucepan.
- Sift flour and baking powder together. Add to melted ingredients along with vanilla essence. Stir to combine.
- Add chopped walnuts.
- Press lightly into a greased 20 cm x 30 cm sponge roll tin.
- Bake at 180C for 15 minutes or until golden brown.

- Pour icing over slice and cut while still warm.
- Icing: Heat icing sugar, butter and condensed milk in a saucepan. Bring to the boil stirring constantly.

Chapter 8: Baked Cheesecake Recipes

***

---

233. Baked Black Cherry, Vanilla And Dark Chocolate Cheesecake

Serving: 12 | Prep: 20mins | Cook: 75mins | Ready in: 95mins

Ingredients

- 250 g chocolate biscuits
- 70 g unsalted butter melted
- Cheesecake filling
- 500 g cream cheese softened
- 3/4 cup caster sugar
- 100 ml thickened cream
- 3 egg
- 3 tbs black cherry and vanilla jam
- 1 tbs vanilla essence
- Decoration
- 200 ml thickened cream whipped
- 50 g dark chocolate shaved

Direction

- Preheat fan-forced oven to 150C degrees. Grease and line 22cm springform tin with baking paper.
- In a food processor, process biscuits until fine crumbs. Add melted butter and combine.

- Press biscuit mixture into the base of the prepared tin and flatten using the bottom of a glass. Place in fridge while filling is prepared.
- Beat cream cheese in an electric mixer until smooth, add the sugar and vanilla and beat until combined. Add the cream and mix through. Add the eggs one at a time, beating in between each addition until combined. Add the jam one tablespoon at a time and fold through the cheesecake filling until swirled though. Pour the filling onto the prepared biscuit base.
- Place tin on a baking tray and place in a preheated oven for 60-75 mins (depends on your oven). The cheesecake should have a slight wobble in the centre. Turn the oven off and allow the cheesecake to cool completely in the oven with the door ajar to prevent cracking. Once cooled place in fridge to cool completely.
- Remove from tin and pipe whipped cream around the edges. Top with grated dark chocolate. Enjoy.

234.   Baked Pineapple Cheesecake Recipe

Serving: 10 | Prep: 30mins | Cook: 50mins | Ready in: 80mins

Ingredients

- 125 g butter melted
- 250 g Nice biscuits crushed
- 500 g cream cheese brought to room temperature
- 410 g (crushed) canned pineapple drained reserve liquid
- 1 tbs cornflour
- 3 egg brought to room temperature
- 3/4 cup sugar
- 1 tsp vanilla essence

Direction

- Combine crushed biscuits and melted butter or margarine.
- Press onto base and sides of greased 20-22 cm springform pan.
- Combine reserved syrup and cornflour and heat gently in a medium saucepan, until thick.
- Add pineapple and mix well.
- Pour thickened pineapple over biscuit base.
- Beat cream cheese until smooth.
- Add sugar, eggs and vanilla and continue beating until mixture is thick and smooth.
- Pour over pineapple in pan.
- Place pan on baking tray, place in centre of oven and bake at 180C for 25 minutes.
- Turn oven off and leave cheesecake in oven with door ajar until at room temperature.
- Refrigerate, then serve with whipped cream.

235.   Baked Raspberry Cheesecake

Serving: 10 | Prep: 45mins | Cook: 180mins | Ready in: 225mins

Ingredients

- 350 g cream cheese
- 530 g ricotta
- 4 egg
- 1 lime juiced zested
- 300 g caster sugar
- 1/2 tsp vanilla extract
- 1 1/2 tbs cornflour
- 3 tbs water
- Raspberry Sauce
- 150 g frozen raspberries
- 1/2 cup caster sugar
- 2 tsp cornflour
- 2 tbs water
- Base
- 50 g almond meal
- 100 g plain flour
- 50 g caster sugar
- 100 g butter

Direction

- Base: Process all ingredients, combine into a soft crumb.
- Line the base of a 24 cm springform cake tin with cooking paper. Press crumb mix onto base forming an even, compact base.
- Bake at 150C for approximately 20 minutes or until light brown. Set aside to cool.
- Filling: Mix cornflour and water into a runny paste.
- Combine all other ingredients in a food processor and mix to smooth paste. Then add the cornflour mix and combine to create a creamy texture. Set aside.
- Raspberry Sauce: Add frozen raspberries and sugar to a saucepan over medium heat and bring to a simmer, reduce heat and simmer for 5 minutes. Add cornflour mixed with water slowly to make a thick sauce. Stop adding the cornflour mix if the raspberries thicken too much. Set aside and cool.
- Line the sides of tin with baking paper.
- Carefully spoon the raspberry sauce around the top of the base evenly.
- Add the cheesecake filling over the raspberry sauce. The cake tin should be about ¾ full.
- Bake for 1 hour at 150C, turn off oven and leave in hot oven for another hour with door closed. Refrigerate until cool.

---

236.   Baked Raspberry Cheesecake Recipe

Serving: 8 | Prep: 30mins | Cook: 60mins | Ready in: 90mins

Ingredients

- 14 Arnott's milk arrowroot biscuits
- 125 g butter melted
- 600 g cream cheese softened
- 3/4 cup caster sugar
- 2 tbs plain flour
- 1/2 tsp vanilla essence
- 1/2 cup sour cream
- 2 eggs
- 1 egg yolk
- 300 g fresh raspberries
- 1 tbs icing sugar
- 1 1/2 tbs raspberry jam

Direction

- Preheat oven to 180C.
- Place biscuits in a food processor and crush until the texture of breadcrumbs.
- Mix with the melted butter, press into a well-greased 20cm springform pan and bake for 5 minutes. Set aside to cool while making filling.
- Using an electric beater, beat the cream cheese, caster sugar, plain flour, vanilla, sour cream, eggs and extra yolk until light and fluffy.
- Using a spatula, gently fold in half the raspberries and pour over the top of the biscuit base.
- Bake for 40 minutes and then check. Cheesecake should be set but slightly wobbly in the middle. If it appears too runny after this time, continue to bake and check every 5 minutes. Leave in the pan to cool.
- Place the remaining raspberries into a saucepan with the icing sugar and raspberry jam. Heat until the juice starts to come out of the fruit and is slightly thick.
- Remove from heat and then mash with a fork or potato masher.
- Sieve the raspberry mixture, then pour over the cheesecake in pan and refrigerate for at least 4 hours.
- Serve with whipped cream or ice cream.

---

237.   Baked Rhubarb Cheesecake

Serving: 10 | Prep: 360mins | Cook: 90mins | Ready in: 450mins

Ingredients

- Rhubarb
- 1/3 cup sugar
- 2 tsp cornflour
- 1 1/2 cup rhubarb finely chopped
- 1 tbs water
- Crust
- 250 g ginger biscuit crushed
- 1/3 cup butter melted
- Cream cheese filling
- 500 g cream cheese room temperature
- 1/2 cup caster sugar
- 2 tbs cornflour
- 3 large egg
- 1 1/2 tsp vanilla extract
- 1 cup sour cream room temperature

Direction

- In a small saucepan, mix together sugar, cornflour, rhubarb and water. Heat over medium heat, stirring occasionally, until mixture starts to bubble.
- Reduce heat and simmer for 5-6 minutes until rhubarb is softened. Do not burn. Remove from heat and cool to room temperature.
- Combine biscuit crumbs and butter. Add a little extra butter if needed.
- Line base of pan with grease proof paper.
- Press evenly into 23 cm spring-form pan. Refrigerate for approximately 30 minutes.
- Cream cheese filling: In large bowl with electric mixer, beat cream cheese, sugar and cornflour until smooth.
- Beat in eggs, at low speed, one at a time.
- Add vanilla and sour cream and mix just until smooth.
- Pour half the cheese mix into crust.
- Spoon approximately half of the rhubarb mix in dollops over the top. Using a knife, swirl rhubarb through cream cheese mixture, being careful not to hit the bottom and stir in crumbs.
- Repeat with remaining cream cheese mix and rhubarb, and swirl again.
- Bake at 160C (150C fan forced) for 50–60 minutes or until almost set in centre but still a bit wobbly.

- Run knife around edge to prevent cracking and return cheesecake to oven.
- Make sure oven is off and cool in oven with door ajar until completely cool.
- Remove from tin, cover and chill in refrigerator for approximately 6 hours or overnight.

238.   Basic Baked Cheesecake Recipe

Serving: 18 | Prep: 20mins | Cook: 85mins | Ready in: 105mins

Ingredients

- 250g biscuits
- 1 tsp mixed spice
- 100g butter melted
- Filling
- 500g cream cheese
- 2/3 cup caster sugar
- 4 eggs
- 1 tsp vanilla essence
- 1 tbs lemon juice

Direction

- Grease a 20cm springform tin.
- Crush biscuits in food processor and add mixed spice and butter.
- Line base of tin with foil and brush sides with oil. Press crumbs over base and sides of tin. Place in fridge for 20 minutes.
- Meanwhile, to make the filling, preheat oven to 180C.
- Beat cream cheese until smooth. Add sugar, vanilla and lemon juice. Beat until smooth.
- Add eggs, 1 at a time, beating well after each addition.
- Pour mix into tin and bake for 45 minutes or until just firm to the touch.

239. Best Mini Cheesecakes Recipe

Serving: 10 | Prep: 15mins | Cook: 25mins | Ready in: 40mins

Ingredients

- 250 g Arnott's butternut snap biscuits
- 250 g cream cheese softened
- 1/2 cup caster sugar
- 2 eggs
- 1 cup fresh blueberries *to decorate

Direction

- Preheat oven to 140C.
- Arrange patty papers in a muffin tray.
- Place a biscuit in the bottom of each patty paper.
- Beat cream cheese, gradually adding sugar until mix is smooth.
- Add eggs, one at a time, mixing until smooth.
- Spoon mixture into the patty papers.
- Place berries on top and bake for approximately 25 minutes, or until cooked.
- Refrigerate when cool.

240. Bistro Cheesecake Recipe

Serving: 10 | Prep: 60mins | Cook: 30mins | Ready in: 90mins

Ingredients

- 187 1/2 g sweet plain biscuits crushed
- 125 g butter melted
- 750 g cream cheese softened
- 2 eggs
- 3/4 cup sugar
- 1 tsp vanilla essence
- 300 ml whipped cream
- 1 pinch nutmeg

Direction

- Preheat oven to 150C.
- Line a spring-form pan with baking paper.
- Combine melted butter with crushed biscuits. Press biscuit mixture into base of pan, refrigerate until firm.
- Using an electric mixer, mix cream cheese and sugar until combined.
- Add eggs one at a time, continue to mix until combined.
- Add vanilla essence and mix thoroughly.
- Pour cheesecake filling over biscuit base, spread evenly.
- Bake on middle shelf of oven for 30 minutes.
- Turn oven off after 30 minutes, allow cheesecake to cool in the oven.
- Refrigerate to chill.
- Spread all the whipped cream over cheesecake.
- Sprinkle nutmeg lightly over the cream, serve.

241. Caramel Crunch Cheesecake

Serving: 0 | Prep: 80mins | Cook: 70mins | Ready in: 150mins

Ingredients

- Base
- 1 cup biscuits crumbed
- 60 g butter melted
- 1 tsp water
- Filling
- 500 g cream cheese room temperature
- 1/3 cup caster sugar
- 2 tsp lemon rind grated
- 3 egg
- 1/3 cup cream
- 1 tbs self-raising flour
- 30 g butter
- 1/4 cup brown sugar
- 4 tbs condensed milk
- 1 tbs golden syrup
- 2 tbs hot water

- 90 g chocolate honeycomb bar crushed

Direction

- Pre-heat oven to 150C and grease a 20 cm springform pan.
- Base: Mix biscuit crumbs, melted butter and water together and press mixture evenly over base of pan.
- Refrigerate for 30 minutes.
- Caramel: Combine butter, brown sugar, milk, syrup and water in a saucepan.
- Heat until sugar is dissolved, continually stirring.
- Bring to boil without stirring until a deep caramel colour develops.
- Cool for a minimum of 10 minutes.
- Filling: Beat cream cheese in bowl until soft.
- Beat in caster sugar, lemon rind, then eggs one at a time.
- Add flour and cream and continue beating until well combined.
- Pour ½ cream cheese mixture over biscuit base and top with crushed honeycomb.
- Drizzle caramel over honeycomb and top with remaining cream cheese mixture.
- Bake in oven for 1 hour.
- Cool to room temperature then refrigerate.

---

242. Cheesecake Brownie Muffins Recipe

Serving: 12 | Prep: 20mins | Cook: 25mins | Ready in: 45mins

Ingredients

- 250 g cream cheese
- 1/2 cup caster sugar
- 2 eggs
- 1 tsp vanilla essence
- 1/4 cup plain flour
- Chocolate Brownie
- 190 g dark chocolate melts
- 160 g butter
- 3/4 cup plain flour
- 3 eggs
- 3/4 cup brown sugar

Direction

- Preheat the oven to 180°C. Grease a 12 hole muffin pan with cooking spray.
- Beat the cream cheese and caster sugar until smooth. Stir in the vanilla and beaten eggs, then add the flour. Mix until to smooth and then set aside while you make the chocolate brownie mix.
- Put the chocolate melts and butter into a large glass bowl and melt in the microwave in short bursts of 30 seconds until smooth. Add the brown sugar and eggs, mix well. Stir in the flour.
- Divide the chocolate brownie mixture across the 12 muffin holes. Spoon the cheesecake mixture over the top. Use a skewer to swirl the mixture in each muffin cup so that it marbles.
- Cook for 25 minutes, until they are just set but still gooey in the centre.

---

243. Cherry Ripe Baked Cheesecake Recipe

Serving: 0 | Prep: 30mins | Cook: 35mins | Ready in: 65mins

Ingredients

- 250 g cream cheese
- 1/2 cup brown sugar
- 2 egg
- 1/4 cup thickened cream
- 2 tbs cocoa powder
- 100 g dark chocolate melted cooled slightly
- 2 Cherry Ripe chocolate bar chopped
- Base
- 1/2 packet chocolate ripple biscuits
- 40 g unsalted butter melted

Direction

- Preheat oven to 140C, fan forced.
- To make base: Process chocolate ripple biscuits until fine crumbs. Add melted butter and combine. Press into base of 6 heart molds. Pop in fridge while preparing filling.
- To make filling: Place cream cheese in mixer with paddle attachment and mix until smooth.
- Add brown sugar and mix until combined well.
- Add eggs one at a time, beating between each addition until combined.
- Add cream and cocoa powder and mix.
- Add slightly cooled, melted chocolate and mix well.
- Add chopped cherry ripe bars and mix through mixture gently with a spatula or wooden spoon.
- Pour filling evenly into prepared bases and pop in oven for 30-35 minutes, or until the middle has a slight wobble. Cool in oven with door ajar.
- Once cooled, place in fridge for at least 2 hours or overnight and prepare topping.
- To serve, put extra melted chocolate into a ziplock bag and snip the corner. Remove cheesecakes from molds and drizzle the dark chocolate over the cooled cheesecakes. Return to fridge until set.

---

244. Chocolate Cheesecake Brownie Recipe

Serving: 12 | Prep: 15mins | Cook: 50mins |Ready in: 65mins

Ingredients

- 1 cup plain flour
- 1 cup caster sugar
- 1/4 cup cocoa
- 2 egg
- 170 g butter
- 100 g dark chocolate
- Cheesecake

- 285 g cream cheese softened
- 5 tbs caster sugar
- 2 egg
- 1 tsp vanilla essence
- 100 g white choc bits optional

Direction

- Preheat oven to 160C.
- Brownie: Melt butter and chocolate together.
- Combine flour, sugar and cocoa. Add eggs and melted butter and mix together.
- Cheesecake: Process cream cheese, sugar, eggs and vanilla until smooth. Add choc chips if using.
- In a lined slice tin, dollop brownie mixture and cheesecake mixture alternatively.
- Using a knife or stick drag through mixture to create a marbled effect.
- Bake at 160C for 45-50 minutes or until set. Best served chilled.

---

245. Christmas Choc Peppermint Cheesecake Recipe

Serving: 12 | Prep: 45mins | Cook: 50mins |Ready in: 95mins

Ingredients

- 250 g chocolate ripple biscuits
- 125 g butter melted
- 500 g cream cheese
- 1 1/2 cups thickened cream
- 3/4 cups caster sugar
- 3 eggs
- 3 drops peppermint essential oil
- 1/2 cup chocolate sprinkles *to decorate
- 1 packet M&Ms, *to decorate
- 1 packet candy canes *to decorate

Direction

- Preheat oven to 180C (160C fan-forced). Line the base of a 22cm springform cake tin with baking paper. Grease the sides with a little butter.

- In a food processor, blitz biscuits to form a fine crumb. Add butter and process to combine. Tip into prepared tin and use the back of a spoon to line the base with an even layer of biscuit, coming 2-3cm up the sides as well. Refrigerate for 30 minutes.
- Wipe out bowl of food processor. Place in cream cheese, 1/2 cup cream and sugar and process until smooth. Add eggs one at a time, processing between each addition. Add peppermint oil or essence a little at a time, tasting as you go.
- Remove cake tin from fridge and place on an oven tray. Carefully pour in filling. Bake for 50 minutes until just set. Turn off oven and leave cheesecake in while it cools for 1-2 hours. Place in fridge to cool and set completely.
- Just prior to serving, whip remaining cream until thick. Carefully remove cheesecake from tin and place on serving platter. Spread cream over the top and decorate with chocolate sprinkles, M&M's and candy canes.

---

246. Classic New York Baked Cheesecake Recipe

Serving: 12 | Prep: 30mins | Cook: 90mins | Ready in: 120mins

Ingredients

- 325 g sweet plain biscuits crushed
- 250 g unsalted butter melted
- 750 g full-fat cream cheese room temperature
- 215 g caster sugar
- 1/2 tsp vanilla extract
- 2 tsp lemon rind, finely grated
- 1 tsp lemon juice
- 2 tbs plain flour
- 4 eggs room temperature
- 300 ml sour cream
- 125 g fresh blueberries
- 2 tbs icing sugar sifted

Direction

- Preheat oven to 160C (140C degrees if using fan-forced). Grease and then line the base and of a 23cm springform pan with non-stick baking paper.
- Finely crush the biscuits in a food processor and then place into a large bowl. Add the melted butter and mix thoroughly until well combined.
- Spoon half of the biscuit crumbs onto the base of the prepared tin. Use a glass to press the mixture town evenly (you will also need to use a spoon to press the edges down firmly). Press the mixture firmly up the sides of the pan (leaving a small 1cm gap near the top). Chill in the fridge for 30 minutes.
- Beat the cream cheese, sugar, vanilla and lemon rind with electric beaters until just combined (don't over-beat). Gently beat in the flour followed by the eggs (1 at a time). Beat until just combined. Stir through the sour cream.
- Gently pour the cream cheese mixture into the base of the tin.
- Place the the tin onto a baking tray and bake for 1.25 - 1.5 hours or until just set in the centre. Do not open the oven during the cooking time or the cheesecake will crack and sink.
- Turn the oven off and leave the cheesecake in the oven, with the door slightly ajar, for 2 hours. Place the cheesecake onto the bench until completely cooled before placing into the fridge (still in the baking tin).
- After a minimum of 4 hours in the fridge (preferably overnight), carefully remove the cheesecake from the baking tin and take off the baking paper.
- Top with fresh blueberries and icing sugar to serve.

247.   Fudge Truffle Cheesecake Recipe

Serving: 16 | Prep: 270mins | Cook: 70mins | Ready in: 340mins

Ingredients

- 18 wafers
- 1/3 cup cocoa powder unsweetened
- 1/3 cup white sugar
- 100 g butter melted
- 750 g cream cheese softened
- 440 g sweetened condensed milk
- 375 g milk chocolate chips melted
- 1 tsp vanilla extract
- 4 large egg

Direction

- Preheat oven to 150C.
- Place vanilla wafers between 2 layers of greaseproof paper. Crush wafers with a rolling pin to make about 1½ cups of crumbs.
- Combine crumbs, cocoa, sugar, and melted butter in a medium bowl and mix well.
- Press onto the bottom of a 22 cm springform pan. Bake crust for 10 minutes. Remove from oven and put aside.
- Place softened cream cheese in a large bowl. Beat with electric mixer set at high speed until light and fluffy.
- Gradually add condensed milk to the cream cheese, beating well after each addition.
- Add melted chocolate, eggs and vanilla extract and beat well. Spoon mixture over the baked crust base.
- Bake cheesecake for about 1 hour or until set.
- Cool to room temperature and then chill for at least 4 hours.
- Serve with fresh whipped cream and strawberries.

248.   Gluten And Lactose Free Baked Cheesecake Recipe

Serving: 16 | Prep: 15mins | Cook: 60mins | Ready in: 75mins

Ingredients

- 1 1/2 cups Freelicious gluten-free tea biscuits
- 1/3 cup Liddell's lactose-free butter melted
- 4 tubs Liddell's lactose-free cream cheese
- 3/4 cup sugar
- 1 tsp vanilla essence
- 4 eggs

Direction

- Preheat oven to 160C or 150C if using a dark non-stick spring form pan. Alternatively for a fan forced oven 140C (whether dark non-stick spring form pan is used or not).
- Crush 15 - 20 biscuits into crumbs, ideally using a rolling pin and chopping board. Mix crumbs and melted butter together. Press mixture onto the bottom of the spring form pan.
- Beat cream cheese (4), sugar and vanilla essence with electric mixer until blended well. Add eggs one at a time, mixing on low speed until blended. Pour cream cheese mixture over biscuit crumb mix.
- Bake between 50 - 60 minutes (times may vary depending on ovens) or until centre is almost set. Loosen cheesecake from rim of pan. Allow to cool before removing rim and refrigerating (about 10 - 15 mins). Refrigerate for 4 hours.

249.   Lactose Free Sticky Date Ricotta Cheesecake Recipe

Serving: 8 | Prep: 40mins | Cook: 300mins | Ready in: 340mins

Ingredients

- 5 Scotch Finger biscuits
- 1/3 cup walnuts
- 3 tbs butter melted
- 450 g ricotta
- 1 1/2 tbs caster sugar
- 2 tbs maple syrup
- 1/2 cup Pauls lactose-free Zymil regular thickened cream
- 8 medjool dates
- 2 eggs large
- Toffee Sauce
- 4 tbs brown sugar
- 1 1/2 tbs butter
- 1/2 cup Pauls lactose-free Zymil regular thickened cream
- Walnut Praline
- 3 tbs caster sugar
- 1 tbs water
- 2 tbs walnuts finely chopped
- Ricotta
- 4 L Pauls lactose-free Zymil full cream milk
- 160 ml lemon juice
- 2 tsp salt

Direction

- Ricotta: Bring the milk to the boil, remove from heat. Add lemon juice and salt, then stir. Allow to stand for 10 minutes until the curd and whey separate. Line a sieve with a cheesecloth and place over a large bowl. Gradually pour milk mixture into a sieve and allow to drain. Twist the cheesecloth to enclose the curds, hang over a clean bowl, using a wooden spoon for support. Drain for 30-40 minutes.
- Walnut biscuit base: Process walnuts, they should resemble coarse breadcrumbs. Process biscuits to a fine crumb, then melt butter and mix well. Line the base of a 20cm spring form pan with baking paper, press the mixture firmly onto the base. Bake for 5 minutes in a preheated oven at 160C, then set aside to cool.
- Process ricotta, cream, maple syrup, caster sugar and eggs until smooth. Chop the dates into bite-sized pieces, then stir into the mixture. Pour over base and bake for 40

minutes at 160C or until the centre is just cooked. Leave in the oven to cool, with the door slightly open for 2 hours. Chill for 3-4 hours.
- Toffee sauce: Place brown sugar and butter in a small pan, heat until the butter is melted and sugar is dissolved. Simmer for a few minutes, then remove from the heat. Add cream and simmer for another 5 minutes, or until thickened, cool. Pour over the chilled cheesecake and place in the fridge to set.
- Praline: Sprinkle chopped walnuts onto a baking paper covered, heat proof surface. Place caster sugar and water in a small pan, bring to the boil without stirring, and cook until the mixture turns golden brown. Pour over the walnuts and allow to cool. When hard, break up with a rolling pin.
- To serve, cut into wedges, and drizzle with Pauls Zymil Cream. Finish with a sprinkle of walnut praline.

---

250.   Lemon Baked Cheesecake Recipe

Serving: 10 | Prep: 20mins | Cook: 480mins | Ready in: 500mins

Ingredients

- 250 g sweet plain biscuits crumbed
- 125 g butter melted
- 3 eggs lightly beaten
- 1/2 cup caster sugar
- 3 x 250 g cream cheese softened
- 3 tsp lemon rind grated
- 1/4 cup lemon juice

Direction

- Lightly grease a 22 cm springform tin.
- Combine biscuit crumbs and butter in a bowl.
- Using a glass, press crumb mixture evenly over base and side of tin.
- Refrigerate biscuit crust for 1 hour.

- Beat eggs and sugar in a bowl with an electric mixer until pale and thick.
- Add cheese, rind and lemon juice. Beat until mixture is smooth and creamy.
- Pour mixture into prepared tin and bake in moderate oven for about 45 minutes.
- Cool in oven with door ajar, then refrigerate for several hours or overnight.
- Decorate with cream and strawberries if desired.

251. Lemon Coconut Pie Maker Cheesecake Mooncakes Recipe

Serving: 0 | Prep: 10mins | Cook: 16mins | Ready in: 26mins

Ingredients

- 250g cream cheese
- 1/4 cup caster sugar
- 1 lemon, zested, juiced
- 1 egg
- 1 cup desiccated coconut
- 3 sheets frozen puff pastry, defrosted

Direction

- In a food processor, combine cream cheese, sugar, lemon zest and juice, egg and coconut until smooth.
- Preheat pie maker according to manufacturer's instructions. Use cutter to make six bases and six tops. Use a mooncake mould to press patterns into the top pieces. Line pie maker plates with bases. Fill with cream cheese mixture. Top with patterned pieces. Close lid and bake for 8 minutes until golden.
- Repeat with remaining ingredients.

252. Mini Cookies And Cream Cheesecakes Recipe

Serving: 0 | Prep: 20mins | Cook: 25mins | Ready in: 45mins

Ingredients

- 26 Oreo biscuits
- 500 g cream cheese room temperature
- 2/3 cup caster sugar
- 1 tsp vanilla essence
- 3 eggs beaten
- 1/3 cup sour cream
- 100 g white chocolate melted
- 1 pinch salt

Direction

- Preheat oven to 135C. Line 19 cupcake pans and place a whole Oreo in the base of each liner.
- Beat cream cheese until soft. Gradually add sugar and beat in, the beat in vanilla.
- Gradually beat in eggs.
- Continue beating and add sour cream and salt. Beat in white chocolate.
- Gently stir through chopped Oreos.
- Divide batter equally between pans, leaving enough room for mixture to rise slightly.
- Bake for 20-25 minutes or until filling is just set.
- Allow to cool and refrigerate for at least 4 hours.

253. Mini Oreo Cheesecakes Recipe

Serving: 0 | Prep: 30mins | Cook: 180mins | Ready in: 210mins

Ingredients

- 3 puff pastry thawed
- 250 g cream cheese softened

- 1/2 cup cream
- 1/4 cup caster sugar
- 100 g mini Oreo biscuits
- 100 g white chocolate melted
- 1/2 tsp vanilla essence
- 1 tsp gelatine powder
- 0.125 cup water boiling
- 25 g dark chocolate melted

Direction

- Preheat oven to 180 degrees. Grease a 12 hole muffin tin and set aside.
- Using a 10cm round cutter, cut 12 rounds from the puff pastry. Ease each round into a hold of the muffin tray. Place some baking paper over the top and fill with baking weights or rice.
- Place muffin tin in oven and bake for 15 minutes. Remove weights and paper and bake for a further 10 minutes or until the bottom of each pastry case is browned. Note: The pastry will puff up a bit once weights have been removed. Carefully press down to remove air, being careful of the steam.
- Remove from oven and allow to cool.
- Place boiling water in a coffee cup and sprinkle gelatine over the top. Stir with a fork to dissolve. Set aside to cool slightly.
- Place white chocolate in a microwave safe bowl and microwave in short bursts until melted. Set aside to cool slightly.
- Place softened cream cheese into a mixing bowl and mix on medium speed with electric beaters until smooth.
- Add cream, vanilla essence, sugar, gelatine mixture and white chocolate to the cream cheese. Mix with electric beaters until combined.
- Reserve 12 Oreo biscuits for decoration. Chop each remaining mini Oreo biscuit into 4 pieces and gently fold them through the cheesecake mixture.
- Leaving the pastry cases in the muffin tin, carefully spoon cheesecake mixture into each pastry case. Top with a mini Oreo biscuit and place in fridge for 30 minutes.

- Remove mini cheesecakes from fridge. Place dark chocolate in a microwave safe bowl and microwave in short bursts until melted. Using a spoon or fork, drizzle chocolate over the cheesecakes. Place back in fridge to set for a further hour.

---

254.   New York Baked Cheesecake

Serving: 10 | Prep: 120mins | Cook: 360mins | Ready in: 480mins

Ingredients

- 15 crackers crushed
- 2 tbs butter melted
- 250 g cream cheese
- 1 1/2 cup white sugar
- 3/4 cup milk
- 3 egg beaten
- 250 g plain yoghurt
- 1 tbs vanilla extract
- 1/4 cup self-raising flour

Direction

- Preheat oven to 175C and grease a 23 cm springform pan.
- Mix in a medium bowl, the crushed crackers with the butter until no butter lumps remain.
- Press onto the bottom of the springform pan. Place in freezer to set.
- In a large bowl, mix cream cheese with the sugar until smooth.
- Blend in the milk and then the eggs. Mix in the yoghurt, vanilla extract and flour until mixture is smooth.
- Pour the batter onto the crust, and bake for 1 hour. Switch off the oven and let the cheesecake cool in the oven for 5-6 hours with the door closed.
- Chill in the refrigerator and serve cool.

255.   Oreo Cheesecake

Serving: 16 | Prep: 45mins | Cook: 330mins | Ready in: 375mins

Ingredients

- 570 g Oreo biscuits crushed
- 1/3 cup unsalted butter melted
- 3 x 250 g cream cheese brought to room temperature
- 3/4 cup sugar
- 4 egg brought to room temperature
- 1 cup sour cream brought to room temperature
- 1 tsp vanilla extract
- 6 Oreo biscuits halved

Direction

- Reserve some cookie crumbs for the filling.
- Add melted butter to the cookie crumbs and mix well.
- Press mixture into a 23 cm spring form pan and press mixture 5 cm up the sides of the tin.
- Beat cream cheese and sugar with an electric mixer on medium until creamy. Add lightly beaten eggs, one at a time, mixing by hand.
- Stir in sour cream and vanilla. Fold in reserved cookie crumbs.
- Pour mixture onto the prepared cookie crust.
- Bake at 170C for 55-60 minutes or until set.
- Cool on a wire rack at room temperature for 15 minutes.
- Use a flat blade knife to cut around the edge of the cake to help it slide out of the pan. Don't cut into the cake.
- When cooled to room temperature, put it in the fridge for at least 4 hours.
- Remove side from pan and garnish with cream, cookie halves or cookie crumbs.

256.   Oreo Cheesecake Slice Recipe

Serving: 24 | Prep: 30mins | Cook: 430mins | Ready in: 460mins

Ingredients

- 4 x 150 g Oreo biscuits
- 60 g butter melted
- 1 kg cream cheese brought to room temperature
- 1 cup sugar
- 1 tsp vanilla extract
- 1/2 tsp salt
- 1 cup sour cream
- 4 egg

Direction

- Preheat oven to 160C. Line 23 cm x 33 cm pan with a layer of foil, then baking paper extending over sides.
- Process 30 cookies in food processor until finely ground. Add butter, mix well. Press onto bottom of pan.
- Beat cream cheese in large bowl of an electric mixer until smooth. Add sugar, vanilla and salt. Continue beating until well blended.
- Add sour cream, mix well.
- Add eggs, 1 at a time, beating after each just until blended. Process remaining cookies until roughly chopped. Stir through cream cheese mixture.
- Spread mixture over crust.
- Bake for 40-45 minutes or until centre is almost set.
- Cool completely. Refrigerate 4 hours or overnight.

257.   Ricotta And Custard Apple Cheesecake Recipe

Serving: 8 | Prep: 10mins | Cook: 45mins | Ready in: 55mins

Ingredients

- Filling
- 500 g smooth ricotta
- 500 g cream cheese
- 4 eggs
- 1/3 cup granulated sugar
- 2 tsp lime juice
- 1 tsp lime zest
- 1 tsp vanilla essence
- 1 pinch sea salt
- 1/4 cup plain flour
- 1 custard apple medium
- Crust
- 6 ginger biscuits
- 1 tbs butter melted
- Decorate
- 1/2 cup custard apple *extra
- 1 tsp lime zest
- 1 tsp lime juice
- 2 ginger biscuits crumbled

Direction

- Preheat oven to 180C. Brush a round 23cm springform tin with a bit of the melted butter.
- Crush or blitz the ginger biscuits to a fine meal. Scoop 2 tbs of crumbs into the buttered tin and spread the biscuit meal around the sides, allowing any extra to settle in the base. Combine remaining butter and biscuit crumbs in a bowl and stir until just mixed. Press the mixture into the base of the tin, then pop the pan into the refrigerator while you make the filling.
- In a food processor, blend ricotta and cream cheese until smooth. Add eggs, sugar, juice, zest, vanilla and salt to the processor – blend again until thick and smooth. Stir through custard apple, then fold in flour.

- Pour mixture into prepared pan and gently crisscross a knife through the batter to break any air bubbles. Smooth the top of the cheesecake and place tin on a baking tray.
- Bake cheesecake for 45 minutes, then turn the heat off, prop the door open a centimetre or so with the end of a wooden spoon, and leave the cheesecake to cool in the oven for a further 1 hour.
- Remove cake from oven, place on a rack and cool completely before releasing the side of the pan. Top cake with extra custard apple segments, zest and crumbled biscuit to serve.

258.   White Chocolate Baked Cheesecake Recipe

Serving: 6 | Prep: 20mins | Cook: 210mins | Ready in: 230mins

Ingredients

- 300 g chocolate biscuits
- 125 g butter melted
- 200 g white chocolate
- 500 g cream cheese brought to room temperature
- 300 g sour cream
- 1/2 cup caster sugar
- 1 tsp vanilla essence
- 3 egg

Direction

- Preheat oven to 160C.
- Process biscuits in food processor until fine.
- Add melted butter and mix well.
- Spoon mixture into the bottom of an unlined 22 cm springform pan and bake for 10-15 minutes.
- Put white chocolate into a bowl over boiling water and stir until chocolate melts. Cool slightly.

- Put cream cheese, sour cream, sugar and vanilla in a bowl and beat well with electric mixer (mixture will be slightly lumpy).
- Add melted chocolate and beat until combined.
- Add eggs and beat on very low speed until just combined (do not overbeat).
- Pour into cooled pan.
- Bake in oven for an hour and 10 minutes.
- Turn off oven and leave door ajar for 1 hour or until almost cold.
- Put into the fridge to set.

Chapter 9: Easy Cake Recipes

***

259. 6 Egg Pavlova Recipe

Serving: 8 | Prep: 15mins | Cook: 75mins | Ready in: 90mins

Ingredients

- 6 egg whites large
- 3 tsp white vinegar
- 3 tsp vanilla essence
- 1 pinch salt
- 3 cups caster sugar
- 3 tsp cornflour
- 4 tbs boiling water

Direction

- Place all ingredients into a large mixing bowl, adding the boiling water last.
- Beat on full speed until very stiff.
- Spread on a pavlova plate or baking sheet and cook for 15 minutes at 160C, then approximately 1 hour on 150C.

- Cool in the oven with the door ajar.
- Top with whipped cream and fruit of choice.

260. Anne's Cake Recipe

Serving: 8 | Prep: 10mins | Cook: 50mins | Ready in: 60mins

Ingredients

- 2 cups sugar
- 2 cups self-raising flour
- 2 tbs cornflour
- 2 tbs custard powder
- 250 g butter softened
- 1 tsp vanilla essence
- 1 cup milk
- 4 eggs
- 1 dash glycerine

Direction

- Combine all ingredients in large bowl and beat together for 10 minutes.
- Pour mixture into pan of choice.
- Bake at 180C for approximately 50 minutes or until cooked.

261. Apple Cake Recipe

Serving: 8 | Prep: 15mins | Cook: 40mins | Ready in: 55mins

Ingredients

- 2 apples chopped peeled
- 1 cup sugar
- 1 cup sultanas
- 1 1/2 cups self-raising flour
- 125g butter melted
- 2 eggs lightly beaten
- 1 tsp mixed spice

Direction

- Mix all ingredients together with a wooden spoon.
- Bake at 180C for approximately 40 minutes.
- Spread with butter while hot, and sprinkle with cinnamon and sugar.

262. Apple Crumble Cake

Serving: 8 | Prep: 15mins | Cook: 40mins | Ready in: 55mins

Ingredients

- 1 1/2 cups self-raising flour
- 1/2 cup caster sugar
- 115g butter
- 1 egg lightly beaten
- 440g canned pie apples sliced
- 1/4 cup icing sugar *to decorate

Direction

- Sift flour and sugar.
- Quickly break the butter into the dry mixture until it resembles crumbs.
- Add egg and gently mix through with a fork until it resembles crumbs.
- Press just under half the mixture into a greased and lined 20cm round tin.
- Top with apple.
- Sprinkle over remaining crumbs.
- Bake at 180C for 40 minutes. Cool on wire rack.
- Dust with icing sugar and a dollop of thickened cream to serve.

263. Apple Teacake In A Mug Recipe

Serving: 1 | Prep: 10mins | Cook: 2mins | Ready in: 12mins

Ingredients

- 3 tbs self-raising flour
- 2 tbs brown sugar
- 1/4 tsp ground cinnamon
- 1/2 egg beaten
- 2 tbs apple grated
- 1 tbs milk
- 1 tbs oil
- 1 pinch white sugar *to decorate
- 1 pinch cinnamon *to decorate *extra

Direction

- Place dry ingredients in a large coffee mug and mix well with a fork. Add egg.
- Add remaining ingredients and combine well. Make sure there are no pockets of dry flour in the bottom of the mug.
- Cover loosely with cling wrap and microwave on high for 2 minutes. Allow to stand for a minute, then run a knife around the inside to loosen.
- Tip cake out onto a plate. Serve with butter and a sprinkle of cinnamon and white sugar.

264. Apple, Caramel And Custard Poke Cake Recipe

Serving: 8 | Prep: 30mins | Cook: 50mins | Ready in: 80mins

Ingredients

- 180 g butter room temperature
- 1 cup caster sugar
- 2 egg lightly beaten
- 1 1/2 cup self-raising flour
- 2/3 cup milk

- 1 Granny Smith apples coarsely grated cored cored unpeeled
- 250 g cream cheese room temperature
- 1 1/2 cup icing sugar
- 3 tsp lemon juice
- 2 tbs Woolworths salted caramel dessert sauce warmed
- 1/2 cup custard
- 2 tbs pecans chopped *to decorate

Direction

- Preheat oven to 180C or 160C fan-forced. Grease and line base and sides of a 20cm square cake pan.
- Using an electric mixer, beat 150g butter and caster sugar until light and fluffy. Beat in eggs 1 at a time until combined.
- Stir in flour and milk until combined. Stir through grated apple. Spoon into prepared pan. Bake for 50 minutes or until a skewer inserted in centre comes out clean.
- Stand cake for 5 minutes in pan. Turn onto a wire rack to cool completely.
- Meanwhile, using an electric mixer, beat cream cheese and remaining butter until smooth. Beat in icing sugar and lemon juice until combined.
- Using the handle of a wooden spoon, make 16 holes into top of cake (evenly spaced over whole cake, about 1cm wide and 3cm deep).
- Pour warmed caramel into holes.
- Pour custard over caramel and into remaining holes.
- Dollop cream cheese mixture over cake. Using a spatula, spread frosting to cover cake. Decorate with chopped pecans. Chill for 1 hour. Serve.

---

265. Aussie Pavlova Recipe

Serving: 8 | Prep: 20mins | Cook: 60mins | Ready in: 80mins

Ingredients

- 4 egg whites extra large
- 0.125 tsp cream of tartar
- 1 cup CSR caster sugar
- 1 tbs cornflour
- 300 ml cream
- 2 tbs CSR pure icing sugar
- 1 cup mixed berries fresh
- 1 block milk chocolate shaved *to decorate

Direction

- Pre-heat oven to 120°C (100°C fan-forced). Line a large baking tray with baking paper, drawing a 20cm circle on the paper.
- Place egg whites and cream of tartar into the bowl of an electric mixer. Beat until firm peaks have formed. Gradually add sugar a little at a time, until all has been incorporated. Continue beating for 2 minutes once all of the sugar has been added.
- Reduce mixer to slow speed and add cornflour, mixing until just combined. Spoon mixture onto baking paper and spread within the circle. Bake for 1½ hours and turn oven off. Leave pavlova to cool in the oven. Keep in a sealed container once cooled prior to decorating and serving.
- Use an electric mixer to whisk the cream and icing sugar in a medium bowl until firm peaks form. Spoon cream onto the top of pavlova. Decorate pavlova with berries and shaved chocolate.

---

266. Basic Butter Cake Recipe

Serving: 12 | Prep: 15mins | Cook: 85mins | Ready in: 100mins

Ingredients

- 185 g butter softened
- 1 cup caster sugar
- 1 tsp vanilla essence
- 3 eggs large
- 2 cups self-raising flour

- 1/4 cup milk

Direction

- Preheat oven to 180C and grease a 20 cm cake tin well.
- In a large bowl, beat the butter, sugar and vanilla together with an electric mixer until light and creamy.
- Add the eggs one at a time and beat well after each addition.
- Sift the flour over the mixture alternately with the milk, adding a third at a time. Stir in lightly.
- Spoon batter into prepared tin and bake for 50-60 minutes or until a skewer pulls clean from the middle of the cake.
- Cool cake in tin for a few minutes before turning out onto a wire rack.
- Cake can be iced or dusted with icing sugar if desired.

267. Carrot Cake Recipe

Serving: 10 | Prep: 20mins | Cook: 90mins | Ready in: 110mins

Ingredients

- 1 tbs olive oil *to grease
- 2 carrots grated peeled
- 1 cup self-raising flour
- 1/2 cup plain flour
- 1 tsp bicarbonate of soda
- 1/2 tsp ground cinnamon
- 1/2 cup brown sugar
- 3/4 cup oil
- 1/2 cup golden syrup
- 3 eggs
- 1 tsp vanilla essence
- 3/4 cup walnuts
- 3/4 cup sultanas
- Icing
- 250 g cream cheese
- 1/2 cup icing sugar

- 1/2 tsp vanilla essence
- 1 tsp buttermilk
- 3/4 cup walnuts *to decorate

Direction

- Preheat oven to 170C. Grease a 20cm round cake pan lightly with oil and line with non-stick baking paper.
- Cake batter: Sift the flours, bicarbonate of soda and cinnamon into a large bowl.
- Place the brown sugar, oil, golden syrup, eggs and vanilla in a separate bowl and whisk until combined.
- Pour the oil mixture into the dry ingredients and stir gently with a wooden spoon until just combined. Stir in the grated carrot, sultanas and walnuts.
- Pour the mixture into the pan and bake for approximately 1 hour.
- Set aside for 5 minutes before turning out onto a wire rack to cool completely.
- Icing: Place cream cheese, icing sugar, buttermilk and vanilla in a bowl and mix well with a wooden spoon until smooth.
- Spread icing over cake.
- Decorate with walnuts.

268. Carrot And Pineapple Cake Recipe

Serving: 12 | Prep: 10mins | Cook: 50mins | Ready in: 60mins

Ingredients

- 3 cup plain flour
- 2 cup sugar
- 1 1/2 tsp bicarbonate of soda
- 1 tsp salt
- 2 cup carrot grated peeled
- 450 g (crushed) canned pineapple
- 1 1/2 cup sunflower oil
- 4 egg
- 1 cup pecans

Direction

- Sift dry ingredients into a bowl.
- Add carrot, undrained pineapple, oil, eggs and pecans.
- Mix well.
- Pour into a greased and lined lamington pan.
- Bake at 180C for approximately 50 minutes or until cooked.

---

269. Cheat's Berry Pudding Recipe

Serving: 6 | Prep: 15mins | Cook: 50mins | Ready in: 65mins

Ingredients

- 1 butter cake
- 2 egg
- 200ml berry fruit yoghurt
- 300g frozen mixed berries

Direction

- Empty cake mix into bowl. Beat in eggs and yoghurt.
- Fold in fruit.
- Pour into a greased 28cm round cake tin.
- Bake at 180C for 40 minutes.

---

270. Citrus Buttercake

Serving: 8 | Prep: 30mins | Cook: 35mins | Ready in: 65mins

Ingredients

- 125g butter
- 2 eggs
- 1 cup self-raising flour
- 1/2 cup plain flour
- 2 tsp lemon rind grated
- 2 tsp orange rind grated
- 1/3 cup freshly-squeezed orange juice
- 2/3 cup white sugar
- 1/2 tsp vanilla essence

Direction

- Preheat oven to 190C. Grease and line base of a 20cm cake pan with baking paper.
- Place all ingredients into a mixing bowl. Blend on low speed until all ingredients are combined, then beat on medium speed for one minute.
- Pour mixture into prepared cake tin and bake for 30-35 minutes.
- Allow to cool slightly in pan before inverting onto cake cooler.
- Once cool, ice with lemon frosting, or dust with icing sugar.

---

271. Classic Pavlova Recipe

Serving: 0 | Prep: 10mins | Cook: 90mins | Ready in: 100mins

Ingredients

- 5 egg whites
- 1 1/4 cups caster sugar
- 1 1/2 tsp vanilla essence
- 1 1/2 tsp white vinegar
- 1 1/2 tbs cornflour
- 1 pinch salt

Direction

- Preheat oven to 120C.
- Beat eggs whites until stiff.
- Add caster sugar slowly and then salt.
- Beat for a further 5 minutes until thick, stiff peaks form.
- Beat in vanilla and vinegar, then fold in cornflour.
- Spoon mixture onto a baking paper covered tray, shape into a 20 cm circle and pile high.

- Bake for about 1-1½ hours and let cool in the oven with door ajar.
- When cool cover top with whipped cream and toppings of choice.

272. Condensed Milk Fruit Salad Cheesecake Recipe

Serving: 12 | Prep: 25mins | Cook: 0S | Ready in: 25mins

Ingredients

- 200g plain sweet biscuits
- 100g butter, melted
- 500g cream cheese, at room temperature
- 395g tin condensed milk
- 1 tsp vanilla essence
- 3 tsp gelatine powder
- 300ml thickened cream, whipped
- 820g tin fruit salad in jucie

Direction

- Lightly grease a 24cm springform cake tin with butter and line the base and sides with baking paper. In a food processor, blitz biscuits into a fine crumb. Add butter and blitz until just combined. Pour into the prepared tin and use a large spoon to press into an even layer in the base. Refrigerate for 30 minutes.
- Wipe out the bowl of the food processor, then add cream cheese, condensed milk and vanilla. Process until smooth.
- Place 2 tbs boiling water in a small bowl and sprinkle over gelatine powder. Whisk with a fork until gelatine is completely dissolved. Add to cream cheese and blitz to combine. Fold through whipped cream.
- Pour half the cream cheese mixture into the prepared tin on top over the biscuit base. Drain fruit salad well and layer over the cream cheese. Top with remaining cream cheese mixture and smooth over the top. Refrigerate for at least an hour, or overnight, to set.

- Just before serving, release the cheesecake from the tin and carefully remove baking paper and transfer to a serving plate. Slice and serve.

273. Custard Sponge Cake

Serving: 10 | Prep: 20mins | Cook: 40mins | Ready in: 60mins

Ingredients

- 4 egg separated
- 1 tsp vanilla essence
- 3/4 cup caster sugar
- 1/2 tsp bicarbonate of soda
- 1 tsp cream of tartar
- 3/4 cup cornflour
- 1 tbs custard powder
- 2 tbs hot water
- 1 pinch salt
- 1 tsp icing sugar
- 1 tsp cornflour

Direction

- Prepare 2 x 20 cm deep round cake tins. Grease with butter and dust with combined icing sugar and cornflour.
- Preheat oven to 180C.
- Add vanilla to egg yolks.
- Sift all dry ingredients, except salt and sugar, twice.
- Beat egg whites and salt until stiff. Gradually add sugar. Beat in yolks.
- Fold in sifted dry ingredients, then the hot water.
- Pour into prepared tins and bake for approximately 20 minutes, or until cakes shrink from the sides of the tin. When the cakes are ready they will also spring back when touched in the middle with a finger.

274.   Easy Apple Cake Recipe

Serving: 12 | Prep: 30mins | Cook: 60mins | Ready in: 90mins

Ingredients

- 150g butter melted
- 2 cups stewed apple
- 1 cup sugar
- 2 eggs
- 2 cups self-raising flour
- 2 tsp baking powder
- 2 tsp ground cinnamon
- 1/2 cup mixed nuts chopped optional

Direction

- Place all ingredients into a bowl. Stir until well combined.
- Add nuts if desired.
- Pour mixture into a springform tin and bake for 40-45 minutes at 140C.

275.   Easy Fairy Bread Cake Balls Recipe

Serving: 0 | Prep: 20mins | Cook: 5mins | Ready in: 25mins

Ingredients

- 450 g madeira cake store-bought
- 180 g white chocolate chopped
- 2 cups icing sugar
- 2 1/2 tbs boiling water
- 1 cup hundreds and thousands

Direction

- Process the madeira cake in a food processor until coarse crumbs form. Melt the chocolate in a heatproof bowl over a saucepan of simmering water (make sure the bowl doesn't touch the water). Stir until smooth. Add the cake crumbs and stir to combine.

- Roll level tablespoons of mixture into balls, squeezing firmly as you roll. Place the hundreds and thousands on a plate.
- Combine the icing sugar and boiling water in a small bowl. Use 2 forks to carefully dip a truffle into the icing to coat. Tap forks on side of bowl to remove excess (you only need a very thin coating). Carefully roll in hundreds and thousands to coat. Transfer to a tray. Repeat with remaining truffles, icing and hundreds and thousands.
- Set aside to set. Place in an airtight container and store in the fridge for up to 3 days.

276.   Easy Keto Lemon Mug Cake Recipe

Serving: 1 | Prep: 5mins | Cook: 2mins | Ready in: 7mins

Ingredients

- 20 g butter cooled melted
- 1 egg
- 1 tsp lemon rind, finely grated
- 1/4 cup coconut flour
- 1 tbs almonds ground
- 1 tsp xylitol
- 1/2 tsp baking powder
- 2 tbs fresh lemon juice
- 1 pinch lemon rind *to serve *optional *extra
- 1 dollop mascarpone *to serve
- 2 tbs almond milk

Direction

- Whisk together the butter, egg and lemon rind in a small mixing bowl until combined. Add the flour, almond, xylitol, baking powder, milk and lemon juice. Stir to combine.
- Transfer mixture to a 250ml (1 cup) heatproof mug or cup and smooth the surface. Microwave on High for 2 minutes. Set aside for 30 seconds. Top with a dollop of mascarpone and extra lemon zest, if using, to serve.

277. Easy Orange Cake With Orange Icing Recipe

Serving: 10 | Prep: 20mins | Cook: 40mins | Ready in: 60mins

Ingredients

- Orange Cake
- 125g unsalted butter, softened
- 1/4 cup milk
- 1/4 cup orange juice
- 2 eggs
- 3/4 cup caster sugar
- 1 1/2 cups self-raising flour sifted
- 1 tbs orange zest, finely grated
- Orange icing
- 1/3 cup butter softened
- 1 1/2 cups icing sugar sifted
- 2 tbs orange juice *to taste
- 1/2 tsp orange zest, finely grated

Direction

- Combine all cake ingredients and beat thoroughly for 3 minutes.
- Pour mixture into a greased 20cm x 10cm loaf or 20cm ring tin.
- Bake in the centre of an 180C oven for 30-40 minutes.
- Turn onto a wire rack and allow to cool.
- Mix orange icing ingredients together in a bowl, then ice cake.

278. Easy Pavlova Recipe

Serving: 8 | Prep: 15mins | Cook: 80mins | Ready in: 95mins

Ingredients

- 6 egg whites
- 1 1/2 cup caster sugar
- 1/2 cup white sugar
- 2 tbs cornflour
- 2 tsp lemon juice
- 1 cup cream *to decorate
- 1 cup mixed berries *to decorate

Direction

- Line a baking tray with baking paper.
- Beat eggs whites until stiff peaks form.
- Gradually add the caster sugar to the egg whites and mix until mixture becomes thick and glossy.
- Mix white sugar and cornflour together in separate bowl.
- Fold sugar mixture and lemon juice into egg white mixture.
- Place mixture on baking tray and mould into a circle about a dinner plate size.
- Bake at 150C (fan forced) for 45 minutes to 1 hour. It will be ready when it is dry to touch. Allow to cool in the oven with the door ajar.
- Once cool, decorate with cream and topping of choice.

279. Easy Mix Butter Cake Recipe

Serving: 10 | Prep: 10mins | Cook: 40mins | Ready in: 50mins

Ingredients

- 2 eggs
- 125g unsalted butter, softened
- 1 cup sugar
- 2 cups self-raising flour
- 2/3 cup milk
- 1 tsp vanilla essence

Direction

- Combine all ingredients in a small bowl of an electric mixer.

- Beat on low speed until blended, then beat on high speed for 3 minutes.
- Grease a 28cm x 18cm lamington tin, and line the base with greaseproof paper.
- Pour mixture into tin and bake in a moderate oven (180C) for 30-40 minutes.
- When cold, ice with icing of choice and sprinkle with coconut or coloured sprinkles.

280. Egg And Dairy Free Chocolate Cake Recipe

Serving: 20 | Prep: 5mins | Cook: 20mins | Ready in: 25mins

Ingredients

- 3 cups self-raising flour
- 2/3 cup cocoa
- 2 cups caster sugar
- 1 tsp salt
- 2 cups water
- 2/3 cup canola oil
- 2 tbs lemon juice
- 1 tsp vanilla essence

Direction

- Preheat oven to 180C.
- Sift flour, cocoa, caster sugar and salt into a large bowl.
- Add remaining ingredients and combine well.
- Pour mixture into a greased cake tin.
- Bake until cooked through.

281. Gluten Free Pumpkin Cake Recipe

Serving: 12 | Prep: 10mins | Cook: 45mins | Ready in: 55mins

Ingredients

- 1 cup pumpkin cooked drained mashed
- 1/2 cup rice bran oil
- 2 eggs
- 1 cup caster sugar
- 2 cups White Wings gluten-free plain flour
- 1 tsp bicarbonate of soda
- 1/2 tsp salt
- 1/2 tsp ground cinnamon
- 1/4 tsp gluten-free baking powder

Direction

- In a large bowl, mix wet pumpkin, oil and sugar.
- Add eggs and mix well with a wooden spoon.
- In another bowl, mix flour, bicarbonate of soda, salt, cinnamon and baking powder.
- Add dry ingredients to wet and stir with a wooden spoon until well mixed and free of lumps.
- Pour into a greased loaf tin.
- Bake at 180C for 45 minutes.

282. Grandma's Pavlova Recipe

Serving: 6 | Prep: 0S | Cook: 90mins | Ready in: 90mins

Ingredients

- 4 egg whites
- 1 cup caster sugar
- 1 tsp white vinegar
- 1/2 tsp vanilla extract
- 1 tbs cornflour
- 300 ml thickened cream
- 1 punnet fresh strawberries halved hulled *to serve
- 1 punnet fresh blueberries *to serve
- 1 handful edible flowers *to decorate

Direction

- Preheat oven to 200°C. Line a large baking tray with baking paper. Draw a 20cm-diameter circle on baking paper and place it, circle-side down, on tray.

- Using an electric mixer, whisk egg whites in a clean, dry bowl until firm peaks form. Gradually add caster sugar, 1 tablespoon at a time, whisking well after each addition. Whisk until sugar has dissolved and meringue is thick and glossy. Add vinegar and vanilla, and whisk until combined. Sift cornflour over meringue. Using a large metal spoon or spatula, gently fold cornflour into meringue.
- Spoon meringue into circle on prepared tray and smooth into a disc. (Keep edges of disc high and don't smooth out too far.)
- Reduce oven temperature to 125°C. Bake pavlova for 1½ hours. Turn off oven. Leave pavlova in oven to cool completely. (Do not open oven door until pavlova is completely cooled — it's best to leave it overnight.)
- Using a balloon whisk, whisk cream in a large bowl until soft peaks form. Top pavlova with whipped cream, strawberries and blueberries. Decorate with edible flowers.

---

283. Jaffa Cake Recipe

Serving: 8 | Prep: 40mins | Cook: 25mins | Ready in: 65mins

Ingredients

- Cake
- 1 cup self-raising flour
- 3 tbs cocoa
- 1/2 tsp bicarbonate of soda
- 1/2 cup brown sugar
- 1/2 cup caster sugar
- 2 eggs
- 3/4 cup milk
- 60g butter melted
- 1 orange zested
- 1/4 cup orange juice
- Ganache
- 3/4 cup cream

- 150g dark chocolate chopped
- 200g Jaffas

Direction

- Preheat oven to 200C (180C fan-forced). Grease and line the base of two 20cm round sandwich tins.
- Sift flour, cocoa and bicarb soda into a large bowl. Stir through sugars. Add remaining ingredients and stir to create a smooth batter.
- Divide equally between prepared cake tins. Bake for 25 minutes or until a skewer inserted into the centre comes out clean. Invert onto cake racks to cool completely.
- To make ganache, heat cream in a small saucepan until almost boiling. Remove from heat and stir through chocolate until melted and smooth. Refrigerate until cool and starting to firm.
- Place in a stand mixer or use hand-held beaters to whip for 1-2 minutes until pale and thick.
- Place Jaffas into a ziplock bag on a wooden chopping board, cover with a tea towel and whack with a rolling pin to roughly crush.
- Combine ganache with two-thirds of the crushed Jaffas, reserving the remainder. Spread about half of the crushed Jaffa ganache onto one of the cakes. Top with second cake. Spread the remaining ganache on top. Sprinkle reserved Jaffas on top.

---

284. Lamington Cake Balls

Serving: 0 | Prep: 20mins | Cook: 25mins | Ready in: 45mins

Ingredients

- 200g butter
- 4 eggs
- 200g sugar
- 2 tbs vanilla essence
- 400g self-raising flour

- 250ml milk
- For assembling:
- 100g hot chocolate powder
- 100g berry jam
- 300g desiccated coconut

Direction

- To make the cakes: Preheat oven to 180C. Grease and line 2 slice tins.
- Cream butter and sugar until white and fluffy. Add eggs and vanilla and continue to beat. Fold in flour and milk, alternating between the two. Pour into slice tins and bake for 20-25 minutes. Cool cake before assembling cake balls.
- To make the cake balls: Process cake into crumbs. Whisk hot chocolate drinking powder with one cup of water. In a large bowl, combine cake crumbs, jam and chocolate liquid. Squeezing together to form a solid mass. If the mix is excessively wet add some coconut until it holds.
- Portion out mix into 30g balls. Roll in coconut. Chill in refrigerator until firm.

---

285.   Lamington Cheesecake Recipe

Serving: 12 | Prep: 180mins | Cook: 10mins | Ready in: 190mins

Ingredients

- 18 lamingtons
- 250 g white chocolate
- 300 ml thickened cream
- 2 tsp gelatine powder
- 3 tsp water
- 125 g cream cheese
- 250 g mascarpone
- 1/2 cup caster sugar
- 1 tsp vanilla extract
- 250 g dark chocolate
- 1/2 cup thickened cream

- 1/2 cup desiccated coconut *to decorate

Direction

- Grease and line a 17 cm x 27 cm slice pan with baking paper.
- Lay lamington fingers side by side in pan.
- In a heatproof bowl, melt white chocolate and 150 mL of cream in microwave in short bursts, stirring regularly until chocolate is melted and cream is completely mixed into chocolate.
- Mix gelatine and water together. Heat in microwave for 20 seconds or until gelatine is dissolved. Stir into chocolate mixture.
- Beat cream cheese, mascarpone, sugar and vanilla until soft and creamy, then beat in chocolate mixture.
- In a separate bowl, beat remaining cream until soft peaks form. Fold through mixture.
- Pour over lamingtons and set in fridge overnight.
- Once set, melt dark chocolate and extra thickened cream together then refrigerate for 20 minutes to make ganache and spread over cheese cake. Sprinkle with coconut.
- Refrigerate until topping sets.

---

286.   Lemon Meringue Cheesecake Recipe

Serving: 10 | Prep: 20mins | Cook: 180mins | Ready in: 200mins

Ingredients

- 250 g sweet plain biscuits crushed
- 125 g butter melted
- Filling
- 250 g cream cheese
- 440 g condensed milk
- 2 egg yolks
- 2 tsp lemon rind grated
- 1/4 cup lemon juice
- Meringue
- 3 egg whites

- 1/2 cup caster sugar

Direction

- Base: Combine biscuit crumbs and butter and press firmly into base of a springform pan. Refrigerate until firm.
- Filling: Beat cheese until smooth, add condensed milk, lemon rind, lemon juice, and egg yolks and beat until smooth.
- Pour over base and refrigerate for approximately 2 hours or until firm to touch.
- Meringue: Whip egg whites until stiff peaks form. Gradually add sugar and beat until dissolved.
- Spread evenly over filling.
- Preheat the grill to high heat and cook for 4 - 5 minutes, checking regularly or until meringue browns.
- Allow to cool, then refrigerate until required.

287. Lemon Teacake Recipe

Serving: 8 | Prep: 15mins | Cook: 30mins | Ready in: 45mins

Ingredients

- 1 cup self-raising flour
- 1/2 cup caster sugar
- 60g butter chopped
- 1 egg lightly beaten
- Lemon filling
- 60ml lemon juice
- 1/2 cup caster sugar
- 1 egg lightly beaten
- 60g butter chopped

Direction

- Teacake: Preheat oven to 180C.
- Grease a deep 18cm round cake pan and line base with baking paper.

- Sift flour into a medium bowl. Add sugar, then rub in the butter until mixture resembles breadcrumbs.
- Stir in the egg to form a soft dough.
- Press two thirds of the dough over the base of the prepared pan.
- Lemon filling: Combine juice, sugar, egg and butter in a small saucepan.
- Stir over low heat until mixture thickens and coats the back of a spoon.
- Spread the hot lemon filling over base in pan to within 1cm of the edge.
- Crumble the remaining dough over the filling.
- Bake for about 30 minutes or until browned. Cool in pan.
- Serve dusted with sifted icing sugar.

288. Lemon Yoghurt Cake Recipe

Serving: 12 | Prep: 10mins | Cook: 45mins | Ready in: 55mins

Ingredients

- 1 3/4 cups sugar
- 2 eggs
- 1/2 tsp salt
- 3 tsp lemon juice
- 2 lemons grated
- 3/4 cup oil
- 1 cup natural yoghurt
- 2 cups self-raising flour

Direction

- In a bowl, mix rind, oil, eggs and sugar with a fork.
- Add remaining ingredients and combine well.
- Pour into greased ring tin and bake at 180C for 30 minutes.
- Leave to cool then turn out and dust with icing sugar.

289. Lime And Olive Oil Coconut Cake Recipe

Serving: 12 | Prep: 10mins | Cook: 75mins | Ready in: 85mins

Ingredients

- 2 cups self-raising flour
- 3/4 cup caster sugar
- 3/4 cup coconut
- 1 cup olive oil
- 1 cup milk
- 3 eggs
- 3 limes juiced zested

Direction

- Preheat oven to 180C. Grease and line an 8 inch round cake tin with baking paper.
- In a mixing bowl, combine oil, milk, eggs, lime juice and lime zest and whisk until combined.
- Sift self raising flour into another mixing bowl and mix in sugar and coconut. Make a well in the centre and pour in wet ingredients. Stir to combine.
- Pour mixture into the prepared cake tin and bake for approx 1 hour 15 minutes or until a skewer inserted comes out clean. Allow to cool in tin for 10 minutes before turning out on a wire rack to cool.
- Serve with some whipped cream or yoghurt and dust with icing sugar.

290. Lumberjack Cake Recipe

Serving: 12 | Prep: 20mins | Cook: 70mins | Ready in: 90mins

Ingredients

- 2 apples large peeled cored finely chopped
- 1 cup dates chopped
- 1 tsp bicarbonate of soda
- 1 cup boiling water
- 125g soft butter
- 1 tsp vanilla essence
- 1 cup caster sugar
- 1 egg
- 1 1/2 cups plain flour
- Topping
- 60g butter
- 1/2 cup brown sugar
- 1/2 cup milk
- 2/3 cup shredded coconut

Direction

- Grease and line a deep 23cm square cake pan.
- Combine apples, dates and bicarbonate of soda in a bowl.
- Add the water and leave for 10 minutes.
- Beat butter, sugar, vanilla and egg until light and fluffy.
- Add butter to apple mixture and fold in flour.
- Pour into a prepared pan and bake in a moderate oven for 50 minutes.
- Topping: Combine ingredients in a saucepan and stir until butter melts and sugar dissolves.
- Remove the cake from the oven and carefully spoon topping mixture over the cake. Return to oven and bake for further 20 minutes.
- Stand cake for 5 minutes before turning onto a wire rack to cool.

291. Mars Bar Mud Cake Recipe

Serving: 10 | Prep: 20mins | Cook: 110mins | Ready in: 130mins

Ingredients

- 400 g butter chopped
- 400 g dark chocolate chopped
- 1/2 cup cocoa powder
- 1 3/4 cups caster sugar
- 6 eggs lightly beaten
- 1 1/2 cups self-raising flour

- 4 x 53 g Mars Mars Bar chilled chopped

Direction

- Preheat oven to 160C (140C fan-forced). Grease and line a deep 22 cm x 28 cm slab pan.
- Melt butter and chocolate together in large bowl in microwave on 70% for 3-4 minutes, stirring with a metal spoon every minute until almost smooth.
- Add cocoa and whisk until smooth, add sugar and mix well.
- Add half of egg mixture, stir to combine, repeat.
- Sift flour over mixture, stir gently until just combined.
- Pour into prepared pan.
- Arrange chopped Mars Bars over cake batter and press in slightly.
- Bake for 60-65 minutes or until a skewer inserted off centre has moist crumbs clinging to it. Cool completely in pan, then cut into squares.
- To make cupcakes use muffin pans lined with papers, baking for 25 minutes.

292.   Microwave Nutella Mug Cake Recipe

Serving: 0 | Prep: 0S | Cook: 0S | Ready in:

Ingredients

- 2 tbs gluten-free self-raising flour
- 2 tbs brown sugar
- 2 tbs Dutch cocoa powder
- 1/4 tsp gluten-free baking powder
- 1 egg large
- 2 tbs milk
- 1 tbs oil
- 2 tbs Nutella
- 1 scoop ice cream *to serve
- 1 gluten-free chocolate sauce *to serve

Direction

- Combine the flour, sugar, cocoa and baking powder in a bowl.
- Make a well in the centre and add the egg, milk and oil. Use electric beaters to beat until well combined.
- Spoon into a 435ml (1 3/4 cup) mug. The spoon the Nutella into the centre. Microwave on High/1000watts/100% for 70 seconds or until risen. Top with double cream or ice cream and drizzle with chocolate sauce.

293.   Moist Orange Poppy Seed Cake Recipe

Serving: 12 | Prep: 15mins | Cook: 60mins | Ready in: 75mins

Ingredients

- 1 orange roughly chopped
- 185 g butter melted
- 3 eggs
- 1 cup caster sugar
- 1 1/2 cups self-raising flour
- 2 tbs poppy seeds

Direction

- Preheat oven to 170C.
- Grease and line an 18 cm cake pan or a loaf tin.
- Puree whole orange, peel on, in food processor
- Add melted butter, eggs, sugar and mix well.
- Add flour and poppy seeds and mix until well combined.
- Bake for approximately 45 minutes or until cooked when tested.

294.   No Bake Pavlova Recipe

Serving: 6 | Prep: 20mins | Cook: 5mins | Ready in: 25mins

Ingredients

- 2 egg whites
- 1 cup caster sugar
- 3 tsp gelatine powder
- 1 cup boiling water
- 500 ml thickened cream
- 1 cup fresh strawberries *to decorate

Direction

- Dissolve gelatine in boiling water and place in fridge to cool.
- Beat together egg whites, caster sugar and the dissolved gelatine and water. Mix with an electric mixer for about 10 minutes or until very stiff.
- Place in large bowl and refrigerate for at least 2 hours or until set.
- Whip up cream and place on top of pavlova. Decorate with sliced strawberries or kiwifruit.

---

295. Passionfruit Cheese Lova Recipe

Serving: 0 | Prep: 40mins | Cook: 90mins | Ready in: 130mins

Ingredients

- 4 egg whites
- 1 cup caster sugar
- 1 tsp cornflour
- 1/2 tsp lemon juice
- 1 tsp vanilla extract
- 1 tub cream whipped *extra
- 1 cup mixed berries *to serve
- 1 cup passionfruit *to serve
- 1 mango *to serve
- For filling
- 300 ml cream
- 2 tsp gelatine
- 500 g cream cheese
- 3/4 cup caster sugar
- 170 g tinned passionfruit pulp seeds removed

Direction

- Preheat oven to 140C (120C fan-forced). Remove the base from a 22-24cm springform tin and set aside. Line the sides with baking paper, coming up a few centimetres above the edge. Place on a flat oven tray lined with paper.
- Whip egg whites until soft peaks form. With the beaters running, add caster sugar one spoonful at a time, mixing well in between each addition. This will take some time, but is important for the finished result. Add the cornflour in with the last spoonful of sugar. Continue mixing for 5-10 minutes until the sugar has dissolved completely. You can test this by rubbing a little of the mixture between a finger and thumb - it should be completely smooth. Add lemon juice and vanilla and continue mixing for another minute.
- Spoon into prepared tin (the meringue will be sitting directly on the lined tray), smoothing down the top evenly. Place in the oven and bake for 1.5 hours. Without removing pavlova, turn off oven, open the door slightly and allow to cool for a couple of hours or overnight.
- To make filling: beat cream until thick. Set aside. Dissolve gelatine in 1/4 cup boiling water. Set aside. Whip together cream cheese with caster sugar until smooth. Add dissolved gelatine and strained passionfruit and beat well. Fold through whipped cream.
- Spoon filling into tin on top of pavlova base, pushing it right to the edges and smoothing out evenly on top. Refrigerate for 4 hours to set completely.
- Just prior to serving, remove from fridge. Tilt tin and carefully remove paper from base, then place on serving platter. Unlock spring and carefully remove tin - you may need to first slide a knife around between tin and paper to unstick it. Pull off paper. Spread extra whipped cream around the sides to cover any imperfections. Top with fruit and serve.

296.   Pavlova Recipe

Serving: 12 | Prep: 10mins | Cook: 90mins | Ready in: 100mins

Ingredients

- 4 egg whites
- 1 cup caster sugar
- 1 tsp lemon juice
- 2 tsp cornflour

Direction

- In a small electric mixer bowl, beat egg whites until soft peaks form.
- Add sugar, lemon juice and sifted cornflour, and beat until stiff and glossy (at least 10 minutes).
- Cover a baking tray with baking paper.
- Pile meringue onto paper and shape into a large circle, leaving the centre slightly hollowed.
- Bake in at 130C for 1½ hours or until crisp on the outside.
- Turn oven off and leave pavlova to cool in oven with door ajar.
- Decorate with whipped cream and fruit in season.

297.   Pear Upside Down Cake Recipe

Serving: 8 | Prep: 15mins | Cook: 70mins | Ready in: 85mins

Ingredients

- 50g butter
- 1/3 cup brown sugar
- 3 pears firm medium peeled sliced
- 150g butter
- 1 cup brown sugar lightly packed
- 3 eggs
- 1 1/3 cups self-raising flour
- 1 tsp baking powder
- 2 tsp ground ginger optional

Direction

- Preheat oven to 180C or 160C fan forced. Line the base of a 22cm spring form cake pan with baking paper.
- Melt 50g butter and 1/3 cup brown sugar together and pour over the baking paper. Cover with sliced pears in a circular pattern.
- Beat together butter and sugar until pale and creamy.
- Add eggs, one at a time, beating well after each addition. Stir in the combined flour, baking powder and ginger.
- Spoon the cake batter over the pears. Bake for 40 minutes until a skewer inserted comes out clean.
- Leave to rest for 5 minutes and then invert onto a serving plate.
- Serve with custard, whipped cream or caramel sauce.

298.   Raspberry, Orange And Almond Simnel Cake Recipe

Serving: 11 | Prep: 25mins | Cook: 60mins | Ready in: 85mins

Ingredients

- 1 orange large
- 1/2 cup sultanas
- 1/2 cup mixed peel
- 150 g unsalted butter room temperature
- 3/4 cup caster sugar
- 4 eggs
- 1 cup plain flour
- 1 1/2 cups almond meal
- 1 tbs baking powder
- 1 1/2 cups frozen raspberries defrosted
- 500 g marzipan
- 11 white chocolate truffles

Direction

- Preheat oven to 180C (160 degrees fan-forced). Grease and line the base and sides of a 20-22cm springform cake tin.
- Remove zest from the orange, then juice it to yield half a cup. Pour over sultanas and mixed peel in a bowl and allow to soak for 10 minutes.
- Meanwhile, cream butter and sugar until pale and fluffy. Add eggs one at a time, beating well between each addition. Fold through flour, almond meal and baking powder. Add soaked sultanas and mixed peel with the juice, zest and raspberries, and fold until just combined.
- Roll out one packet of marzipan between two sheets of baking paper to form a circle the same size as your cake tin. Pour half the batter into prepared tin. Gently place marzipan circle onto batter, then pour over remaining batter and smooth the top. Bake for approximately 1 hour until a skewer inserted partially into the top comes out clean. Allow to cool in the tin.
- Roll out second packet of marzipan to the same diameter as the cake. Remove cake from tin and place on serving platter. Drape marzipan over the top of the cake and smooth down. Place truffles evenly around the edge of the cake. Decorate with extra Easter eggs as desired.

---

299. Sponge Flan With Cheesecake Cream And Strawberries

Serving: 8 | Prep: 20mins | Cook: 0S | Ready in: 20mins

Ingredients

- 200 g sweet flan pastry cases
- 80 ml orange juice to coat
- 125 g soft cream cheese
- 1 tbs orange rind, finely grated
- 2 tsp orange juice
- 2 tbs icing sugar mixture
- 250 ml thickened cream
- 250 g fresh strawberries thinly sliced
- 1/3 cup strawberry jam sieved warmed

Direction

- Place flan case on a serving plate and brush all over with the orange juice to soften.
- Beat cream cheese, orange rind, extra juice and icing sugar in a small bowl with an electric mixer until smooth.
- Beat the cream in a separate bowl until soft peaks form; fold into the cream cheese mixture.
- Fill the flan case with the cream mixture.
- Arrange sliced strawberries over the cream and brush strawberries with the jam.

---

300. Strawberry Pavlova Roll Recipe

Serving: 8 | Prep: 15mins | Cook: 1470mins | Ready in: 1485mins

Ingredients

- 4 egg whites
- 3/4 cup sugar
- 1 tsp white vinegar
- 1 tsp cornflour
- 1 tsp vanilla essence
- 300 ml whipped cream
- 250 g fresh strawberries
- 2 passionfruit optional

Direction

- Grease a Swiss roll tin and line with baking paper. Preheat oven to 170C.
- Beat egg whites until soft peaks form.
- Add sugar gradually and continue beating until mixture is stiff and glossy and all sugar is dissolved.

- Gently fold through vanilla, cornflour and vinegar.
- Spread meringue evenly into prepared tin. Bake for 12-15 minutes.
- Allow to cool completely before turning out onto sugared baking paper.
- Spread with whipped cream and top with sliced strawberries.
- Roll up from long side and place on serving plate, still covered with the baking paper.
- Refrigerate for 24 hours.
- Decorate top with strawberries and passionfruit if desired.

301. Super Moist Coconut Lemon Cake Recipe

Serving: 12 | Prep: 20mins | Cook: 45mins | Ready in: 65mins

Ingredients

- 2 cup self-raising flour
- 1 cup caster sugar
- 1 cup macadamia oil
- 1 cup natural yoghurt
- 1/2 tsp salt
- 2 egg
- 1 lemon juiced
- 2 lemon zested
- 1 cup shredded coconut

Direction

- Beat sugar, oil, eggs and juice.
- Add yogurt and rind and mix.
- Add flour, salt and coconut and mix.
- Double line a round cake pan and pour in batter and top with left over coconut.
- Bake at 180C for 45 minutes or until an inserted toothpick comes out clean. Decorate with some extra coconut.

302. Sweet Potato, Custard And Sultana Cake Recipe

Serving: 10 | Prep: 30mins | Cook: 120mins | Ready in: 150mins

Ingredients

- 300 g sweet potato chopped peeled
- 1 cup custard
- 250 g sultanas
- 3 cups self-raising flour
- 250 g butter chopped
- 1 1/2 cups caster sugar
- 2 tbs honey
- 4 eggs
- 1/4 cup icing sugar for dusting

Direction

- Grease a 25 cm round cake pan.
- Place sweet potato in a pan with a little water.
- Boil until tender, then drain and cool. Mash sweet potato with custard.
- Coat sultanas with 1 tablespoon of the flour, and set aside.
- Beat butter, sugar and honey in a large bowl with an electric mixer until light and fluffy.
- Beat in eggs, one at a time, until combined.
- Lower the mixing speed, beat in sweet potato mixture, then gradually beat in flour until combined.
- Use a wooden spoon to stir in sultanas, then pour mixture into prepared pan.
- Bake at 150C for about 1 hour 40 minutes or until a skewer inserted in the centre comes out clean.
- Serve cake warm or cold, dusted with sifted icing sugar.

303. Zucchini Cake Recipe

Serving: 16 | Prep: 15mins | Cook: 45mins | Ready in: 60mins

Ingredients

- 2 cups zucchini grated
- 3 eggs
- 2 cups caster sugar
- 2 1/2 cups self-raising flour
- 1/3 cup canola oil
- 1 cup walnuts chopped
- 3 tsp vanilla essence
- 1/4 tsp baking powder
- 1 tsp salt
- 2 tsp ground cinnamon

Direction

- Beat eggs, add sugar, vanilla and oil.
- Beat until mixture thickens slightly and add remaining ingredients.
- Mix together and pour into 2 log tins.
- Bake for 45 minutes at 180C.

Index

Conclusion

Thank you again for downloading this book!

I hope you enjoyed reading about my book!

If you enjoyed this book, please take the time to share your thoughts and post a review on Amazon. It'd be greatly appreciated!

Write me an honest review about the book – I truly value your opinion and thoughts and I will incorporate them into my next book, which is already underway.

Thank you!

If you have any questions, **feel free to contact at:** _author@chardrecipes.com_

Eva Taylor

chardrecipes.com

Printed in Great Britain
by Amazon

52483767R00086